THE MYTH OF FRANCE

By the same Author
MONSTERS: STUDIES IN FEROCITY

RAYMOND RUDORFF

The Myth of France

"Il faut qu'on sache et qu'on sache complètement, ce que c'est que la Belle France: ce qu'elle a été, ce qu'elle est, ce qu'elle peut devenir. On le saura."

GEORGES DARIEN, *La Belle France*, 1901

COWARD-McCANN, INC.
New York

Copyright © 1970 by Raymond Rudorff

FIRST AMERICAN EDITION 1970

All rights reserved. This book, or parts thereof, may not be reproduced in any form without permission in writing from the Publisher.

Library of Congress Catalog Card Number: 72-81005

PRINTED IN THE UNITED STATES OF AMERICA

To My Wife Patricia

Acknowledgements

The author expresses gratitude for help given during the writing of this book by M. Claude Angeli, M. Paul Gillet, M. Francis Hamon, M. Jean-Jacques Pauvert and Mrs. Robin Smyth. For constant encouragement, help and much wearisome retyping of the manuscript of this book, his wife. For editorial advice he would particularly like to thank Mr. Christopher Sinclair-Stevenson of Hamish Hamilton Ltd. In addition, grateful acknowledgement is made to Calder and Boyars Ltd. for permission to quote from André Pieyre de Mandiargues, *La Marge,* in the writer's own translation; to Editions Gallimard, for permission to quote in its entirety 'L'exécution du testament de Sade' from Alain Jouffroy, *Une Révolution du Regard,* 1964; to Jarrolds Ltd. for permission to use extracts from Pierre Alix, *My France,* 1939; and to Editions Jean-Jacques Pauvert, for permission to quote from Georges Bataille, *Madame Edwarda,* 1967, and *Ma Mère,* 1967, and from Boris Vian, *L'Herbe Rouge,* 1962.

Contents

PART ONE
MARIANNE

The Ideas of France	3
The Missionary in Arms	15
Mother of Liberty	39

PART TWO
PARIS

The Capital of the Spirit	67
The Idols	102
The Byzantines	128

PART THREE
FRANCE

The Foremost Cultural Country	153
The Image and the Word	176
Anti-France	194
The Republic, One and Indivisible	219
NOTES	233
INDEX	237

PART ONE
MARIANNE

I

The Ideas of France

'You speak to me of the idea I have of France. The subject is not new. It is quite true—I would say it is my *raison d'être*—it is altogether true that always, and today more than ever before, I have had a certain idea of France. By this, I mean to say that to my mind she is something that is very great, very special. Moreover, I think that this is felt by the whole world. There is even something quite extraordinary in all this: in our misfortunes it is seen at once, and when we are happy, prosperous, glorious and strong, it may also be seen by the extent to which people look at us with envy . . . France . . . must have a role of her own . . . to play her role she must be France.'

Ex-President Charles de Gaulle, television interview with Michel Droit, December 13, 1965.

LONG BEFORE De Gaulle ever expressed his own idea of France which was to inspire him as a national leader, there existed among his countrymen two different but related ideas of *la patrie* and its role in the world. These ideas were symbolized by two aspects of a female figure, representing the Republic, and popularly known as Marianne.

One Marianne was warlike, the other peaceful. The first expressed martial glory, the second, spiritual radiance. They are powerful symbols and they perfectly express two of the most frequent ways in which generations of Frenchmen have seen and been taught to see their homeland, both in its past and in its present. They are both figureheads for great myths which have been repeated for so long that they have been taken for realities, and like most myths they have a basis of historical truth.

As the French Republic began its existence in a series of wars, it is only fitting that we should look first at the warlike symbol—Marianne in arms, whose concrete, artistic representation may be studied on the Arc de Triomphe in Paris.

The Arc is one of Paris's best known monuments. It was set up to commemorate Napoleon I's battles and some 386 generals of the First Republic and Empire. It was under its arch that France's

Unknown Soldier of the First World War was buried, with the Sacred Flame burning on his tomb. It stands massive and imposing at the top of the long avenue of the Champs-Elysées, a symbol of France's military grandeur, a reminder of past victories and the fitting background to the great military parades of July 14, which is known as Bastille Day when it might more appropriately be called 'Arc de Triomphe Day'.

For many Frenchmen, the Arc has a political significance. A chauvinistic monument, it is not surprising that it attracts so many French ultra-patriots who usually belong to what is known as the Right. It is there that ex-servicemen's associations, reactionaries of various tendencies, conservatives and right-wing extremists will congregate on special occasions while their opponents of the Left, long distinguished by their anti-militarism, will gather in the eastern quarters of the city, at the Bastille which is their symbol, or in the Place de la Nation. Many outbursts of nationalistic fervour of the more martial kind have been witnessed by the Arc. In 1938, as Alexander Werth described in his book, *The Twilight of France*, after the Prime Minister Daladier had returned from Munich and what was presumed to have been a diplomatic victory, a vast patriotic ceremony was held at the Arc which was floodlit and draped with a huge tricolour flag. Many ex-servicemen attended the occasion and while Daladier rekindled the Sacred Flame, vast crowds sang the *Marseillaise*. At the same time, many young French Fascists could be seen giving the Hitler salute in the Champs-Elysées, thus demonstrating that ultra-patriotism could be accompanied by admiration for a foreign system which violated every noble ideal that France had proclaimed.

Thirty years later, the ultra-patriotic Gaullists and Rightists converged towards the arch in a huge demonstration of support for the régime after the riots and strikes of May 1968. By rallying around this monument, they proved that it had lost none of its attraction as a symbol of a nation which prided itself as much on its military as on its cultural grandeur.

The personification of military France is to be found among the bas-reliefs which decorate the sides of the arch. It is François Rude's famous 19th-century composition known as *La Marseillaise* or *Le Départ*. This striking work represents the Republic going into battle. The main image, a warlike woman symbolizing the nation in arms, illustrates a notion of France which has been immensely influential ever since the *Marseillaise* anthem was first sung and which has remained particularly dear to the Right for whom exaltation of France's military past is essential to the myth which is part of its creed.

Let us examine Rude's bas-relief more closely. The bellicose amazon is wearing the Phrygian cap of the Republic. She is seen against a background of outspread wings with which the sculptor endowed her, military emblems of the ancient Roman variety, and spears. Her left arm is flung high, her right hand is thrust forward, grasping a sword, her head is turned back and with eyes almost popping from their sockets and mouth wide open she is obviously shouting some war cry to the legions who must be following her into the fray. To a spectator unaware that she might be commemorating France's Revolutionary wars in the 1790's, she might be an allegory of war and violence—a rhetorical and aggressive figure not unlike the neo-Roman monuments and bas-reliefs with which Mussolini thought fit to adorn the public buildings of his Fascist Italy.

But when the sculpture was placed upon the Arc, the wars of the First Republic had long been ended. Rude completed the work in 1836, the year the Arc was finally inaugurated, during the reign of that very bourgeois and unheroic king Louis-Philippe. Against whom then was this frenzied amazon supposed to be summoning the nation? Against what enemy? Any enemy, presumably, the suggestion being that France will always have an enemy to fight on the battlefield. Although the work may intend a glorification of French patriotism, here equated with bellicosity, it would be difficult to find a greater plastic expression of warlike exultation anywhere else in the world. It is essentially a repellent image for a country that has prided itself on its civilization, and appears to express mindless violence for its own sake. It has little to do with a France that has proclaimed the glory of its culture and its contribution to the sum of human happiness in the world but it is still a famous symbol. It is the visual accompaniment to France's national anthem which, significantly enough, is also a war cry, full of blood and slaughter.

After Rude's stone idea of France, it is a relief to turn to that other female personification of the nation, Marianne the Mother of Civilization and Liberty. This peaceful lady has often been depicted on French postage stamps and is now to be seen on fifty-centime and franc coins. She has exchanged the sword for the task of sowing in the fields. She wears the same Phrygian cap to show that she is a good Republican but instead of going into battle she is shown striding forward, scattering seeds from her upheld apron into the fields of the world with a radiant sun in the background. Like her warrior sister, she is a figure in motion. Whereas England's John Bull or Britannia with her shield are static, Marianne is dynamic. She is a busy person. When she is not engaged in warfare she is doing something practical and beneficial—and not merely for herself. She illustrates the idea that France is a country with a mission which is to contribute to the spiritual and material welfare of the world. Marianne sheds her rays abroad like the sun on the coin, in a process which the French call *rayonnement*, 'radiating', a word that has been much used by France's patriots, politicians and historians. This 'radiating France', *la France qui rayonne*, is an essential part of that form of French patriotism which feeds on historical myths and which is known as chauvinism. The idea is an old one and was used by the monarchy of Louis XIV, the 'sun king'.

The light that Marianne radiates in the world has been given such various definitions as 'culture', 'civilization', 'the art of living', 'liberty', 'human dignity and rights', 'fraternity' and 'spiritual values'. That it has been France's vocation to exemplify these ideals and turn them into realities for other countries as well as herself is something that has been believed by generations of Frenchmen. It has been taught to them at school, they have read it in history books, and every local dignitary hard up for something to say when making his July 14 or school prize-day speech can safely fall back upon this stirring theme of the homeland from whom the idea of *rayonnement* is inseparable.

*

Corresponding to these two symbols of France is that sentiment of exaggerated patriotism of which her people have been so often accused and which is called chauvinism. The word is derived from Chauvin, the name of an officer in Napoleon I's armies who distinguished himself by his fanatical nationalistic and martial fervour. Like excessive national self-glorification in other countries, it arises from the conviction that the homeland is and was the foremost country in the world by virtue of its military abilities and victories, its natural physical beauties and resources, the intelligence of its population, the incomparable refinement and superiority of its way of life and culture, and from the unshakeable belief that the nation has the duty and mission to teach civilization to other, less privileged countries.

Running through French chauvinism like a gleaming silver thread is the feeling that France is vital to the rest of the world and that only France can give it those qualities and benefits for which it must be crying out. France's greatness is not only in itself but in its missionary vocation, hence the emphasis on the idea of France as a spreader of enlightenment. The idea is common to Frenchmen of the most diverse political beliefs and has been expressed time and time again. No other country has ever spoken so much of its supposed mission. In the 1930's, we find France's Socialist Prime Minister, Léon Blum, writing that France could be found abroad in the world in 'the faith in some of the great ideas that France has represented in the world' and that 'what you call our internationalism is the hope, is the certainty, that the whole world will one day be peacefully conquered by those ideas which France represents in history'. (1)

More recently, the same idea that the world will be peacefully conquered by France's great ideas was repeated by De Gaulle and the man he appointed as spokesman for French civilization and culture, André Malraux. It was during the régime that ended with De Gaulle's resignation in 1969, that the myths of France's grandeur were once more consecrated at the highest official level in the country and it is best therefore to study them against the background of this period and in contrast to its realities.

During his career as President of France, De Gaulle seemed to have appropriated the traditional, chauvinistic idea of France for his own personal use in his many speeches to his fellow-Frenchmen. In a book which was a ferocious analysis of De Gaulle's style of language and the mentality behind it, *Le style du Général*, the writer, Jean-François Revel, observed that the General spoke as though this 'certain idea of France' had existed before him but in obscurity. It was as if the idea had been waiting for De Gaulle to discover it and then proceed to draw both France and the world's attention to it by incarnating it in his own person. But engrossed as he was in studying the peculiarities of the language in which De Gaulle elaborated and repeated his themes, Revel did not emphasize its enormous, breath-taking unoriginality.

It is well known that De Gaulle had seen himself as the living symbol of that France already symbolized by the two figures of

Marianne. His belief that he was a kind of new Joan of Arc sent to save his country amused many people but in seeing himself as representing France he was not wholly mistaken. He was perfectly typical of a France that believed in its myths and he also represented the continuity and orthodoxy of a chauvinistic tradition which always spoke the same language, remained faithful to the same creed, and which worshipped both the warlike and the peaceful Marianne while at the same time confusing them in the idea of *rayonnement*. As a political phenomenon, De Gaulle was equally unoriginal. He illustrated the tendency of Frenchmen to rally round a father figure in a time of crisis and to accept him as their representative as long as he accords them the maximum chauvinistic satisfaction. He was also a reminder that, as in other things, the French are conservative in their myths and like to hear them repeated in a traditional language that refuses all change—even stylistic.

*

Shortly after De Gaulle had returned to power in 1958, that same Revel who analysed the General's style declared that France was now governed by two great stylists, the second being André Malraux, appointed as the official spokesman for France's cultural myths. It was to be noted that other pillars of the Gaullist régime were also men of literary achievements and inclinations. Apart from the prolix pair at the top of the state pyramid, the General's leading private apologist and admirer, François Mauriac, was a world-famous novelist. The licensed, homespun philosopher of the régime who broadcast every day on the state radio was Jean Nocher, a compulsive versifier. The Paris Prefect of Police, Maurice Papon, fancied himself as a philosopher and produced two books, and Georges Pompidou, so long Prime Minister and now President, had been a professor of French literature and compiled an excellent anthology of French poetry. The expression Republic of Letters had never seemed more apt.

De Gaulle and his government were supposed to have given a new political style to France after the muddles and incoherences of the Fourth Republic but when it came to elaborating their ideas of France there was no sign that their combined literary abilities had changed the language in which it was communicated. Like their ideas, their verbal style was conservative and completely traditional.

How hallowed by chauvinistic tradition was De Gaulle's view of France may be seen in the opening passage of his *War Memoirs*: 'I came to believe that France, like the princess in a fairy tale, or the Madonna of the frescoes, had an eminent and exceptional destiny.' Apart from believing that he had been providentially sent to renew his country's institutions and save her from what he termed the 'abysses' so that she might again move towards the 'peaks of the world' (2)—convictions common to most army officers who take over their country's government—he fully shared the orthodox chauvinist's belief that the eyes of the world are always fixed upon France. He explained that 'the world ... wishes, even if she sometimes pretends the contrary, to see us playing a role which suits us since it feels that this will be to the advantage of all mankind since France's power and grandeur, aiding her genius, are directed towards the good and the fraternity of mankind' (3). France was 'on the way towards a great destiny' (4) and had shown that 'she is made to live, to raise herself, and to radiate' (5) because 'we are a single people ... we are the great, the only, the unique French people'.

Similar profundities were echoed by André Malraux, from his first television appearances in June 1958 when, with his intense, brooding face twitching with a prophet's fervour, he solemnly evoked identical ideas of France clothed with historical allusions. His France was the one which had built the great Gothic cathedrals, led the Crusades and fought the enemy at Valmy and Jemappes. France stood at the crossroads of history for her latest appointment with destiny, again ready to continue her great mission in the world. Without her mission France could not be France, for as Malraux explained 'France has been ill from not having a mission ... France is France when she assumes a part of the nobility of the world' (6). France could only be herself when she 'is a part of others' hopes' (7) and was 'in charge of man's destiny' (8). The eyes of the world were expectantly fixed upon this nation which was about to perform those actions which would illustrate her mission. For Malraux, as for De Gaulle and so many previous French patriots, France was Marianne in the fields, sowing abroad the seeds of something that could only be French and which the world must find indispensable for its well-being.

Given such pronouncements, it was clear that when it was a matter of defining France's identity and aims, all the Gaullist régime had to do was to turn once more to that well-worn image of Marianne which had been evoked on so many earlier occasions like a sacred talisman. France's rulers had to hand a traditional philosophy, language and catechism of chauvinism. The way these ideas were expressed we may call Gaullese for the sake of convenience, but it had been used long before the latest spectacular interpreters of the France-idea.

Ever since Napoleon I gave France a taste for a military glory and a cultural diffusion that reflected upon the people as a whole instead of, as formerly, upon the monarchy, Frenchmen have been writing books glorifying their country for the twofold military and cultural point of view. Every second-hand bookshop in France, every library, is cluttered up with books, with such titles as *L'esprit de la France*, *L'âme française*, *La civilisation française* and so on. In each such book the tenor is the same and the style all but identical since it is Gaullese or Chauvinese. Their language is a limited one but after all, one trumpet blast sounds very much like another.

We need only dip at random into the pile of these books to find one which already contains the full Gaullist philosophy. Many were written between the two world wars. After France had lost the flower of her young manhood in those massacres she was convinced were her Victory, there was a mania for publishing all the hoary old clichés which passed for original thought on the nature and destiny of the country.

One of the many writers who preceded De Gaulle in voicing a personal idea of the homeland was Pierre Alix, author of *Les destins de la France*. A glance at its long bibliography of books on France shows that Alix was by no means alone in this literary domain. Nevertheless, his book must have attracted considerable attention when it was published since it also appeared in English (9) and included a glowing preface by the veteran Radical minister Edouard Herriot.

Herriot stated that Alix's study was inspired by that 'humanity' which is the 'pre-eminent virtue of the French spirit' and agreed that 'our nation, the mother of liberty, should be a nation of the elect, capable of safeguarding Western civilisation'. The author's reasons for writing the book were that he felt the need for such a picture of his country at a time when many people thought that France was 'finished' and 'decadent' and because she had been passing through a period of 'intellectual crisis' when it was fashionable to be pessimistic about her future. What Alix was writing was an expression of faith in France and her democratic future since 'France, whatever her government may label itself, has too strongly democratic a temperament to be anything else but a democracy'. Of this he was certain: that 'France, after being on the point of relapsing to the rank of a second-rate nation and becoming a mere deadweight in European politics, is about to resume her proper position'. Lest his readers might fear that he was about to launch into an exaggerated panegyric, he assured them that he would make no attempt to hide French failings which are many and 'quite incorrigible'. What he was going to do was to tell the world the truth about France.

It is thus that we learn that France is on excellent terms with other races and nations, with whom she maintains relations which are not 'merely relations of good neighbourliness, but rather relations of brotherhood'. France is a country which 'abhors extremes', where there is 'mutual toleration' since France is the 'land of liberty', and where 'a sense of moderation, often an exquisite sense, controls our way of living and our way of thinking'. France has respect for human dignity and 'democracy as we conceive it, is closely associated with charity. We shrink from securing our own comfort at the cost of suffering for somebody else ... Liberty is a congenital necessity to the French peoples. They have never taken any other régime to their hearts'. The present Republic of France may not be the best in the world, but as 'dictatorship does not suit the French temperament at all' it is the one most advantageous to France. If there is one thing that can save the French from absolutism it is their intelligence, for 'French intelligence is no empty word. It is their intelligence which irresistibly urges the French people to see in authority only an emanation of themselves'. Later in the book, Alix expounds the idea of France in the purest Gaullese style: 'The "France-idea" is one of the richest in existence, thanks to the manifold expressions it assumed in the course of its creation, thanks to the diverse aspects whose attraction it offers to everybody's eyes at one and the same time. France is an idea just as the diamond might be called the idea of the soil: in other words, the issue of thousands upon thousands of years of almost imperceptible pressure, a pressure almost imperceptibly crushing, almost imperceptibly creative. What a long labour we represent! What myriads of men died to raise the pyramid on which we stand!'

France seen as something organic, an idea incarnated in a form that slowly matures and reaches fruition—all this is true Gaullese. So is the way in which Alix listed various French achievements in the arts and the sciences as proof of the Gallic genius—just as De Gaulle was later proudly to mention France's Concorde aeroplane and her atomic power projects. When Alix came to the idea of France as the missionary of civilization, everything he said was to be repeated in almost exactly the same form by De Gaulle and Malraux: 'civilization at its purest, its most disinterested; civilization seen as the ultimate achievement of Occidental experience—civilization in this sense is French.' Another remark—'France has acted as a filtre for civilization'—is also pure Gaullese with the accent of Malraux as is 'French thought has not lost its primacy . . . Paris confers consecration . . . Anybody who has not received our baptism can scarcely pretend to universality. Even more than at the time of Voltaire, Paris is the capital of thought'. In his final chapter, after a look at the tensions, rivalries, turmoils and racial hatreds in the world, Alix comes to the conclusion that 'it is our *duty* to provide the world with a solution of its problems which will prove its salvation'.

After all this trumpeting of French supremacy and vocation, it seems almost too cruel to add that Alix published his book a year before France fell to the Nazis and that among the writers he lists at the end of the book, two at least—Marcel Déat and Charles Maurras—were to turn from the image of France the Saviour to that of Germany the Redeemer.

While Alix's tone showed that his book was written largely for foreign consumption, another of the 'idea of France' books that proliferated between the wars, Robert Burnand's *Je suis Français!* (Paris, 1927), was plainly intended for a domestic public. With its large format, its tricolour cover and coloured illustrations of Joan of Arc's statue at Rouen, peasants in the fields, a French soldier at the front and other such stirring subjects, it is the sort of book that must have been handed out to French school-children on prize-days.

De Gaulle's and Alix's theme that the history of France is the history of an idea taking form throughout the centuries soon appears. Burnand rapidly hits the right Gaullese note by declaring that the history of France is the 'most beautiful of all histories' and also the one which is the most 'profoundly national, the most *one*'. Next there enters the familiar figure of Marianne the Mother of Liberty, with a sword in her hand:

> No matter what has been said, the Revolution did not create the idea of homeland: by no longer applying it to the king, in whom it had until

then been incarnated, but to the nation, she made it more accessible. Nor is it enough to say that it created liberty since the latter existed already . . . But out of liberty the Revolution made a dogma, and out of her soldiers, missionaries. With these ragged, superb lads, it was as if there had come the light.

Here the peaceful sower in the fields assumes the guise of Rude's warlike Marianne. Military glory is to be celebrated as much as cultural grandeur. The thought of Napoleon's victories sends Burnand into raptures and his proud reflections before the monuments commemorating them were close to those of De Gaulle in the first volume of his *War Memoirs*:

> When, under the evening skies, I see the arch raised to Napoleon's victories . . . I am proud to be French (Burnand).
>
> Nothing in Paris struck me more deeply than the symbols of our glory: night descending on Notre Dame, the majesty of the evening at Versailles, the sunlit Arc de Triomphe . . . (De Gaulle).

Burnand's thoughts on the end of the First World War, which France has called *la Victoire*, are equally Gaullese in their rhetoric and language:

> Never was the face of France more radiant than on that misty autumn morning when she took off her helmet and when at last, as though worn out by too much glory, she was able to bend down and weep over her dead.

But despite her losses, France is still the France of the armed Marianne for as Burnand says 'the French are not military-minded but they are warriors'. The French army is the best in the world because in it 'there reigns that cohesion, that communion of thought, that fraternity, in the noblest sense of the word, that to my mind do not exist in any other army'.

The amazon is in the ascendant in Burnand's mind as he recalls France's historic mission: 'Since France became aware of herself, she has felt that radiating force which is one of the characteristics of her genius . . . After our mourning in 1870, France, wounded but passionate, felt the need to act, to make use of her strength, that warlike ardour that she feels throbbing in her blood . . . that life force . . .'

Rayonnement thus begins with the army but once the fighting is over, France is able to show 'the different populations what French peace is'. France may conquer but she brings liberty and 'this is why, when the tricolour is raised under the skies of Africa or Asia or over the West Indian seas, it is everywhere saluted as the emblem of liberty'. Then comes the accompanying theme of the Mother of Culture: 'I am proud to be French because French culture is the most beautiful'. As Malraux was to repeat when he spoke on behalf of the Gaullist régime, 'French art has always gone beyond our frontiers and radiated over the world' and 'France is the aristocracy of the world' (Malraux: 'France is France when she assumes a part of the nobility of the world'). And as De Gaulle was to reiterate so often, France might have its troubles and lapses but 'the hour always comes when France raises herself, pure and serene, and when the world recognizes her'.

What De Gaulle was to call the 'summits of the world', towards which he was to direct France, Burnand called 'the peaks'. France might not be the largest nor the most powerful nation in the world but 'she is, despite everything, the highest' and, as befits a nation that has reached such eminence, 'the world cannot forget that the call to liberty has always come from France'.

The diffusion of culture and liberty—such was France's traditional conception of her role in the world. The idea of military grandeur might be in eclipse after two catastrophic world wars but the memory lingered on. The idea of a civilizing mission remained and was reinforced after De Gaulle took power. The spread of France's civilization and the maintenance of her lofty position was to be accomplished peacefully for as François Mauriac wrote in the *Figaro* on July 7, 1946, 'it is . . . thanks to the spirit that countries remain dominators . . . France is opening up again and, as she has always been, she remains offered to other peoples; she proposes the means, she defines the aims, she has recovered her vocation'.

But a few years later, the battlefields of Indo-China and North Africa were reminding the world that too often in her history, France's *rayonnement* had been accompanied by the sword, the bomb and the machine-gun. Marianne was still a warrior. Rude's statue still expressed a reality.

2

The Missionary in Arms

LIKE ANCIENT Rome, which inspired the neo-classic movement in her arts and even the forms of her constitution, the First Republic began France's civilizing mission abroad in the simplest and most direct way: by armed force. In the process France became for a long time the most military-minded country in the western world.

Every French schoolchild has learned of the heroic battles fought in defence of the new Republic, of the victories at Valmy and Jemappes when a new type of army, an 'army of the people' came into existence. It was at this time that there arose a new conception of the motherland coinciding with the adoption of a singularly bloodthirsty and dynamic song for a national hymn and the idea that an army was a nation in arms, defending and exporting the national genius, instead of being a force of hired mercenaries. Created at a time of crisis and national emergency, the army was seen as representing the quintessence of the national spirit and as the depository of the people's noblest aspirations. Later, even when many hopes had been disappointed, there remained to the army its conviction that it incarnated all that was best and most virtuous in the nation which had created it. This conviction never died. There are still generals and officers in France who resemble other soldiers in African or Latin American states (not to mention Spain and Greece) by believing that they represent the *real* nation as opposed to that false nation of self-seeking politicians and anti-military opposition parties.

The same ideas appeared as recently as February 13, 1969, in the *Figaro*, in an article called 'Unease in the Army', written by General Beaufré. After discussing the main theme—equipment and men for the French army in an age of the thermonuclear bomb—and lamenting the fact that the army is now without a properly defined purpose in France, General Beaufré wrote:

> But what is hardest for the soldiers, is the feeling that the country is turning away from them ... It is *esteem* that the military need above all.

On the contrary, they see themselves calumniated by young men who have no idea of what the national duty represents ... What is serious is that the country has become alien, on the whole, to the idea that the survival of a people may depend on its ability to defend itself, arms in hand ... We still celebrate the anniversaries of the last war, but the virile tradition is being lost if we do not take care.

Yes, the Army is undergoing a period of unease, but beyond contingent causes, this unease is that of our country, dazed by prosperity, disorientated by propaganda, misled by an easy present even if it is filled with tasks, and willingly forgetful of the recent lessons of History ... the Army is the Conservatory of the instinct of defence of the nation. It suffers from seeing this instinct lose its virtue. Without the moral support and confidence of the country, the Army feels its *raison d'être* disappearing and risks becoming simply a foreign body in the nation ...

The 'virile tradition', the 'national duty', the Army as the 'Conservatory' of the nation's instincts of survival and defence, and the idea of the nation and the army being one—all this is part of the classic national philosophy of the revolutionary years. Underlying General Beaufré's words is the conviction that at certain times, the army is the highest expression of the *patrie* in its purest state. That the army represented the country's mission, was a belief that survived and became even stronger in Indo-China and Algeria as recent French history shows. That, in the final resort, the *real* France was to be found in the army would even appear to have influenced De Gaulle during his sudden disappearance from Paris during the May riots of 1968. Only a month previously he had been heard to say: 'if the eventual elections were not to show themselves to be favourable to the majority, I would never entrust the opposition with the task of forming the government.' (10) When the régime seemed on the point of collapse, we find him conferring with his generals, to make certain of their support if necessary. De Gaulle has never been an ardent admirer of other generals and his pronouncements on the French military mind have been far from flattering in the past. But when assuring himself of the eventual help of generals like Jacques Massu, self-confessed torturer* and rabid *ultra* in Algeria, he was reverting to the tradition that in an emergency the Army could represent the real nation. As we have said, he had often made it plain

* Joseph Alsop in the *New York Herald Tribune*, June 12, 1958, reported that the definitive decision to use torture in the French army depended at a certain moment on General Massu who gave his consent after 'submitting' himself to various 'treatments' and recommending his officers to do the same so that they could not be reproached for inflicting upon others that which they could not bear themselves!

that he regarded himself as a kind of incarnation of France. On this occasion the France that he was incarnating was the Army as the guarantor and defender of the legitimate power. The Republic had become the Amazon again and the President was once more the General.

As in the past, every time that the civilian nation of France has seemed 'decadent', a man of the Army has stepped forward as the incorruptible representative of a legitimate as opposed to a false France. It happened with Napoleon Bonaparte, Napoleon III, General Boulanger and even with the ardent right-wing extremist Colonel de la Rocque* in the 1930's. On each occasion, a large section of the French people was ready and willing to regard such a man as the symbol and protector of the France they believed in. After all, had not the Army *made* France during the First Republic?

The idea of France as a bellicose divinity has certainly undergone a battering since the end of the First World War. Militarism, thank heavens, is now mostly confined to the military and the more rabid (and unfortunately numerous) ex-servicemen's associations in France. But even if militarism lost its appeal in the last fifty years, it is worth noting that for a whole century it was one of the most powerful forces at work in the nation and its influence upon a widely held idea of France among the people was immense. We have only to look at a French school history book to read how the French people 'hungered for glory' during the 'dull reigns' of Charles X and Louis-Philippe, how they enthusiastically applauded Napoleon III's martial ventures in Mexico, Italy, the Crimea, and how, after 1870, large sections of the population and their leaders were clamouring for the 'war of revenge' to recapture the 'captive provinces' of Alsace-Lorraine. Even today, the rulers of France can find no better way of celebrating July 14 (the anniversary of a Revolution in the name of 'Liberty'!) than by holding a gigantic military parade in Paris.

A quick survey of militarism in France between the First Empire and 1914 is enough to show that Prussian militarism was nothing but a pale shadow compared to the French product—especially in the late years of the nineteenth century. It was as if a great part of the French people was incapable of visualizing France as anything other than an armed warrior, spoiling for a fight—almost any fight with almost any enemy who happened to be handy.

* Founder of the extremist right-wing nationalist organization, *La Croix de Feu*.

The glamour of militarism was encouraged under Napoleon, and the myth of *la France rayonnante* was reinforced by the Revolutionary wars. The French who so enthusiastically followed Napoleon on his campaigns were encouraged to see themselves as armed missionaries called upon to bring happiness to their neighbours by making them acquainted with the principles of the Revolution, just as a Maoist today cannot but believe that bringing revolution to the peoples unfortunate enough to live in a 'capitalist' country is the highest good that he can confer upon them. How widely convinced the French people were of the importance of their mission it is impossible to say. What we do know is that the idea of wars and military victories for their own sake very soon became an attractive one in France. The Bonapartist myth that grew to such proportions after Waterloo was essentially militaristic. When seven and a half million Frenchmen voted during the plebiscite of December 1851 to ratify the future Napoleon III's *coup d'état* (the opposition only polled some 650,000 votes), they were voting, among other things, for a memory of past military glories and a hope of more to come. In 1870, a mere telegram relating what was presumed to be an insult was enough to rouse France into a warlike fury after she had long been feasting her eyes on all the panoply and splendour of the Emperor's uniforms and regiments. Enough eye-witnesses have left accounts of how crowds surged through Paris crying warlike slogans. They were often not surprised since 'it is in the nature of the French to prick up their ears at the sound of a drum and to quiver with joy at the blast of a bugle'. (11)

When, during the insurrection of the Paris Commune in 1871, the Communards wished to symbolize their detestation of the past régime, the greatest symbol they could find to destroy was the Vendôme column, celebrating the first Napoleon's military exploits. After the army had showed them in no uncertain manner who was the 'real' France by shooting some 20,000 Parisians, militarism and a longing for the next war of revenge was a passion felt just as strongly by violent anti-Republicans, Bonapartists and monarchists as by staunch Republicans.

The years between 1875 and 1914 were the golden age of French militarism: everything that had come before was nothing compared to the relentless wave of bloodthirsty flag-waving, uniform-adulating chauvinism that relentlessly rolled over Third-Republic France. France was deluged by warlike prints and lithographs, bellicose books and newspapers, countless reproductions of war paintings by famous artists and war-glorifying books for small boys. The popularity of General Boulanger, who came so close to overthrowing the Republican régime, was enormous all over France even if ephemeral for reasons that have nothing to do with any sudden revulsion from bellicosity.

The young were often indoctrinated with martial ideas—at school and by such writers as the army captain Driant, Boulanger's son-in-law who wrote best-selling, enormously lengthy war sagas with such titles as *The War of Tomorrow* with lurid jackets and bold letters on the front announcing that the work had been 'crowned by the French Academy'. Driant's works (written under the pseudonym 'Captain Danrit') were constantly reprinted and praised to the skies by elderly schoolmasters and writers who should have known better, like the poet François Coppée. One of Danrit's books was dedicated to the Academician Jules Clarétie, himself the author of a book called *The Flag*. Here is part of the preface which this man of letters enthusiastically wrote for Danrit's *War of Tomorrow*:

> My fingers tremble with emotion as they write to you, but your sword will not tremble in your hand... No human condition, in our present society, so divided, so turbulent, seems to me to be superior or even equal to that of the soldier. To spill one's ink is to give of one's labours but to spill and give one's blood—what is more noble and more proud? And resolved, disciplined as they are, only thinking of the country, how many are ready to offer their existence to the homeland!

This was written some twenty-five years before the First World War. At the same time, academic painters were churning out vast compositions featuring every incident of the war of 1870 from the (futile) charge of the French hussars at Reichshoffen against the German rifles to the defence of some obscure farmhouse in a minor skirmish. When they ran out of Franco-Prussian-war subjects to paint, they returned, like Meissonier, to the battles of Napoleon I. Some eye-witnesses of this intoxication with the idea of war that seemed to be contaminating the whole French nation have left a graphic picture of France at the time:

> At the café-concert, in between couplets about mothers-in-law and couplets about cuckolds, some buffoon will bellow verses about the war of revenge to thunderous applause... Prize-givings resound with patriotic speeches addressed to young pupils by official personalities who never wore a uniform but know how to get their sons or nephews out of

military service. In picture galleries, these last twenty-five years, more German corpses have strewn the battlefields and more German prisoners have trailed across paintings than all the men Germany ever put into the front line during the war.(12)

To nourish this war mania, a pathetic image of the captured provinces of Alsace-Lorraine was kept in the public mind by a deafening propaganda barrage, led by the ferocious Deroulède* who never failed to plague the Republican government with his insane calls to arms and his ludicrous attempt to persuade a general, Roget, to seize power in 1899. When Rémy de Gourmont wrote an exasperated article in the *Mercure de France* in 1891, attacking this sabre-rattling conception of patriotism and demanding an end to this stale 'joke of two little enslaved sisters, kneeling in mourning robes at the foot of a frontier post and weeping like heifers instead of going to milk their cows', he was promptly dismissed from his post at the Bibliothèque Nationale as a result of the fury he aroused in the 'patriotic' press. He was yet another victim of a France for whom the idea of homeland revolved around a never-ending procession of uniforms, flags and fixed bayonets—an idea that was almost exclusively taken over by the powerful Right after the Boulanger and Dreyfus affairs.

Right-wing monopoly or not, the truth was that at least half France—a very conservative estimate—was passionately in love with its army and the idea of military glory. Patriotism was to be measured by the degree of a person's militarism. *Patrie* and army were one and the same thing and military activity abroad coincided with the idea of cultural diffusion. The schoolmaster or doctor who went overseas to one of France's half-conquered colonies was never so much applauded as was the soldier in uniform. During the colonial wars of the nineteenth century, those in power responsible for them might speak of France's civilizing mission, but the fact that there was glory to be won on the battlefields of a foreign nation in the process of being conquered was a prospect with popular appeal.

After the war-weariness and disillusionment that came with the 1914–18 War, the French people at home turned in their great majority away from the warlike image of their country but their governments still waged wars in the colonies. The peoples who were supposed to receive the benefits of *rayonnement*, in Africa and the Far East, could be forgiven if their main idea of France was that

---

* Founder of the ultra-chauvinistic *Ligue des Patriotes*.

of a nation in arms which had descended upon them to conquer, to
kill and to repress while expecting them to be grateful for elements
of a foreign culture which stronger countries were free to choose
without looking down the muzzle of a gun.

*

No country's colonial history is edifying. France's is simply more
tragic than most others'. Culture apart, French *rayonnement*
throughout the world has had a smell of gunpowder and high
explosive from the 1830's until the 1960's.

The last colonial drama in Algeria which caused so much death
and suffering and which came so close to poisoning France's life and
institutions between 1954 and 1962 was being enacted in much the
same way over a hundred years previously. The tortures that Frenchmen were practising in Algeria in the 1950's were already being
practised in Indo-China in the 1930's in similar circumstances. The
divorce between, on the one hand, an army resentful of its lack of
support and appreciation by the civilian population and, on the
other, a civilian nation almost totally ignorant of what its armies
were doing overseas, dates back to the first campaigns in Algeria,
the Indo-Chinese expeditions of the 1870's and '80's, and the
African and Madagascar campaigns of the 1890's. The quaint idea,
so often expressed in France, that France was, on the whole, a
generous and beneficent colonizing power bringing such elements of
French culture as schools, Molière performances, Sorbonne scholarships, fine roads and hospitals after a sharp but brief period of
military campaigns, followed by a long peace and prosperity only
rarely interrupted by a few misguided local rebellions put down by
glamorous foreign Legionaries led by dashing officers, scarcely bears
examination. But it is closely tied to that myth of French *rayonnement* which was so essential to the representatives of a people who,
as the German Marshal Von Moltke remarked, are always ready to
accept words as facts.

That similarity between De Gaulle's and Malraux's utterances
and those of French writers between the two World Wars with
regard to France's vocation in general is again to be found in
references to France's colonial mission and its history. For the
natives of France's empire, *rayonnement* was the advent of culture,
material and spiritual, and lessons in Liberty—such was the theme.
It was often linked with that idea of *patrie* which was accompanied

by the image of a glory-hungry army. As late as 1950, in a little history of Indo-China published in a series selling hundreds of copies to students, a historian describing the first conquest of Indo-China was able to write such phrases as 'thanks to Admiral de la Grandière, France's *rayonnement* in Indo-China went beyond the limits of Cochin-China'. (13) A highly respectable professor at the Sorbonne, writing a volume in a highly respectable series of histories of 'French colonies and the expansion of France throughout the world' (14), gave the following rosy description of the memories left in the Algerian native mind by the conquering campaigns of Generals Bugeaud and Lamoricière in the nineteenth century:

> What is generally ignored in France and what must be known is that the memories of the battles that these populations waged against us count among those that the natives most willingly evoke even today . . . They are proud of having fought heroically against us at first, and then of later having fought by our side in the colonial or European wars. The names of Bugeaud, De Lamoricière, etc., have remained as dear to them as to ourselves. It was thus that our ancestors the Gauls honoured the memory of Julius Caesar.

As we might expect the book is liberally strewn with the usual key-words and clichés: 'the work of France', 'her civilizing mission' and, words that were more true than he realized of a certain France, a 'France which re-discovered its own image in Algeria'.

De Gaulle won a reputation as a great decolonizer after 1958 but it is too frequently forgotten that when he first came to power he was no less ardent a champion of France Overseas than his literary precursors in the language of *rayonnement*. Did he not say 'we must remain in Indo-China' (15), 'France is here for ever' (16), and speak of France 'pursuing her great work in Algeria' (17)?

For Malraux too, when France was the colonizer there was no need to speak of any struggle for liberty in her territories since 'France's colonization has always been that of justice and truth' (18). No clearer, more classical, or more traditional exposition of the theme of beneficent colonization, even if tempered by one or two qualifications, is to be found than in De Gaulle's speech at his press conference on January 31, 1964, when he referred to the 'third world' and the role played by France in the 'vast evolution' of that world:

> This is also due, above all, to the nature of her genius which has made of her, at all times, a leaven and a champion of human liberation. Despite

interruptions in our action in this domain, we have always returned to our general line. Even apart from the many interventions and encouragements which we have lavished for centuries in order to help the enfranchisement of so many peoples or oppressed men, and apart from the spiritual and cultural influences which have radiated out from us in the same direction throughout all regions of the universe, the sign of what we gave to others to raise their condition, wherever we were to be found, is imprinted in striking fashion in many souls and on many soils. To be sure, at a time when colonization was the only path permitting us to penetrate to people withdrawn in their slumber, we were colonizers, and sometimes imperious and rough ones.

'Imperious and rough' was an understatement.

*

It was when, as so many French school histories tell us, the French people were dissatisfied with the placid rule of Louis-Philippe and hungering for glory, that France began her conquest of Algeria. The same school textbooks will tell us that the immediate pretext for this war was the insult proffered by the Bey of Algiers in 1827 when he struck with a fan at the face of the French ambassador who had come to his court to complain about the Moorish pirates operating from his port. A few years later, a large French expeditionary force was engaged in waging a bitter war throughout northern Algeria.

Thiers, when Prime Minister under Louis-Philippe, soon showed himself to be favourable to the idea of a vastly increased French military involvement in that unhappy country. He was not thinking in terms so much of economic benefits to France but rather of an enterprise which could 'save France from her base materialism'. To French parliamentarians and objectors who told him that such a war would ruin France in peacetime and weaken her should she become involved in another European war, his reply was clear and succinct. France needed something to do: she needed a war abroad. To his opposition he said:

> You are fortunate indeed to have something which touches, which stirs, which moves. Is it our ill-tempered debates, is it our representative government in its present poor state, which will lift up souls from the trifling passions which possess them, from this scepticism which gnaws away at them? No, what we are doing in Paris, what we cry in our Chambers does nothing to the country, but when the country learns that we have been fighting at Mazagran and that we have vanquished at Misserghin, children are moved and women weep. Is sixty million francs too much to maintain what remains of moral sentiments and

disinterested passions, to prevent France from squatting down over her foot-warmers? (19)

From the start, the war was represented from above as good, just and eminently moral. Even the opposition, Republicans and Bonapartists hostile to Louis-Philippe, urged the king to conquer all Algeria for France and satisfy their craving for fresh military glory. But to undertake the task of conquest properly the right man had to be found. The war was too static. French commanders were on the defensive. The general in charge of the Algerian expedition, Valée, was practising a policy of limited occupation with fixed garrisons and outposts, and of understanding and good-neighbourliness. It was not enough and in Abd-el-Kader, Algeria had thrown up a brilliant and dangerous enemy leader.

The right man was found: Thomas Robert Bugeaud, Marquis de la Piconnerie, Duc d'Isly and later Marshal of France. He was to become a school history-book hero and the most popular general in France between 1815 and the political appearance of General Boulanger.

From the beginning of his command in Algeria, the war closely foreshadowed the one fought 110 years later. Almost every detail was the same: the same propaganda in favour of the war and the same hostility for the civilians who protested against it; the same military resentment against a civil population in France, the same scorched-earth policies in the field. Everything was there that was to be found in 1954-62, and the mind of Bugeaud himself was the mind of such generals as Salan and Massu.

What sort of man Bugeaud was may be seen from his own utterances and from his lengthy correspondence with Thiers. His contempt for the French working class and for civilians generally was tremendous. He had led the military repression of the Paris insurrection of 1834, celebrated by Daumier's famous lithograph of the *massacre dans la Rue Transnonain*. When ordered to move into the city and put down the rising he had proclaimed to his soldiers:

> We must kill everyone. Friends, be pitiless. We must make giblets out of 3,000 factious men.

Fifteen years later, his opinion of the Paris populace was no kinder:

> The miseries reported in the cities, especially in the largest, are principally due to the irregular, immoral life of the workers. What brutish, ferocious beasts! How can God permit mothers to make such beings! Ah, there is the real enemy and not the Russians and the Austrians!

Bugeaud's opinion of writers, journalists and intellectuals was equally unflattering. The very mention of a journalist or writer was enough to make him foam with rage. Writing to Thiers in 1836 (20) he had declared that writers and their kind did nothing but stay in Paris to organize riots and assassinations instead of fighting Arabs. All they were doing was to defame the generals conducting the war. Oh, if only they could be sent to him—he would soon see to it that they all were killed in Africa! War and the army were all that really counted. He longed for a great European war as a heroic remedy which could save the social order and the dynasty. Later, when he had enough of the dynasty he wrote that the only way to save France was to make the President at the time (Louis Bonaparte in 1849) a dictator. But even better, why not make the whole of France into an army? If only, he cried, 'we could apply that admirable military discipline to the whole of French society!' As for writers who prated about liberty, they could be pushed willy-nilly into the ranks for 'there is more real liberty in our 14,000 *gendarmes* than in all the writers and advocates of liberty' and there could be no greater instrument for 'social education' and for 'purging disturbing elements' than his beloved army.

Led by such a firebrand, the war soon gave rise to a right-wing offensive on the 'bad French', those 'Bedouins of Paris' as they were contemptuously called for not being in favour of the conquest. But happily, Bugeaud had little time to deal with the 'enemy' in France: he was too busy subjugating Algeria by the ruthless means which he had learned as a young officer in the Napoleonic campaigns in Spain (he was born in 1784). He was well qualified to deal with guerrillas and had learned that the best way to do so was to move from the defensive to the offensive. This he did immediately after taking up his command. With his advent the war became one of 'frightfulness': even the more chauvinistic French history books have depicted him at the head of his columns, destroying everything in their path that might nourish an enemy, moving inexorably across the Algerian landscape, grim and silent on his charger, against a background of flaming crops and villages, charred corpses and suspected guerrillas shot out of hand. The list of atrocities lengthened as in all colonial wars in which the barbarian methods of the resisting natives and the reprisals of the so-called 'civilizer' culminate in a gigantic catalogue of horrors.

The scorched-earth policy as a system for the mass destruction of native crops, including the uprooting of acre after acre of fig trees, upon which the natives depended for their livelihood, began in 1841. The government in France had to sanction Bugeaud's methods but, as in the 1950's, it did not dare to proclaim them to the rest of the world and took care that certain passages in reports of operations were suppressed before they could be communicated to a wider public. Some of the atrocities were too great to be concealed. There was an immense sensation in France in 1845 when it was learned that some 600 tribesmen had taken refuge in the caves of Nekmaria in northern Algeria and had been burnt and suffocated to death slowly by a Colonel Pélissier. Naturally Bugeaud defended his subordinate. The opposition might cry 'enough!' in France but there was nothing they could do about it. The army continued its mission as before. For many officers, to take part any longer in such a war became an affair of conscience. Some wrote home saying that they were sickened by what they had seen and done. Doubts became more frequent. There were reports of thousands of unarmed Arabs being shot and beheaded, of French officers paying ten francs for each pair of human ears cut off. A Colonel Smidt of the 53rd regiment of the line wrote from the captured town of Medeah on May 18, 1841:

> The Duke of Nemours has visited my capital. It is fortunate that France is ignorant of how we have treated this poor town which is no more than a heap of ruins... (21)

The great poet Lamartine declared that the Algerian conquest was 'an atrocious, impious war'.

As Bugeaud advanced towards the mountains of Kabylia he complained ever more bitterly about attacks made on him by the parliamentary opposition and of the weakness of the government. Not for the only time in French history, there was a beginning of an army revolt in Algeria against the 'spineless' governments in the homeland who would not let them get on with their task. And not for the only time did French objectors like the Abbé de Pradt write that the generals in North Africa 'had wanted the war in Algeria in order to turn with all the more strength against the liberties of France'.

After de Tocqueville had visited Algeria, he wrote in his *Notes sur l'Algérie* of the hostility he had noticed between the French military and civilians. Many army officers had become possessed by an intense hatred of the civilian settlers who were coming over to obtain land and wealth, ignorant of the fact that it was the army that had made it all possible, and which, as Bugeaud wrote to Thiers in 1846, had 'created everything in Algeria'. Meanwhile, the settler population was growing. After the revolution of June 1848, the Paris government had thought it advisable to encourage the more unruly elements among the proletarian population to emigrate across the Mediterranean. Credits were voted to establish thousands of colonists. Those who went from Paris were solemnly harangued and blessed by the Archbishop.

Many economists and politicians thought that Algeria could help to solve the unemployment problem. What the attitude towards the conquered population was to be was made clear enough by theoreticians of colonization like Raousset Boulbon who stated that 'to deliver Algeria up to civilization France must for the public good appropriate the totality of the soil owned by the natives'. (22) Furniture-makers and weavers from the Faubourg Saint-Antoine who had fought on the barricades and roared revolutionary slogans in 1848 suddenly found themselves acquiring a pleasing taste for land and profits to be made with cheap native labour in a foreign, conquered country.

With the work of conquest and 'pacification' virtually ended, the generals felt free to turn to politics. General Saint-Arnaud, who had campaigned in Algeria under Bugeaud and who succeeded him after his death in 1849, became Louis-Napoleon's Minister of War and helped him to become Napoleon III by participating in the anti-Republican *coup d'état* of December 2, 1851. He was later made Marshal of France for his pains.

The work of *rayonnement* continued with French generals in command. In 1871, there was another rising against the French. Colonists were massacred at Palestro by Kabyle tribesmen and the same dreary history of repression, village-burning, destruction of crops and mass shootings began again. When the rising was quelled, an enormous indemnity was exacted from the rebellious tribes who lost nearly 450,000 hectares of their land as well as a quantity of gold and several 'privileges'. To command a punitive expedition, the Paris government sent General Galliffet, a man notorious for having had Parisians shot in thousands during the 'bloody week' that had brought the Commune to an end. As ardent an enemy of 'civilians' as Bugeaud had ever been, he was no less zealous in carrying out his task which involved shooting practically everything that moved in the path of his forces. He also was generously rewarded for his services, becoming military governor of Paris in 1880, Minister of War in 1899, a lion of Paris society and a good friend of the Prince of Wales.

An admiral, de Gueydon, was appointed governor of Algeria in the same year. He lost no time in making his colonial philosophy known:

> The French element must be the dominant element; it is to it alone that the direction of the country's administration belongs. Neither the native, the Arab nor the Israelite element, nor even the foreign (*European*) element can claim to any influence or any part in the political or administrative management of the country. (23)

Such were the beginnings of French Algeria. For a time, while Algeria slumbered—the sleep of the vanquished—roads and hospitals were built and fortunes were made. The country provided an exotic background for Foreign Legion stories and her products were proudly and lavishly displayed in various international exhibitions. But by 1945, when the propaganda of a newly liberated France was celebrating the 'victory of free peoples' over the forces of tyranny, a combination of economic distress among the native population, hunger, Arab xenophobia and frustrated nationalistic hopes that had been raised by the Allies' victories resulted in the Setif rising in the province of Constantine. There were the usual atrocities on the native side, the usual blasting of entire villages to smithereens by French warships and planes, and the usual brutalities committed by the Legionaries and French colonial troops from Senegal (who had an appalling reputation for ferocity) as they moved into the region. Nine years later, it all started again, more savagely than ever before. Today the results of France's 130 years of 'mission' in Algeria may be seen in the *bidonvilles*, in the mean streets of Belleville and Paris's northern suburbs, in the dejected faces of France's Algerian workers, scorned or ignored by the population, reviled by the Right-wing press. It is not a story of which France can be proud.

*

After Algeria came Indo-China, Senegal, Madagascar and Morocco. The French army continued to distinguish itself by shooting the native population, by imprisoning and exiling their leaders and by destroying towns and harvests, while politicians and chauvinists at home preached the war of 'revenge' against Germany. Well might the writer Urbain Gohier (echoed by so many other writers of his time like Mirbeau, Jaurès and Darien) cry out that

> murder and rape, arson and pillage are the first benefits of conquest on all the exotic lands where France 'faithful to her mission in the world, carries the torch of civilization'.

Was this too partisan a view? There are enough records left to show how France acquired her empire. The fearful massacres committed in Senegal by native troops under French command have been described by eye-witnesses. Generals like Galliéni, the hero of the battle of the Marne, were well known for their harshness and their ruthless shooting of suspected rebels, were they in North Africa, Central and West Africa or Madagascar where, in 1894, over 7,000 French soldiers died during a campaign. Even more were sent to their deaths in the Tonking delta while the Prime Minister Jules Ferry exhorted Parliament to vote him more credits for the Indo-Chinese expedition for the 'grandeur of the country and the honour of the flag'.

In 1898, the Marchand mission's setback at Fashoda nearly precipitated a war with England. A year later such a ferocious propaganda campaign was being waged against England for her 'atrocities' in the Boer War that the British ambassador in Paris was recalled for several weeks by Queen Victoria. The French press and caricaturists made much of concentration camps in the veld, the use of dum-dum bullets and shooting of hostages while the embattled Boer nation was presented as a kind of Dutch version of Marianne standing over her children and gallantly fighting a bloodthirsty horde of Tommies encouraged by hypocritical missionaries and a joyful John Bull gloating over his gold heaps. Seven years later, the massacre of a few foreign workmen in the Moroccan port of Casablanca led to the landing of French soldiers after a ferocious bombardment and the beginning of the country's conquest.

The horrors of the Moroccan conquest were described graphically by the Socialist leader Jean Jaurès and even by the conservative press. The very bourgeois newspaper *Le Matin* gives some idea of how the native quarters of Casablanca were treated after the attack of August 1907:

> Casablanca . . . is a vast cemetery . . . The Arab town is no more than a heap of smoking ruins. Everywhere you come across the corpses of Moroccans swollen by decomposition . . . The Legionaries have taken

possession of the town while singing the *Marseillaise*, geraniums and laurel leaves at the tip of their rifles ... (24)

Later, even that unusually intelligent general Lyautey—another hero of the school-books—forbade journalists to accompany his units, and in France the campaigns led to another explosion of chauvinistic pride.

Even worse was to come as the twentieth century progressed. Of the so-called 'civilized' Western nations, it is France, after Germany, which has earned the melancholy reputation of a conquering power that has allowed torture to be used systematically in her territories. The paratroops and officials of the *Sûreté* in Algeria after World War II were certainly not the first Frenchmen to have committed acts of torture against political detainees and 'suspects'. In 1935 a French journalist of impeccable professional reputation published a book on Indo-China which caused a sensation in France (25). Her findings were never officially contested and never disproved.

Andrée Viollis, the author, was correspondent for the *Petit Parisien*. In the autumn of 1932 she went to Indo-China accompanying Paul Reynaud, later Prime Minister and then Minister for the Colonies, on an official 'study mission'. What she found makes terrifying reading. She managed to visit prisons, to talk with detainees, Indo-Chinese students, police and military officials. What she could not see for herself she checked. She gave references to accounts published by the French press in Indo-China—a press which was hardly likely to be over-partisan on the side of France's 'enemies'. In other words, her account is authoritative.

Conditions in local prisons were revolting. Everywhere, she was given accounts of tortures practised. The French *Sûreté* in the town of Cholon was one of the most notorious. At the Binh-Donj police station in that town, prisoners were interrogated with the use of electrodes attached to the most sensitive parts of their body (as in Algeria later), beaten, half-suffocated, half-strangled, half-drowned. Students who had been to Paris told her how their books were examined and their luggage searched after their return from the 'mother of generous ideas'. It is hard to see how they could have been exaggerating when a colony like Cambodia had an article dating from 1924 in its penal code which laid down a scale of penalties ranging from three months' to three years' imprisonment and a fine of ten to a hundred piastres for 'any injurious criticism of the actions of the French or Cambodian administrations'.

With Reynaud, she visited the scenes of famine. The sight of starving peasants, kept back by police, pleading for their rice rations deeply shocked Paul Reynaud who spoke of the horror he felt when he was back in France some months later. The local administration was corrupt and any attempt at resistance or exasperated rebellion was soon crushed by the Foreign Legion who, on several documented occasions, had bombed and machine-gunned unarmed demonstrators. Legion outposts in the wilds were virtually independent from all government control: tortures, humiliations and massacres could take place with impunity. The French public at home would never know. Now, however, we are aware that there had been massacres of civilians at Son Tinh in December 1930, and of the total devastation of villages like Thanh-Dan, Yen-Tho and Yen-Phu in the province of Vinh in September 1930.

How the French Foreign Legion behaved in Indo-China during the 1930's came out in the famous trial of the 'Hanoi Legionaries' which is referred to by Andrée Viollis and reported *in extenso* in the press (*Tonkin presse*, the *Ami du Peuple indochinois*, June 12, 14, 1933). Five Legionaries were accused of murdering natives on various occasions, after they had been taken into custody, but more than these murders was mentioned during the trial. Witnesses and the accused spoke of French officers cutting off the heads of dead victims. One of the accused, a Legionary named Layon, admitted that operations against 'rebels' in North Annam were 'war' and not 'police operations' and that the Legion did not take prisoners. He had fought previously for nine years in Morocco. There, too, the Legion did not take prisoners. As for the *Sûreté* in Indo-China, Layon said that it 'knew how to make prisoners speak by every means, even with the aid of electric current'. Another accused stated that they had received vague orders to hunt out and summarily execute the four 'most guilty' rebels in each village they visited. Giving evidence, a French army captain, Joseph Doucin, spoke of overflowing prisons:

> The prisons were overflowing and arrests were always being made; on October 8, 1930, we had precise instructions. We were obliged to carry out repression. These people were communists and with regard to communists—we haven't killed enough of them.
> *The President of the Court:* There were evidently many that were innocent.
> *Captain Joseph Doucin:* Above all, innocent.

Three of the Legionaries were acquitted. A month previously, a monster trial of 120 political suspects, 'communists' and 'rebels', was held at Saigon. Six of the accused were condemned to death, nineteen to life imprisonment as convicts, seventy-nine to terms of imprisonment of between five and twenty-six years. One of the accused was said to have died under torture—a point taken up by the *Presse Indochinoise* of May 13 and 14, 1933. The same newspaper also mentioned the curious discrepancies between sentences imposed for 'offences' that were substantially similar. This was the background to Ho Chi Minh's career of rebellion. As for General Giap who has been giving Americans and South Vietnamese so much trouble these last few years, how many know that his wife and small child were imprisoned in 1939 by the French authorities and died in prison in 1943? His revenge certainly came at Dien Bien Phu but even he could not stop the French press and radio from launching a tremendous barrage of praise of the heroism of a 'French' garrison which had maintained the honour of the Army by fighting so nobly until the bitter end—a garrison of which a third were German (many ex-Wehrmacht), and which included many Vietnamese and African colonial troops.

*

Two years after the Setif rising in Algeria and its repression, even more terrible massacres occurred in Madagascar. In many ways this was the ghastliest episode in all French colonial history. The number of victims that was estimated, and mentioned in Parliament, was horrifying: 80,000. But perhaps even worse was the travesty of French justice on the island and the obscurity—the terrible, troubling obscurity—which still shrouds so much of the whole affair.

It is still difficult to find out very much about what exactly happened as the result of a rising and massacre of French settlers and officials in Madagascar in March 1947. Newspaper accounts in the French press are sketchy, biased and undoubtedly censored. Even in so authoritative a newspaper as *Le Monde*, the reports dealt mostly with military operations. After a few weeks, French military spokesmen are quoted as saying that the anti-French rising had been definitely crushed and that calm had been restored. A few months later, new operations are mentioned. Not until September 1948, in the course of a parliamentary debate, did the truth begin to emerge. A few books were published. A scandalous trial continued to draw attention in the press and in parliament and that was all. In books in English about Madagascar or Africa in general the rising is dismissed in a few lines. In France at the time, French public opinion was unmoved. In the first place, it was almost totally uninformed. And then Madagascar was so far away and the war had only ended in Europe two years before . . .

The story begins on March 29, 1947. During the night a series of local risings broke out in various parts of the island, a French colony which had been handed back to the Free French forces by the English in 1942. The end of the war had seen a rapid increase in the growth of a native, Malagasy movement known as the *Mouvement Démocratique de Renovation Malgache*, which had been founded in 1946 by the Malagasy deputies in Paris. The *M.D.R.M.* was campaigning for a programme based upon Malagasy independence within the French Union—a programme encouraged by the Constitution of the Fourth Republic. Madagascar had members of parliament to represent the island in the French National Assembly. Some were strongly in favour of independence-with-association with France. Others favoured the existing status. But nothing in 1947 pointed to an armed rebellion against France. It was completely unexpected.

A number of French settlers and officials were massacred by armed bands who came out of the great forests of the island. Revolting atrocities were committed by the rebels in several cases and the insurrection was most developed in the region between the high inland plateaux and the east coast where the natives were known to be working in plantations and in the forests under particularly poor conditions. The immediate reason for the risings was hard to determine. Some secret societies active at the time and a few of the more headstrong, irresponsible elements in the *M.R.D.M.* had probably concerted plans for the attacks. If they were trying to invite a fierce repression in order to give more impetus to the movement for independence, they succeeded beyond all expectations. Witnesses, many French, later testified that the counter-measures had been incredibly ferocious.

Villages were destroyed, populations gunned down and bombed, suspects were rounded up in their hundreds and sometimes shot without semblance of a trial. Foreign Legionaries and Senegalese troops showed little or no mercy. The scale of the massacres must have been enormous. Despite a few feeble government attempts in Paris to convince critics that many of the alleged 80,000 killed were victims of the rebels, the number was never officially denied. Some of the dead must have perished from the famine and outbreaks of plague which accompanied the worst reprisals, but the vast majority seem to have died as a result of military operations.

All this was bad enough but what happened in the sphere of 'French justice' was even worse. In the history of the judicial repression, arbitrary imprisonment, irregular conditions of detention and the frequent, systematic use of torture are all prominent.

On March 30, 1947, a judicial investigation opened at Tananarive, the capital of Madagascar. Instead of searching out the murderers of the French settlers and officials, the investigatory commission began by assuming the complicity and guilt of the *M.D.R.M.* and the Malagasy members of parliament. Without the slightest proof, the Governor, General de Coppet, broadcast on the (government-controlled) radio that the *M.D.R.M.* was responsible for what had happened. The Director of the *Sûreté* at Tananarive, M. Baron, was given full backing by the Governor who could also feel sure of support from Paris—all the more so as the Minister for France Overseas had sent him a telegram the previous September, ordering the administration on the island to fight the *M.D.R.M.* by every means.

On 31 March, two of the Malagasy members of parliament, MM. Ravoahangy and Rabemananjara, came to see the Governor and requested permission to broadcast. This request was refused. A few days later, many members and officials of the *M.D.R.M.* were arrested and imprisoned. After they were charged, the examining magistrate sent them to the *Sûreté* for questioning—a practice illegal in France but allowed in Madagascar. Extorted 'confessions' were used to implicate both the *M.D.R.M.* and the Malagasy members of parliament. Despite the latter's parliamentary privilege they were arrested. Three months later, faced by a *fait accompli*, the French Parliament voted to lift their immunity from arrest, after an uneasy debate. The fact that two days before the rising they had sent a telegram to local sections of the *M.D.R.M.*, warning them to 'avoid manoeuvres and provocations of any nature likely to provoke disturbances among the Malagasy population and sabotage the peaceful policy of the *M.D.R.M.*, was taken as evidence of their complicity in the risings. Three days before the trial opened at Tananarive on July 22, 1948, the main witness for the prosecution,

Rakotondrabe, an extremist well-known for the violence of his views and suspected of having been one of the real instigators of the risings, together with the leaders of secret societies outside the *M.D.R.M.*, was shot before he could be confronted in Court with the accused—on the orders of the French High Commisioner and despite official instructions to the country from the President of the French Republic.

During the trial, constant mention was made of what had been well known to all involved in the affair over a year previously: Baron had behaved outrageously towards the prisoners and had personally inflicted tortures on them. The Vice-President of the Provincial Assembly of Tananarive, Stanislas Rakotonirina, later mayor of the city, gave a long account of the brutalities and humiliations he had suffered at Baron's hands. He had been humiliated, whipped, punched, kicked and half drowned by having his head thrust into a bucket of water again and again until he was unconscious. Other similar statements followed.

Witness after witness for the prosecution retracted their earlier statements, alleging that these had been forced out of them by the same methods. All spoke of tortures inflicted by Baron and his subordinates. Some of those questioned were in such a state after leaving the *Sûreté* premises that they had to be taken to hospital at once. Tortures had been witnessed by a French delegate of the National Commission for Scientific Research (*C.N.R.S.*) who had been working in an adjoining building.

The presiding judge was so impressed by these accounts that he ordered an army doctor to examine the accused. The report was damning: sixteen months after the 'interrogations' the accused still bore signs of savage beatings, whip lashes and burns. Baron appeared before the Court (in the meantime he had been relieved of his post) and denied everything. The Prosecutor General simply dismissed all the allegations, stating that the detainees might have been 'somewhat jostled'.

On October 4, 1948, the criminal court of Tananarive gave its verdict: ten death sentences, including two for the parliamentary members Ravoahangy and Raseta, and three sentences of forced labour for life. The deputies had been acquitted of the charge of murder but had been found guilty of 'moral and political responsibility' for the risings. The death sentences were later commuted to detention in a fortified precinct but years were to pass before the prisoners were finally amnestied, and what appeared to be a conspiracy of silence on the part of the French authorities, both in France and in Madagascar, all but buried the affair for ever.

In Paris, a debate on Madagascar was held in the National Assembly on 22 September, 1948. Deputies including the socialist ex-minister André Philip and Gaston Defferre, who had been sent as an observer to Madagascar, spoke of tortures and evidence that Baron had been deliberately 'framing' the leaders of the *M.D.R.M.* They declared that Baron and his men had extorted false confessions from the prisoners by using 'methods worthy of our enemies but intolerable for France'. No attempt was made to deny these and other grave charges. M. Paul Coste-Floret, Minister for the Colonies, declared that he was personally convinced of the fact that torture had been used. But strangely enough, although Baron had been suspended he had later returned to Madagascar where he took up an important job in a trading firm. He was never prosecuted and his behaviour was never officially investigated. As for police brutalities and allegations that prisoners and suspects had been shot down in cold blood, the Minister reminded André Philip that, when they had both served in Algeria together, they had signed a petition *asking that police brutalities should be stopped in that country*. The debate was sterile but the significance of what was not denied was enormous. Constantly in the debate there arose the plea that France should 'show her true face' overseas. As had occurred so many times in the past, Frenchmen stood up in Parliament to declare that France stood for 'liberty and justice'.

*

With France's soldiers there not only came French civilization to the colonies but also the police. With the approval and consent of the authorities, they had tortured in Indo-China in the 1930's and in Madagascar in the 1940's. Even worse was to come in Algeria in in the 1950's, with the participation of an important part of an army still widely believed to be representing the honour and virtue of the homeland.

As readers of so many newspapers published outside France were to learn, torture became part of the system of repression in Algeria from 1955 onwards. Police powers were either delegated to Army paratroops or assumed by officers and Legionaries. By December 1955, the Director-General of the *Sûreté Nationale* had admitted in his own report that the police in Algeria were using methods of interrogation which 'belonged far more to the Gestapo than to a democratic police force'. Such frankness was rare, coming from such an authoritative source. Successive governments contented themselves with denying such reports and with banal protestations that 'France is the nation of the rights of man, etc'. Meanwhile, the Army had become infected by the disease of torture and counter-terrorism.

But the Army was sacred. Mention tortures or shootings and you were a traitor or an enemy of France. Anyone who, like this writer, was living in France during the last two years before De Gaulle's accession to power will remember the sickening barrage of praise lavished on the Army by successive governments, the right-wing and conservative newspapers and the radio, and how those who protested against what was being done in the name of French civilization were reviled when not stifled.

Even the French army of the past had to be defended from its detractors. Stanley Kubrick's film about the case of the 'deserters' from the French front in 1917, *Paths of Glory*, was banned in France in 1958. In June that year, it was also prohibited in the French sector of Berlin by the commander, General Gèze, who found it 'offensive to the memory of our soldiers'. In Brussels, where it won a prize, the film was hissed and booed by a number of French ex-servicemen who had gathered for the occasion and successfully forced it off the screen. This writer remembers watching King Vidor's version of *War and Peace* in a French country town at about the same time, and noticing the absence of scenes which had been shown in Italy where he had previously seen it: the shooting of straggling Russian prisoners accompanying Napoleon's retreating army and the summary execution of Muscovites accused of burning their city. While there was a war in Algeria even Napoleon's army had to be saved from taint. Had it not been the one that had given so many Frenchmen pride in their country's achievements and in a *rayonnement* in which cultural diffusion was accompanied by military conquest—always in the name of civilization?

In the last Algerian war as in the first, France was asked by its leaders to applaud what was being done in the name of *rayonnement* by its armies. For those who saw a contradiction between the idea of France's mission and the reality of her deeds abroad, that 'admirable military discipline' which Bugeaud wished to see applied to the whole of the French people seems also to have been in the mind of the President of the Fourth Republic. Speaking at Verdun on June 17, 1956, René Coty had spoken of the army's task in Algeria and added:

> Over there the homeland is in danger; over there, the homeland is engaged in combat. This being so, duty is clear and plain. Those who are not called to military service have the duty at least to observe that minimum of civic discipline which prohibits any action or words likely to trouble the minds of the children of the homeland whom the Republic has summoned to arms so that abominable acts of violence may be opposed by that French strength which is inseparable from French generosity.

No attack could be permitted on the army for 'our men there arouse the admiration of all by their valour as by their discipline and also by that human kindness which truly makes pacifiers out of these warriors'.

Six years later, by the decree of March 22, 1962, French generosity made sure that those who might have been accused of defiling their country's ideals and making a mockery of her mission were safe from all pursuit in the name of justice. There was an amnesty for persons who had committed 'infractions' during 'operations for the maintenance of order directed against the Algerian insurrection until March 20, 1962'. On June 18, 1966, another decree amnestied those persons who had committed 'infractions' in the course of the 'operations of the administrative or judiciary police' during the Algerian war. In other words, all those who might have been accused or suspected of having tortured, murdered and raped under the cover of the French flag abroad were henceforth to be made safe from any risk of investigation and punishment. The honour of the French army was upheld. The myth remained intact.

Still, a price had to be paid for the honour of the flag representing this civilization whose spreading abroad had cost so much blood and suffering. The self-styled Mother of Liberty and Human Rights was soon only to have her culture left to her to radiate. But she still had her Army and a President who was always to be known as the 'General' even if, as a veteran of Verdun remarked, 'his military exploits are not in danger of filling the history books'. (26)

3

Mother of Liberty

IN 1944, France recovered her liberty and independence thanks to foreign armies. A few years later she was using her own armies to suppress demands for freedom and self-determination in her overseas territories. By the late 1950's, those democratic principles and ideas of human dignity and justice she claimed to have spread abroad were in danger of being stifled on her own soil. The Republic which had made a dogma of liberty was fast becoming a travesty of a democracy. It was moving towards another period of personal rule which, as in the past, was to revive the myths of grandeur while violating those noble ideals which would have made the former a reality if the latter had been put into practice.

The degree to which the Declaration of the Rights of Man has been respected in the country which proclaimed it has varied greatly since the Revolution. There were times, particularly during the Third Republic, when France really did appear to offer those who lived in it every kind of political, spiritual and cultural freedom, but never did she extend it to those countries under her flag. Once only had France made a positive, concrete contribution to another country's independence and that was during the *ancien régime* when Lafayette went to the aid of Britain's rebellious American colonies.

Despite the fact that France had endured several dictatorships or near-dictatorships—under the two Napoleons, Pétain and De Gaulle—as well as periods of reaction and anti-liberal conservatism, the myth that she was the homeland of liberty and the standard-bearer of democracy persisted. Foreigners came to France to imbibe the ideas of revolution and democracy and each outbreak of revolutionary activity or insurrection in the streets of Paris was seen as proof that Frenchmen could not endure life without liberty and were prepared to fight at the barricades in defence of human rights. The idea that France would always champion the cause of liberty and justice endured for 160 years. In that period the country was constantly oscillating between personal rule and a parliamentary democracy which was often under vicious and sustained attack by many of its own people.

The myth is still widespread. For all the horrors of France's colonial past, leaders of many newly independent states have paid homage to her allegedly democratic spirit. Democrats in Spain, Portugal and Greece have turned to France or found refuge there from tyranny. The hope that France would take up the cause of freedom abroad has been voiced on innumerable occasions. As recently as March 1969, in a letter to *Le Monde* about police terror in Greece, the writer, the Reverend Father Bruckberger, stated that the Greeks had been hoping that 'a single word from France in their favour would make their masters tremble'. But he sadly added that 'this word, they no longer expect it . . . and it is the image of France the homeland of the rights of man that darkens and becomes effaced in them'. It had also darkened and become effaced in France.

*

One of the direct consequences of France's last colonial war was that violations of human liberties and dignities were no longer confined to the overseas domain. The Algerian war came close to turning France into a police state.

As soon after the Liberation as 1949, some Frenchmen were pointing out that police of various kinds had never been so numerous on French territory, and that there was nothing to prevent the supposition that tortures similar to those favoured by the S.S. and Gestapo were being practised in France. Torture, arbitrary arrest and detention, *la gangrène*, the 'cancer of democracy'—all these soon reappeared in post-Occupation France. Once more liberty and respect for human rights were under attack. There had been internment camps in France in 1939; in the 1950's there were concentration camps for Algerians in France and North Africa. By a decree of October 7, 1958, 'persons dangerous to public safety by reason of the direct or indirect material aid they might give rebels in the Algerian departments' could be interned without condemnation by any tribunal being necessary. Meanwhile, books and newspapers denouncing the abuses and the tortures that were being reported with increasing frequency were confiscated and suppressed.

When De Gaulle came to power, he was praised at the time for having recognized that tortures were being committed by the army in Algeria. But a year later, after the book *La Gangrène* (27) had been seized, the Prime Minister, Michel Debré, called it 'an assembly of lies ... an infamous book written by two infamous authors'(28) despite the fact that evidence of tortures had never been so overwhelming. What sort of allegedly democratic government was this that could allow an army tribunal in Paris in January 1961 to acquit three officers who had already admitted to having tortured an Algerian woman *to death* (29); and which could allow three provincial gendarmes who had confessed to torturing Algerians with electricity on *French soil* to go free after being fined the derisory sum of 150 francs? (30) What kind of homeland of the rights of man was this in which the police could beat up and murder Algerian civilians in Paris in October 1961, with both the government's Minister of the Interior and the Prefect of Police denying such acts and alleging that they were lies spread by France's enemies? And what kind of democracy was this which could, for seven years after the Algerian 'events', maintain such a vast army of policemen and para-military police auxiliaries in the country that foreigners might be excused for thinking that parts of France, and notably Paris, had been transformed into vast police camps in a constant state of alert?

The extent to which a country may be judged democratic and free depends in part upon the behaviour and nature of its police. The way the police had behaved during the Fourth and Fifth Republics had been notoriously savage. No free nation can afford to have a police force acting as an army of repression or an instrument of autocratic rule or even as a semi-autonomous power which might either support a régime or connive at its destruction. And yet this is what happened in France. Well might François Mauriac have complained in his weekly column (31) that although the army was 'close' to De Gaulle after he had come to power, 'the police depends on the Minister of the Interior. He himself has to put up with it like all of us. If he could not bear what has been happening, it would only remain to him to withdraw but that too is forbidden to him.'

Long before its spectacular development under the Gaullist régime, the French police had a sorry record of behaviour. During Vichy, many policemen had served their Fascist masters with diligence if not enthusiasm. French post-war history is full of instances of arbitrary police brutality with special police brigades and, in particular, the *Compagnies Républicaines de Sécurité* or 'CRS' clubbing, brutalizing and terrorizing strikers and students and protesters against the Algerian or Indo-Chinese wars with impunity if not with open government approval.

Sometimes the use of violence by the police has been justified. At many other times, it has simply seemed to reflect to an abnormal degree that capacity for hatred, sadism and the desire to humiliate which Frenchmen have often shown in their behaviour in times of crisis.

The brutalities committed abroad in the colonies by some of France's police officials need no further emphasizing. But with the Algerian war, police violence and illegal behaviour reached a climax on both sides of the Mediterranean. Tortures were practised in police stations inside France as well as in Algeria. North Africans were attacked and savaged with horrifying regularity and generally treated with a contempt and cruelty that not even the worst *F.L.N.* attacks on the French police could justify. In October 1961 there occurred the massacre of Algerians in Paris with corpses found hanging in the Bois de Boulogne and dozens more being fished out of the Seine after Arab demonstrators emerging from métro stations had been viciously bludgeoned by the police lying in wait for them. On December 19, 1961, an anti-*O.A.S.* demonstration had been attacked by police. Members of the Paris Municipal Council, wearing their scarves and badges of office, as well as unfortunate passers-by, had been clubbed, punched and kicked—incidents that were confirmed by many witnesses. On February 8, 1962, police violence near the Charonne métro station in the eastern quarters of Paris caused eight deaths during an anti-Fascist demonstration. For the next six years there were dozens of minor clashes between police and citizens and always there were fully documented accounts of police brutalities and illegalities. Towards the end of the Gaullist régime, when all communication between a large part of France's youth and the authorities had broken down, the government that had so far managed to avoid giving France the appearance of an outright police state could find no other solution in a crisis than to allow its police to run wild in the streets of its capital and celebrate ten years of Gaullist grandeur by clubbing, kicking, gassing and terrorizing young men and women and innocent passers-by.

The violent riots in Paris in May and June 1968 caused a new and even greater outburst of police sadism. Apologists for the régime and its police have stated that violence was far from one-sided, that certain foreign *provocateurs* and professional 'revolutionaries' had infiltrated the demonstrators, and added that the police did not shoot—as though this was a point in its favour. That professional troublemakers had been active is certainly probable and that bricks and other missiles had been hurled at the police, often causing severe injuries, is beyond doubt. But it must be added that had there been shooting, the Gaullist régime might well have found itself embroiled in a civil war situation; that not to shoot was in its own interest; that the behaviour of the police towards injured, unarmed, and captive demonstrators was sadistic on a horrifying scale, and that hundreds of complete non-participants had been set upon outside the scene of the riots. In other words, the nation's police had gone berserk in the streets and even in private dwellings in the capital, and had been allowed to do so.

There is much evidence and a wealth of certified statements (32) to show how barbaric and arbitrary was police violence on these occasions. Press photographers and journalists wearing distinguishing armbands issued by the Paris Prefecture of Police were set upon and beaten. People far from the scene of the rioting were attacked by roaming police squads; the police fired tear-gas bombs directly at individuals and through the windows of private apartments. Homes were invaded and their inmates brutalized; ambulances were obstructed; injured students were clubbed inside ambulances, on stretchers, and torn away from doctors and first-aid volunteers. No one was safe from arbitrary brutality. People on their way home from work were attacked; idlers, spectators and even people sitting over drinks in cafés were beaten, punched, insulted and humiliated. Foreign journalists of highly respectable newspapers like the London *Sunday Times* wrote of the vicious way the police went about their task of 'keeping order'. The photographer Bryan Wharton (33) described how the police aimed tear-gas shells at individuals, how they clubbed and struck with rifle butts, lashing at students' legs, beating up casualties on stretchers and in improvised ambulances and how they 'systematically drove rifle butts and clubs into the heads of anyone who lay injured' and kicked defenceless young women in the back.

No matter what the authorities declared afterwards, there was no doubt that such horrors were neither isolated nor few. Newspapers and books the world over have published some of the many photographs taken, and even the briefest examination of these photographs will show at once that the demonstrators being 'repressed' were ordinary and mainly middle-class young people—certainly not hired thugs or the products of Cuban or Chinese training camps for 'international subversionists'. Looking at such terrible pictures as that of a young man, his face streaming with blood, lying on the ground and trying to ward off the truncheon blows being dealt him by four or five helmeted policemen; a young woman being struck as she lies unconscious in the middle of a road; of screaming civilians cowering in a doorway under a rain of blows and kicks, and of the faces of the armed phalanxes of the 'forces of order', their clubs, shields and tear-gas rifles at the ready, is to look at a France poisoned by officially condoned brutality.

France is unfortunately not alone in being a nation where rioting students and ferocious police breed violence and counter-violence, but what certainly distinguishes her from other countries is the zest and the frequency with which her police forces gave vent to their sadism in completely unprovoked circumstances, long after the riots had been quelled. What photographs could not show, since they could not be taken, eminent and authoritative witnesses described. Thus, in a letter to *Le Monde* (May 11, 1968), a court lawyer, Maître Camille Dubois, described how passers-by were allowed to move freely along the streets by police until some were picked out at random and beaten up in full public view, without any consideration for their age or sex. He had seen police attempting to disfigure people with the liquid from their tear-gas projectiles which could be poured out by simply unscrewing a cap; he had seen 'a young girl disfigured who was taken in a state of collapse towards the Saint-Michel fountain, and an old man being aimed at as he was about to enter the métro'. Doctors sent in letters to the papers to say how they had seen young girls beaten up; they testified that they had seen gassed people in a dangerous state being torn away from ambulances and being beaten up by the *C.R.S.* squads before being thrown into police vans and carried off to detention centres. The medical review, *Tribune Médicale* (issue of June 21, 1968), carried an article describing the fearful and often desperate state of victims of gas attacks. The doctor, F. Kahn, vainly begged the Minister of the Interior to investigate the matter of toxic gas-shells that had been used, and mentioned cases of old people, asthmatics and children whose lives were directly threatened by such poisons. A student died after being wounded by a fragment of a gas shell; another had his hand blown off. Families gave evidence to investigatory tribunals, set up by students and teachers (34) shortly after the events, of how gas-shells had been fired through the windows of their flats. The police had fired gas-shells in métro stations and at people's faces. Young girls were blinded; horrible injuries were caused by the dozen. And perhaps even worse, detainees in various centres and police stations had been humiliated, tortured and made to run the gauntlet of jeering, truncheon-wielding policemen.

Police violence was directed at everyone who was young, in the first place. Cases of racism and xenophobia expressed in insults and brutality were reported all over central Paris. Again and again there were lengthy, detailed reports which were cross-checked and which tallied, even though coming from different witnesses, and which were afterwards confirmed by medical reports of the way in which even the *ordinary* Paris police had treated those in their custody. A young boy had tear-gas liquid poured over the lower part of his body before being snatched from a first-aid squad and had then been beaten up in detention. Girls and boys were subjected to sexual humiliations of the worst kind.

And what was the reaction to the publication of the accounts and photographs of these atrocities? The authorities' first reaction was when the Paris Prefect, Maurice Grimaud, sent a letter to the municipal police stating that for a policeman to strike a fallen demonstrator was to 'strike oneself' and added that to strike someone in a police station after his arrest was 'even more serious'. Otherwise, all he could do was to express his admiration after 'having seen you at work during twenty-five exceptional days' (letter of May 29, 1968). On June 28, 1968, the Paris Public Prosecutor's office (the *Parquet*) began proceedings against 'X' for 'defamation of the police'. In November that same year, during the budget debate in the National Assembly and in the course of a speech of more than 7,000 words on the need for extra allocations for the forces of law and order, the Minister of the Interior made much of the activities of foreign subversionists, inspired by the resolutions taken at the Tricontinental conference at Havana, Cuba, in January 1966. When he came to the question of police behaviour, he devoted few words to the subject. They are worth quoting here:

> As for the police brutalities, this was one of the great themes which has been so greatly embroidered upon and so lied about. Certain facts have been reproduced in numerous tracts, diffused throughout the entire country. It is, of course, inevitable that in the course of some hundred

demonstrations, in the course of which policemen have been struck or injured, that isolated brutalities should have been committed under the stress of exasperation and tension due to the ceaseless provocation of which the police was a victim. One could read in Paris, in tracts ceaselessly distributed throughout the demonstrations, this infamous slogan 'if you see a *C.R.S.* on the ground, finish him off'. In general—I must say it loudly—the behaviour of the forces of order has been exemplary. Numerous statements of sympathy and admiration have, moreover, come to the Prefect of Police, and the promotions in the Legion of Honour and in the national Order of Merit have shown in what esteem the President, the Government and the entire nation were holding the police. (35)

In March 1969, during a military ceremony held in the courtyard of the Invalides in Paris, De Gaulle decorated a number of military personalities and the Prefect of the Paris police, Maurice Grimaud himself, whose elevation in the order of the Legion of Honour was confirmed. As for the reaction of the vast mass of France's middle-class population to the way in which so many of their own sons and daughters and those of their fellow-citizens and relatives had been terrorized, humiliated and beaten, it was silence, if not approval. After events which might have been expected to provoke a nation-wide cry of protest in a so-called civilized country, there was mostly apathy. To read some of the right-wing and conservative press, with its alarmist stories of "red" plots to take over the universities, it is clear that many Frenchmen would still applaud the police if they repeated their behaviour. With the atrocities and the failure of so many Frenchmen to condemn them, the nation's disgrace was two-fold—as it had been when only a minority had protested against the tortures and terrorism being committed during the time of the Algerian war.

What was this police force that could act in so horrifying a manner, which could violate the country's laws with impunity, which could escape official investigation and which had suddenly appeared like some terrible *deus ex machina*, from beyond the bounds of all constitutional normality, to terrorize and bludgeon on such a scale? Was it French—was it really a tolerated part of the nation's structures? It gave signs of being a law unto itself. It was like a weapon from some extra-constitutional armoury which was used to defend the régime but remained alien to the nation's body, like a cancer. Who were these Frenchmen behind the goggles and shields, who moved so implacably down the streets of Paris like robots?

Who were their leaders and what legacy of previous grudges had led them to show such open contempt and hatred for the people whose servants they were appointed to be?

A country secure in its institutions and whose citizens are at least united on certain basic national issues and on the overall structure of their country, despite political and other internal differences, can afford to maintain some of its most vital institutions free of political influences and controversies. But if not secure in its institutions, and if the population is divided by issues which compromise the entire fabric of the nation and the structure of its régime, then every aspect of public life will inevitably risk contamination by partisan politics. And so it has happened with France's police.

The extent to which the police so often seemed to escape governmental control, during both the Fourth and the Fifth Republics, indicated how greatly France had been weakened as a democratic country. The behaviour of her police had violated every law and principle of human decency which should have been defended by her rulers. Either it was the direct, tolerated expression of the régime's attitudes towards the exercise of authority and the maintenance of power, in which case it must be condemned of resorting to the tactics of tyranny; or, if it occurred outside the control of those claiming to represent the country, it must be seen as the sign of the fragility of a government which professed to maintain the traditions of democracy. France might not have become a police state in the accepted sense but those who suffered from illegal police behaviour never had any hope of redress and never once did any of France's leaders speak up against the crimes committed in their name. The police had become too powerful to criticize. Like the army, their hostility was to be feared and their support had to be courted.

*

In the beginning, the police was apolitical: its members might hold their political opinions, like any other Frenchman, but they were expected to support and obey the legitimate authority of the nation no matter what its political tendency might be. The chief overall organizing body in the structure of the police forces is the *Sûreté Nationale*, which is directly responsible to the Ministry of the Interior, which in turn assumes entire responsibility for the maintenance of law and order on French territory. The duties of the police, grouped according to various specialized activities, are to maintain order and to assure the respect and protection of liberties, persons, possessions, institutions and the State. Offences committed by the police are defined and punishable by the penal code. They have also had their privileges and rights like other citizens, one being to belong to trade union groups, and for a time they even had a right to strike, like any other public body of state servants.

One of the most powerful and responsible officials in the police force is the Prefect, the head of the Paris Police Prefecture. His powers and range of duties are vast: he must maintain order throughout the department of the Seine, he must deal with traffic problems, shop hours, the granting of various licences, and crime; he must also ensure the safety of the President of the Republic and of the members of the government and is under the immediate authority of the Minister of the Interior. He is therefore one of the most important pillars of the régime. At times he has been its opponent.

In the poisonous atmosphere of French politics in the 1930's, the police were already showing signs of a tendency which was to be accentuated throughout the next thirty years: an adherence to the Right destined to become practically traditional. The Fascist paper *Gringoire* was owned by the two brothers Carbuccia and one of them was the son-in-law of the Paris Prefect at the time: Jean Chiappe. Chiappe's political views were no secret: he favoured a change of régime in France, he was in full agreement with the attitudes and policies advocated in *Gringoire* and he supported the extreme right-wing politicians of the time. In 1934, it had been observed that his police were noticeably gentle in their handling of right-wing and Royalist demonstrators in the streets of Paris and remarkably tough with communist and left-wing demonstrators. In 1940, he, together with many other policemen of fascist sympathies and racist views, was treated with great favour by the invading Germans who knew his past record and realized how useful a servant he would be.

After the Liberation there was a 'purge' of Vichy and collaborationist policemen but the transition of the police from being State servants to a quasi-independent body which could work either for or against the government was made under the Fourth and Fifth Republics. It was during the Fourth Republic that the strength or political colour of the government in office could be a determining factor in deciding the loyalty of many policemen.

Immediately after the last war, it was the climate of anti-communism and the not wholly unjustified fears of French governments that gave a new character and orientation to the police. The mobile units of the *C.R.S.* were created and placed under the command of the Ministry of the Interior. The members of this force which has so much distinguished itself by its brutality were essentially recruited from among unqualified personnel in the provinces who had begun their careers as equivalents of the English country constable before being attracted by higher pay and prestige. In the *C.R.S.* they had to deal with mountain rescue work, floods and forest fires; but first and foremost they provided a weapon against strikers, rioters and political demonstrations which got out of hand or were judged dangerous by a government making increasing use of this force in political affairs. Their personality was formed by years of repressive activities, the hatred and hostility they aroused among the population, and by their use against movements that were mainly left-wing. With their training in violence and their experience of hard knocks they were conditioned into a state of perpetual, latent aggressiveness which could always explode spectacularly. They became a right-wing police force with a long memory and with many grudges, a tendency to blame right-wing extremism on communist agitators, and a conviction that a right-wing danger was a left-wing myth.

At the same time that the *C.R.S.* were being hardened and politicized, changes were taking place within the more traditional police structure, headed by the *Sûreté Nationale*. The anti-communist fears of the government were shared by high authorities in the police force. Engaged as they were in political actions, they could not logically remain neutral. In the late '40's, the danger of a communist takeover seemed very real to many Frenchmen. The Resistance which had divided France as much as it had united it, the pre-eminent part played by French communists and the grudges of a vast section of the population against the 'other' France which had collaborated under Vichy, gave great impetus to a communist-led movement which convinced many of its members and sympathizers that it represented the 'real' France. At the same time, police chiefs were discovering the extent of their political power and influence on government policies. Their ability to take part in government policy had been helped by the attitude of the Minister of the Interior, Jules Moch, who was known not only as a strike-smasher and a pitiless enemy of the communists, but as a man convinced that the police had to be given a special character apart from that of other state servants. The police had to be made both apolitical *and* political in the direction chosen by the government.

Two successive directors of the *Sûreté Nationale* were engaged in this task. The influence of trade unionism in the police forces was reduced as far as possible. After a stormy debate in the National Assembly in September 1948, the right to strike was suppressed. There was a wave of dismissals and transfers at the beginning of the '50's—particularly of policemen with known left-wing sympathies— no matter how fine their previous record had been. In other words, a MacCarthyite 'witch-hunt' was carried out.

The Prefect of Marseilles, Jean Baylot, who had a great record as an opponent of the communists, was brought to the Paris Prefecture in 1951 by the Prime Minister, Henri Queuille, as a result of alarming reports on 'red' penetration and of the softness of the former Paris Prefect. Baylot not only held the dossiers on Communist police who were to be kept from promotion but did something that no previous prefect had done since the Liberation. He obeyed a governmental decision which had hitherto been resisted by bringing back into the ranks many of the policemen who had been dismissed and suspended for their active, even enthusiastic collaboration with the Vichy government and the Germans. Furthermore, he cultivated links with members of the government, convincing them that their survival depended on an alliance with the heads of the police, and, more significantly, with 'parallel' police forces whose tasks were to be purely political.

There was an alliance between Baylot and a high member of the Gaullist party, the *R.P.F.*, Jean Dides. It was to have far-reaching consequences. Notorious ex-Vichyites were drawn into the network. A former collaborator who had kept files on communist or left-inclined police and who was himself wanted by the police was given a special post and kept in close touch through other officials with the government and, in particular, the Ministry of the Interior. Informers and *provocateurs* with the darkest records were enlisted. There were more purges. Special squads, trained in strong-arm methods were formed and treatment of demonstrators and, in particular, Algerians, became harsher. To increase the power and virtual autonomy of various police bodies was easy: all people like Baylot had to do was to keep the government in a state of alarm over 'communist plots'. Naturally many persecuted and suspended policemen protested. Victims of witch-hunts and witnesses to the reinstatement of so many Vichyist, right-wing police officials, they claimed that the nation's police force were being given an ever-increasing orientation towards the right. Anti-left and racist tendencies were being encouraged even as the danger of a communist takeover subsided. Policemen belonging to trade unions drew attention to such questionable but tolerated methods as the use of plain-clothes men as *agents provocateurs* and the creation of secret, unofficial networks, often at the instigation of such known Gaullist sympathizers who were hostile to the current régime as the *commissaire* Jean Dides, whose later role in the events leading to De Gaulle's accession to power was not unimportant.

A part of the nation's police had already begun to plot against the régime. There were curious incidents and always the same names kept appearing in connection with them. On April 4, 1954, a ceremony had been organized around the Sacred Flame at the Arc de Triomphe by an association of ex-servicemen who had fought in Indo-China, in the presence of the Prime Minister Joseph Laniel and his Defence Minister René Pleven. In the course of this meeting, both ministers suddenly found themselves being booed, jostled, insulted and even kicked by a number of extremely threatening ex-servicemen, reserve officers and members of extreme right-wing groups. Only the few generals accompanying MM. Pleven and Laniel were able to protect them to some extent. The police were absent.

It had been decided beforehand that 400 plain-clothes men were to be stationed under the Arch since the majority of the public there would be composed of ex-servicemen known to be likely to make angry protests against members of a government which they felt was betraying the army in Indo-China. In charge of this police protection was *commissaire* Dides—a man on the best of terms with the Gaullists who were so hostile to the governments of the Republic. For some reason, instead of gathering his men at the Arch he had stationed them along the Champs-Elysées—too far for them to intervene quickly after the members of the government had been humiliated.

After the Laniel administration had fallen, and Mendès-France had been invested as Prime Minister, with François Mitterand as his Minister of the Interior, there was the curious behaviour of the Prefect Baylot in the affair of the 'communist plot'.

In one of the routine daily meetings between the Minister of the Interior and the Prefect, Baylot spoke of the dangers of the forthcoming July 14 demonstrations and processions, which had already had a record of violent incidents, and showed Mitterand printed tracts calling for violence and signed by the Communist Party. Before he granted Baylot's request for permission to search the Communist Party's offices in the Place Kossuth, Mitterand took the precaution of investigating the precise provenance of these incendiary tracts. They were found to have been printed in the Prefecture building itself. Baylot was sacked but by that time the Prefecture and a large section of the police forces had already been transformed into a semi-independent body with a policy of its own that did not always coincide with that of the régime. Moreover, with people like Dides at its head, its links with the Gaullist party were becoming stronger.

Even more revealing was the astonishing demonstration of nearly 2,000 Paris policemen outside the Palais-Bourbon on March 13, 1958, when slogans violently hostile to the government and shouts of *'Dides au pouvoir!'* were heard. When Dides appeared outside the building he was cheered and he was later questioned in the Assembly about his sympathies with the demonstrators and his involvement in the affair. The scandal resulted in the replacement of the Paris Prefect. He was succeeded by Maurice Papon who had been a prefect in Algeria. Soon afterwards, Papon was continuing his career as the servant of a new régime of more dubious legality.

The state now had to hand a formidable repressive weapon which it was to use on many occasions. Under De Gaulle there was an enormous increase in the strength of various police forces. With an army of more than a hundred thousand police of various kinds on its territory, France was the western country most densely populated with police anywhere in the so-called 'free world'. In no other western capital were there so many policemen to be seen as in Paris. Never had France had so many unofficial and unorthodox police forces whose existence was not always officially admitted and whose activities were often liable to escape government control. The very existence of such a politically orientated police army was incompatible with the idea of a true democracy—as was the behaviour of one of its chiefs. One of the pillars of the régime was Paris's Prefect of Police, Maurice Papon. The way the police were seen to behave and, perhaps even more important, the way they were allowed to behave, were revealing of how far France had abandoned her civilised ideals. A régime must be judged by its servants. During Papon's tenure of office, the police frequently conducted itself in a way to shame any nation—even if it has not had a long history of preaching 'human rights' to the rest of the world.

*

The career of the man who became one of the most detested servants of the government under De Gaulle was brilliant from the beginning. Maurice Papon was born near Paris in 1910. He was a successful student, taking a degree in law, a diploma in political science, and had studied both sociology and psychology. He was only twenty-one when he held his first official post, being attached to the Ministry of Aviation. In 1935 he was employed at the Ministry of the Interior, less than a year later he was attached to the cabinet of the Under-Secretary of State to the *Présidence du Conseil* (the Prime Minister's office), and then a year later transferred to the cabinet of the Under-Secretary of State for Foreign Affairs. Moving rapidly from one post to another and staying in none for more than a few months, his vertiginous ascent through governmental and administrative ranks was interrupted by the outbreak of war in 1939. He was called up for a time but late in 1940 he was back in an office job and beginning to hold the first of a number of administrative posts under the Vichy régime.

This is still an obscure period in Papon's career. Where his real sympathies lay it is difficult to determine with any precision. To hold office he had, of course, like all other civil servants in occupied France, to take the oath of loyalty to Marshal Pétain. In June 1942 he became secretary-general for the department of the Gironde and then Prefect of the Landes department near Bordeaux. When France was liberated, he continued his career under the new régime and was never accused of having been a 'collaborator', unlike the Prefect of the Gironde who was shortly afterwards charged and arrested for collaboration, and placed himself 'at the disposal' of the Gaullist Commissary of the Republic who had been sent to the region by De Gaulle. Later, Papon was awarded the commemorative medal for the 1939–1945 war. What had he done during the Occupation?

A newly liberated regional newspaper, the *Sud-Ouest* of Bordeaux, asked him this and published the answer in a short article in a daily column of profiles under the general heading of 'those of the

Renovation'. The paper (issue of October 7, 1944) said that when asked what his role had been in the Resistance, he had answered with 'charming modesty':

> I have not worked in the Resistance to perpetuate the privileges and to prolong the mistakes of 1939; I have worked and I shall continue to work with more faith than ever before so that France may remain a great nation and so that she may become a true democracy.

The way Papon contributed to France's transformation into a 'true democracy' was a curious one, to say the least. He soon became involved with the Algerian question shortly after the Setif rising and its repression. From June to November 1946, he was *chef de cabinet* to the Under-Secretary of State at the Ministry of the Interior. After various other brief posts and missions, he went to North Africa where he was Prefect of Constantine for a time, in conditions determined by Arab nationalist agitation and French repression. In July 1954, he had become Secretary-General of the Protectorate of Morocco which was then in ferment. There, he made one of the many friends who could be so useful to him: his 'technical adviser', René Tomasini who was later to distinguish himself as a well-known, 'hard core' Gaullist and a bitter enemy of the Fourth Republic 'régime of betrayal'. Papon's job was to direct the 'forces of order' to repress all nationalist movements. His zeal in directing the policy of police repression must have been as ruthless as it was outstanding, since when the Prime Minister, Edgar Faure, sent a new Resident General to Morocco in July 1955, to prepare for the return of the Sultan Mohammed Ben Yussef, Papon was one of the few officials removed from their posts as it was calculated that their continued presence would prejudice hopes of an eventual Franco-Moroccan reconciliation.

But after another brief interlude as 'technical adviser' in the Ministry of the Interior, dealing with Algerian affairs, he was back at Constantine in 1956, as Prefect, with a Legion of Honour decoration and with the sonorous title of 'Inspector General of the Administration in Mission Extraordinary to the departments of Eastern Algeria'. This, it should be remembered, was already a time when a widespread use of torture and ferocious police behaviour towards Arabs suspected of nationalist sympathies and activities was being alleged and denounced. The former Prefect whom Papon replaced was reputed to be one of the most feared and hated officials anywhere in French North Africa.

In March 1958, after the anti-parliamentary police demonstration in Paris, the Félix Gaillard government offered him the post of Paris Prefect, one of whose duties is, as already mentioned, to defend the integrity and security of the government. Two months later, we again find Papon making an easy transition from one régime to the next.* His long reign as police chief of Paris lasted until January 1967. The period was marked by some of the worst police behaviour and brutality that the city had ever witnessed, such as the killing of Algerians one night in October 1961, the beating up of municipal councillors in the December 19, 1961 demonstration, and the Charonne métro incidents in 1962.

The October 1961 massacre was 'covered' and denied by the Minister of the Interior, Roger Frey. Before Paris's Municipal Council of the Seine, Papon had declared that the Paris police 'had done its duty' and protested against the 'attacks and infamies' they had to bear in language that has been monotonously repeated after later similar incidents and atrocities. When the French students' union, *U.N.E.F.*, published and circulated accounts of the tortures being practised upon Algerians in the notorious police station in the Rue de la Goutte d'Or in the north of Paris, Papon started legal proceedings for 'defamation'.

Eye-witness accounts of police savagery towards innocent citizens were heard at meetings of the Municipal Council of the Seine. In November 1961, its President, M. Georges Dardel, spoke of Papon's 'special squads' and told the Prefect to his face: ' "specialists" have been recruited by the Prefect of Police himself. They were given orders and instructions. They have acted with inadmissible brutality. The pre-war police had other methods which were efficient. The present methods, Monsieur Papon, are to be compared with those of other political régimes'. Papon denied all charges of arbitrary police violence and sadism. The entire Bureau of the General Council of the Seine protested against Papon's 'extraordinary behaviour' but they could do no more. No matter what crimes were committed by the police for whose behaviour Papon was officially responsible, he was untouchable and even after the end of the Algerian war and the *O.A.S.* activities he remained in office, always protected by the government, never disavowed, and never out of favour. He had published a glossy magazine called

---

* According to Raymond Tournoux in his book *Secrets d'Etat* Papon was referred to by the plotters in Algiers as 'Jojo'.

Liaisons which purported to tell Parisians the truth about *their* police; he continued to allow his men to club students whenever they demonstrated; and he survived the Ben Barka affair. When he finally left the Prefecture he was amply rewarded by the government. They wanted a high-ranking civil servant of great experience in authority to overhaul procedures in aeronautical construction. Despite the fact that Papon's only experience of aeronautical matters was his brief time with the Air Ministry, when he was twenty-one, he was appointed President-Director-General of the Sud-Aviation company which was making the Concorde airliner in collaboration with Great Britain. As he left his police post to take up these 'high responsibilities', the Minister of Information, Yvon Bourges, declared that 'the government had rendered homage to the action he had pursued in the happiest manner during eight and a half years at the head of the Prefecture of Police'. The homage rendered to Papon by the Sud-Aviation workmen belonging to the *C.F.D.T.* union was somewhat different, taking the form of a protest.

In the general elections of June 1968, Papon was elected Gaullist member of parliament for the 3rd circumscription of the Cher department, leaving his post at Sud-Aviation a few weeks later. Now free to indulge in his passion for politics, he may still have far to go if the right people can make use of his talents.

*

Papon was not only a state servant: he was a writer and a 'philosopher'. What form his philosophy took is not without interest: nor is it without links with a 'certain France' that is anything but 'democratic' in spirit.

He had taken himself very seriously as a thinker and had published a book called *L'Ere des responsables* which, as the title indicates, dealt at length with the subject of responsibility in modern society—a problem of which Papon must have had much experience. The book had mixed reviews, with the more hostile critics agreeing that it was badly written, often obscure, and often nonsensical. While writing about the 'responsible heads of our time' and the question of leadership in a rapidly changing world, Papon frequently quoted an aphorism by a certain 'Doctor Gros', to whom he had dedicated the work:

> The true élites are cultivated in the earth itself and not in a flower pot (*les vraies élites sont cultivées en pleine terre et non en pot*).

His next intellectual effort in philosophy was published in 1965 under the title of *Vers un nouveau discours de la méthode*. Its aim was 'an analysis of the possibilities of intellectual and moral reform'. The book included a critical survey of Western thinkers, in which Papon attacked the 'absurdity' of existentialism and expressed his approval of Teilhard de Chardin's theories. He declared that the 'crisis of our times is a crisis of method', spoke of the problems of adapting a Cartesian mentality to new and changing realities in the world, and expressed his awareness of the phenomenon of the accelerating rate of change and progress. He also made much use of the word '*prospective*' and the expression 'the construction of the future'.

By a curious coincidence, in May 1958 when Papon switched his loyalties from the Fourth Republic to the Gaullist régime, the first issue of a handsomely printed review called *Prospective* was published by the Presses Universitaires de France. It was the creation of a group of businessmen, bankers and civil servants who declared that their group had been 'constituted for the study of the technical, scientific, economic and social causes which accelerate the evolution of the modern world and for the forecasting of situations which might result from their conjoined influences'. The administrative board heading the group whose interests were so similar to those of Papon included such important personalities as M. Arnaud de Vogüe, President of the glass and chemical products factories and manufactures of Saint-Gobain, Chauncy and Cirey; an Inspector of Finances and Director-General of the *Caisse des Dépôts et Consignations*, M. François Bloch-Lainé; a Treasurer who was M. Marcel Demonique, Director-General of the Lafarge cement firm; a State adviser, who had been *chef de cabinet* to Michel Debré when he was Prime Minister and who was a very close friend of Papon's (36), M. Pierre Racine; and a Doctor André Gros whose resounding titles were 'President of the International Society of *Conseillers de Synthèse*' and 'former Vice-Regent of the French Foundation for the study of human problems'.

As we might expect of a group including Papon's philosophic mentor and a political friend in high places, the articles published in the review were similar in theme and tenor to the Prefect's books (or vice versa). The opening article in the first issue of *Prospective* was by a M. Gaston Berger on 'the prospective attitude' and dealt with the problems of the future. One must look forward—such was the main theme in the various articles. The group gave its views on agriculture, transport, cybernetics, atomic energy, relations with North Africa, the rest of the world, etc. M. Arnaud de Vogüe wrote about such weighty themes as 'industrial enterprise and the permanent values of classical culture' while others shared Papon's absorbing interest in responsibility in high places in the world of tomorrow and the formation of new élites and declared that 'by merely looking at the future we can change it'.

There can be little doubt that one of this new élite whose interest in the future is reflected by *Prospective* is the former Prefect. Together with his friends, we may be sure that he has plans for the future, that he has cultivated his contacts and friendships so that should yet another régime appear in France a group of powerful men will be ready to step out of the shadows to put into application a 'philosophy' far removed from any being debated at universities or among the intellectuals of Saint-Germain-des-Prés.

*

That a state servant whose period of office had been marked by so many instances and charges of police brutality and violation of the nation's laws should be promoted and defended by the government was one of the prices that France had to pay for allowing its republic to be annexed by one man.

In seeing himself as the incarnation of France, De Gaulle was representative of a powerfully anti-democratic tendency in France's history since the end of the *ancien régime*. Every time that France has been afflicted by its recurring 'Bonapartist fever' (37) liberty and human rights have suffered unnoticed by a vast majority of citizens.

With De Gaulle as with Napoleon Bonaparte, Napoleon III and Pétain, there occurred one of those periods in French history when the nation seemed for a short time to achieve some semblance of unity by handing over its destinies to a single individual whose appearance appeared to have been stage-managed by Providence. Just as the language of Gaullese existed before De Gaulle, so Gaullism existed before the General. Generals have always enjoyed remarkable popularity in France since the Revolution, and the idea of calling upon one to conduct the nation's affairs is not a new one. In each case there is no precise doctrine. In 1936, in Gustave Hervé's book *C'est Pétain qu'il nous faut!*, a long pamphlet in which the author demanded full powers for the Marshal, press censorship, lock-outs, purges of teachers and a full reconciliation with Germany, we find the idea plainly expressed:

> It is simply and plainly a matter of bringing the Marshal to power—to full powers—by the legal means of a great popular wave as we tried in the time of Boulangism, but this time with a chief whom we know in advance to have something in his head and his belly. With anyone else we would be obliged to ask his programme first for in France, a country of clear ideas, we rather like to know where we are going. With Pétain there is no need to ask for a programme in advance; his name alone is a programme.

In Gaullist France, a nation whose régime had become so personal and whose political institutions were so dominated by a single figure, there would also seem to have been no need to ask for a government since the Head of State himself was the government. No clearer statement of the personal assumption of all power and responsibility by one man is to be found than in De Gaulle's press conference of January 31, 1964, when he described the President of the Republic as the source and holder of all power in a long exposé which, wrote André Passeron, the collector and publisher of his speeches, 'by its breadth, contains in reality the General's doctrine regarding the exercise of power' (38) and which 'can be considered as the true unwritten Constitution'.

After saying that 'a constitution is a spirit, institutions are a practice', De Gaulle spoke of the necessity to give public powers an efficiency, stability and *responsibility* (the author's italics) which they did not have under the Third and Fourth Republics. Power was no longer to be the 'thing of partisans' but to proceed directly from the people which implied that the head of the state which they elected should be its source and holder. The prime minister was to be a kind of super-valet, although the President did not use quite these words. He was to look after the various details of the President's overall plan which he had not the time (nor the inclination, we might add) to attend to himself, for the President was the man of the Nation and 'evidently the one to hold and delegate the authority of the State. But, precisely, the nature, the range, the duration of his task imply that he should not be absorbed without respite and without limit by the political, parliamentary, economic and administrative situation'.

But far more significant was the admission that there was no longer any separation between such powers as the executive and the judiciary:

> ... if it must evidently be understood that the indivisible authority of the State is entrusted in its entirety to the President by the people who elected him, *that there exists no other* [authority], *neither ministerial, nor civil, nor military nor judiciary, which is not conferred and maintained by him* (the author's italics), lastly, that it belongs to him to adjust the supreme domain which is his own with those of which he delegates the management to others, everything makes it necessary, in ordinary times, to maintain the distinction between the function and the field of action of the Head of the State and those of the Prime Minister, etc.

In other words, to use those attributed to President Harry Truman during his term of office, 'the buck stops here'. De Gaulle had admitted that he had virtually monopolized the powers of the state and responsibility for the way in which they were exercised, and must therefore be held ultimately responsible for brutalities and violations of laws committed during his reign. But again and again, control seemed to escape him, whether in incidents involving the police as in the Ben Barka affair, or the army as during the Algerian war. A solitary autocrat who has become the state in person cannot quarrel with the servants who maintain his power nor can he do without them even if he has merely delegated power to them. It was to be noted that after the Charonne métro incident in which eight civilians were killed and which led to one of the largest public demonstrations of protest ever seen in Paris, not a single expression of sympathy on behalf of the victims was ever uttered by this supposed incarnation of the country. After the events in May and June 1968, there was still not a word of official sympathy forthcoming for the victims of police violence, in what most assuredly was a national disaster.

*

Contemporary with this toleration of police brutality for the régime's purposes, came a vast legislation and a wealth of decrees relating to public order and the security of the state. Slowly but surely the law and those who applied it were brought under the control of the régime which spoke so much of France's democratic vocation but which still refused to ratify the European Convention to safeguard human rights, unlike other Western European countries.

Not only under De Gaulle but ever since 1789, there had been a contrast between the noble ideals of liberty and human rights which France has proclaimed, and the lack of effective guarantees of those rights without which no country is truly democratic. There was no *habeas corpus*, there was state censorship of the most powerful means of public communication, and not until much later was there any legal provision for conscientious objectors. Capital punishment remained, even though only rarely used, and there was still a lack of any great public protest movement against it. An imposing repressive apparatus was built up during the Fourth Republic to deal with grave internal troubles, many resulting from the colonial wars which were part of France's *rayonnement* abroad. This strengthening of repressive machinery was not due to De Gaulle alone. In part it resulted from the continuing crises that menaced France with civil war in the first years of his reign, but his régime continued to evolve in an anti-democratic direction afterwards. There were more policemen, there was more repressive legislation, more rights were violated, laws were twisted and misapplied and attacks on the independence of the judiciary were systematically sustained.

Additions and modifications to the penal codes gave the police wider powers, the most notorious being the increase in the time for which they could hold a suspect *incommunicado* before bringing him before a magistrate—the '*garde à vue*', which was introduced as a regrettable necessity under the Fourth Republic, which fixed its duration at forty-eight hours, and then given legal status under De Gaulle. Under De Gaulle also, the power of the police to decide to make 'verifications of identity' all too often led to completely unjustified and arbitrary detention in police stations. The Prosecutor of the Republic who represents the nation's executive was formerly subject to control by a 'chamber of accusation' composed of magistrates from the Court of Appeal to whom he had to answer. Since the 'reforms' of 1957 and 1958, he was no longer under their control. The *Conseil supérieur de la Magistrature*, which the Fourth Republic had founded in 1946 had been designed to guarantee the independence of the judiciary from political control. It consisted of a number of members, of whom some were elected by the parliament and others by various categories of magistrates, and had the power of appointing all magistrates. Under the Fifth Republic, its powers of appointment became greatly reduced and it is still entirely composed of the President of the Republic's nominees.

But more revealing of the régime's assertion of control over the judiciary machine was the way in which it used the pretext of 'state security'. By the decree of February 13, 1960, the Paris Prefect of Police was given important new powers relating to crimes and offences against 'state security', although only when there is a state of 'urgency'—a state that has never been defined and which has nothing to do with the 'state of emergency' for which provision has been made by the Constitution of the Fifth Republic. More serious was the creation of an 'exceptional court', the Court of State Security (*Cour de Sûreté d'Etat*), which was set up on January 15, 1963, well after the end of the Algerian and *O.A.S.* troubles, when conditions in France could once more be regarded as 'normal'.

This Court of State Security is a completely government-controlled court empowered to deal with anything that might be labelled by the government as an offence against the exterior and interior security of the nation. It was created as a *permanent* institution and is competent to judge many offences and crimes which ordinarily belong to the realm of common law but which can be interpreted as relating to 'any individual or collective enterprise aiming at replacing state authority with an illegal one'. It consists of three civil and two *military* judges all of whom are appointed for two years (renewable) by the ministers-in-council. Suspects in cases held to involve state security may have their homes searched at night upon the orders of the Ministry of the Interior or an examining magistrate, contrary to common law practice, and—far worse and more threatening for the future—may be detained by the police for as long as ten days, or even fifteen if a state of national emergency had been declared. Even minors of sixteen or eighteen were made subject to this law. Thus, of all the 'free' countries it was France which had the melancholy distinction of being a 'democracy' in which a suspect in political affairs, arbitrarily considered to concern state security, may be held in a police cell without being charged, without being allowed to contact his family, his lawyer or even a priest, in complete secrecy at the mercy of police interrogators, his whereabouts known only to the authorities who had ordered his arrest, for *ten days* in 'normal' times before appearing before a judge. And if he is put on trial before this special, government-controlled court, should his defending lawyer be considered by this same court to have in any way 'failed in his obligations', this lawyer could be suspended and replaced by another, new to the case, to the obvious disadvantage of the accused.

In view of such repressive Gaullist legislation, the debate on whether France had become a 'police state' or not was meaningless. People were not arrested *en masse* for political reasons, opposition papers continued to appear, people could still advocate a change of régime by constitutional means, elections could still be held without being unduly rigged, and the amount of information damaging to the régime's public image that could be put into print was impressive; but all the machinery for an eventual, sudden transformation of this semi-democracy into a police state was there, ready to be used in a crisis. Even minor common law offences could, in certain circumstances, be arbitrarily estimated to endanger state security, and would therefore come within the competence of this special Court; the independence of the judiciary was diminished, television and radio were in the hands of the rulers and the police had become an instrument of a régime and one part of the nation whose hold over the other was not always maintained by constitutional and legal means and who was able to tamper with the nation's laws in a climate marked as much by apathy as by an almost mystical regard for a ruler who posed as the incarnation of every ideal that was being flouted. Such was part of the price to be paid for the Gaullist notion of *grandeur* and 'renovation'.

*

But if France, by the time she surrendered to Gaullism, was no longer in a position to give lessons in democracy and human rights, did there not still remain to her that culture which is the only real *rayonnement* that endures, and was she not still the Mother of the Arts?

At times, the shadow of repression fell over France's artistic life. A film like *Les Liaisons Dangereuses* might be banned for a time lest the world be given a bad impression of French middle-class morals; Jacques Rivette's film version of *La Réligieuse*, Diderot's story of a nun's tribulations in eighteenth-century France, might be banned in 1966 on the grounds that it might 'seriously offend a very large part of the population' and 'harm the reputation or authority of communities, many of which are involved in a work contributing to the cultural or humanitarian *rayonnement* of France'; leading writers and actors might be prohibited from appearing on radio or television for protesting against their country's policies; certain books and newspapers might be seized or censored, but artistic and intellectual life continued. There was a Minister for Cultural Affairs who had a world-wide reputation as a man of letters and who passionately believed in France's cultural mission in the world. And there was

Paris—there was always Paris. If nothing else, Paris at least could be depended upon to bring admiring foreigners to France and to keep alive the idea that France was still pre-eminent in the arts, the mother of the human spirit, and the most cultured, graceful, intelligent and creative country. It was from Paris that France began her conquests of the spirit and it was Paris that best symbolized the spiritual heart of France. She represented in quintessential form that civilization which was French and therefore universal. Was not her fascination proof of French supremacy and grandeur in things of culture? Was it not there that all the elements constituting French civilization were assembled prior to being exported? With her famous and much-vaunted beauty, her buildings and monuments scrubbed clean, her artistic and literary activity, was not Paris the best sign that France was still radiating beauty and culture if not liberty? And is it not there that we must begin in any attempt to see whether the myth of Marianne the Mother of Arts had any more substance than that of her as Mother of Liberty, during those years in which the world was told that 'France has recovered her vocation'?

PART TWO
PARIS

4

The Capital of the Spirit

TO MOST people outside France, the French nation is first and foremost Paris, that city which has been verbally pawed and fondled for generations like a beautiful whore—an adulation in which the French have heartily concurred. We have only to open a recent guide book in English to see the way in which the charm, importance and radiance of Paris are still being celebrated by writers who expect the reader to fall into an ecstatic trance before the beauty of the Arc de Triomphe and the avenues which radiate from it—for example: 'Paris is the most beautiful city in the world ... Paris is a poem. Look at the grand squares from which wonderful avenues radiate in all directions'. (39) Other statements such as 'France remains the capital of the world of art and intellect, the mecca of painters, sculptors, composers, and writers from every country' (40) are all made with Paris in mind. The more beautiful Paris is believed to be the more convincing is the myth of French cultural radiance. To admire Paris's splendid avenues, buildings and monuments, her great museums and art galleries, bookshops and theatres leads to the conviction that 'France has long been the standard-bearer of Western civilization' (41) and that 'France has proved that she is still the world's leader in the arts, in design, in the art of living'. (42) If it were not for Paris such statements would in all probability never be made. Paris then is the showpiece and figurehead of the French genius and the main attraction in France. Paris dictates and the rest of France, and the world besides, is expected to follow.

France is still under the dictatorship of Paris. Cultural life and the essentials of French 'civilization' are concentrated in the city. For a Frenchman, no career in the arts, the sciences, politics and law can ever be truly successful unless he has come to Paris. To be 'French' is not enough: to be 'Parisian' is the supreme goal. Is not Paris the living heart of the glory and the myth that is France? And for the foreigner, is not Paris the most noble, the most compelling and the most beautiful of all great cities which have created a civilization and a way of life? Is not the adjective 'Parisian' more than a geographical reality? Does it not imply a way of life and that peculiar quality of French (and essentially Parisian) civilization that others may imitate but never find in its authenticity outside those twenty *arrondissements* which enshrine such mythical virtues and enchantments that those who have once seen them can never forget them? What other city has quite the same power to evoke such feelings in the hearts and minds of men all over the world? What other city has such a myth?

High prices, the progressive destruction of old landmarks and charming vestiges of the past, the traffic and the savage events that the capital has witnessed in recent times have all done much to tarnish the lustre of the city in the eyes of many of its former lovers but the myth still survives largely intact. To live in Paris for the *first time* is to risk succumbing to the myth, no matter how convinced you may be that you are at last seeing the 'real' Paris behind the façade. But to become aware of the myth and the ways in which it works its magic is to begin to see a new Paris, perhaps even more fascinating than the first, if somewhat disillusioning.

*

Many great cities have created their myths. That of Paris is that she is a very beautiful and clever woman to whom the homage and lasting adoration of the rest of the world is no more than her due. Paris is the most exciting city in the world. She is the home of good taste, the shameless purveyor of every pleasure known to man, the Mecca of the artist and the place where good Americans go when they die or where they go to be reborn. American writers of world fame have done much to perpetuate and reinforce the myth: for Hemingway, Paris was the 'moveable feast', for Henry Miller, Paris and the rest of France were the antithesis and antidote to the air-conditioned, nightmare civilization symbolized by the cellophane-wrapped loaf of the supermarket. And yet . . . So many disenchanted Parisians will tell you today that Paris is a thing of the past and that you have come too late to see 'their Paris'. The city really was Paris when they were storming the cultural barricades of Saint-Germain des Prés in the heady aftermath of the Liberation, but now 'their' Montparnasse, 'their' Montmartre and 'their' Latin Quarter have gone for ever. A certain quality of life that made the city 'Paris' to its inhabitants and worshippers has gone. What is left for the city's new lovers and would-be worshippers? Only her physical beauty? Her incomparable architectural beauty?

Say what you like about Paris, say that the Parisians are the rudest, most callous, undependable, frivolous or dishonest people on earth, say that the cost of living, or of a mere holiday, is prohibitive, but first acknowledge that Paris is beautiful. It may be widely admitted that Paris is no longer the centre of all that is new and vital in the arts, it may no longer be automatically accepted that Paris is the first home of good taste and the cradle of fashion, but deny that she is ravishingly beautiful, the true 'flower of cities all', and you will be charged with being boorish and insensitive.

After all, was not Paris designed to be beautiful, with her great radiating avenues and tree-lined boulevards, her wide open spaces, squares and gardens, her charming back-streets, her quaysides along the Seine where poets and lovers may wander and dream? Such a well-laid-out city, her admirers will murmur—until caught in the next traffic jam. If you are so rude as to remark that if it is a matter of geometrical lay-out, then Turin must be accounted superior (although it is rather a bore), you will be ignored.

Paris is certainly more than a city of long, straight avenues and great open spaces. It is a city of narrow little streets, villages and backwaters. Paris, to its lovers, may be a corner of Montmartre, a street corner with a café, a few chairs and a gaily striped sunshade on the pavement, an old house in the Latin Quarter or Marais, a fisherman sitting on the quayside in the shadow of Notre Dame, or a beautifully dressed model presenting her glacial profile to the camera in front of a fountain in the Place de la Concorde. All these beauties have become postcard clichés but they still have the power to move the Parish-worshipper who will immediately succumb to what Arthur Koestler wittily called the 'French 'flu' and confess 'I once lived/stayed/starved/made love in the Rue des Martyrs' in a tone so reverential that he might be speaking of the Paradise Lost since Paris is so beautiful.

Paris the Beautiful is roughly one hundred years old. It was not always reputed one of the world's most beautiful cities. Roger Caillois, the anthropologist, has described a different and earlier myth of Paris in his *Le mythe et l'homme*. The city of the first half of the nineteenth century was far from being the beautiful, enchanting lady of the *belle époque*. It was a vast brooding megalopis, a place of mystery and darkness, a ruthless juggernaut crushing the wretched and lonely in its slums, a dark background to poverty, crime and rebellion, a city of hidden splendours behind the high walls of its mansions, aloof from the sullen hatreds and resentments of the streets. It was the city of Balzac, Victor Hugo and Eugène Sue. It was the Paris of the Morgue, the sewers, the street mob, the bandit Lacenaire, the policeman Vidocq, the barricades, and Balzac's Rastignac, exultantly gazing down on the dark roofs with his challenging: '*A nous deux, Paris!*' It was romantic, dangerous, largely medieval, and its beauty was one of decay—the sombre, cancerous beauty of an engraving by Charles Méryon or Doré.

Paris, the *Ville Lumière*, dates from the Second Empire when Napoleon III commissioned Haussmann to renovate and 'beautify' the capital of his Empire. It was in the same period that Paris the Frivolous, the Gay and the Naughty was born. The history of the city became part of world history. After the siege and the Commune, the city entered into its Golden Age when it was not only the world capital of pleasure but the undisputed centre of art and fashion. By the turn of the century it had become the centre of modern art and the home of the unconventional and the rebellious and as such it continued to attract artists, writers, exiles and hedonists throughout the Twenties and well into the Thirties. There was another, briefer period of efflorescence after the Liberation. Paris continued to be an intellectually and artistically exciting city. The Paris of Montmartre and Montparnasse became the Paris of Saint-Germain-des-Prés, of Sartre and Camus, Anouilh and Edwige Feuillère, existentialism and candle-lit caves, jazz in the Rue de la Huchette, Juliette Greco and Boris Vian, Sagan and Dior, Edith Piaf and the Aly Khan.

All this is ancient history. But it is the memory and the legend of these past times, the Nineties, Twenties, Thirties, Forties and Fifties that have created the popular *idea* of Paris and given it its magnetic appeal. For the Peruvian poet, Saint-Germain is still the Saint-Germain of 1947, for the Egyptian painter or exile, Montparnasse is still the Montparnasse of the Twenties, and for the travelling salesman from Coventry or Illinois, Paris is still the place for 'the obvious, old boy', the naughty and the licit illicit. All these are part of the myth of Paris, a myth of physical beauty and spiritual magic. The tragedy is that the myth is rapidly beginning to appear as such. In this respect, as in others, Paris is being crushed down and suffocated by her history. There is too much of it in Paris. Her inhabitants remember too well.

Parisians over the age of thirty tend increasingly to mourn for their city's recent past. Why, they will ask you, did you not come before? Why did you not make your pilgrimage to Paris when it really was Paris? Paris has changed out of all recognition. It is just another big, sprawling, grossly overcrowded city, with its ghosts and its memories of a uniquely *Parisian* quality of life which is widely believed to be in decline. And the physical beauty of Paris—was it a thing of the mind, now vanishing as a result of some complex loss of confidence or crisis whose causes are still to be traced and analysed?

In 1911, Rémy de Gourmont wrote that 'Paris would be a beautiful enough city if only one could demolish some of the absurd buildings which deface it and if one could bend all the rectilinear streets which so stiffen it and which have so dulled it'. There was no greater lover of the city than Rémy de Gourmont and his knowledge of it was vast and encyclopaedic. He was writing of the Paris that first impresses itself upon the eye of the visitor: the Paris that was made officially 'beautiful' to order. He might have added that Paris is two cities: the boulevard, Haussmannesque city and the older Paris of the Middle Ages that was so mutilated in the interests of beautiful and convenient Paris.

Apart from the traffic, central, boulevard-Paris appears to have survived largely unchanged since the time that Haussmann's heavy hand made itself felt on the city. The city escaped serious bombing in the war and the predominant style of architecture is Second Empire and late nineteenth century. The worst damage sustained was during the 1871 Commune but most of the monuments and great buildings have remained intact for tourists and school-parties to contemplate dutifully. Unfortunately, few of them can be called beautiful by any stretch of the aesthetic imagination, and most are heavy examples of an architectural rhetoric as heavy and uninspired as a French headmaster's speech on Prize Day.

The Louvre is crushing and inflated. The museum is crammed with treasures but nonetheless it is a painful experience for any visitor who feels duty-bound to 'do it' since it is rather like the National and Tate Galleries, the British Museum, the Victoria and Albert Museum and the Wallace Collection all rolled into one. Notre Dame is a great cathedral, certainly, and the Sainte Chapelle is the 'jewel of Gothic art' admittedly, but they suffer from their vicinity to the Hotel-Dieu and Police Prefecture, two of the most hideously depressing buildings in all Paris, and the Sainte Chapelle is even tucked away in the middle of the Prefecture so that all you can see of it from outside is the spire. The Invalides is huge, pompous and dispiriting, a vast funeral march in stone. Seen from the back, the great domed chapel appears what it is: a mausoleum. From the front, the long, squat façade faces a few cannon and rusting tanks and an enormous open space which is certainly wide and undeniably open but completely devoid of either interest or charm. The Panthéon is where the great men of France are laid to rest in icy vaults. It has a huge dome, a huge interior, and huge formal paintings by Puvis de Chavannes. It is also a huge bore and deserves no reverence. The Madeleine is an overblown Greek temple which has been scrubbed pink. One look will be enough. A second look and you wonder what it is doing there anyway. If you like Second Empire grandeur, then the Opéra is very grand indeed. There it sits, huge, complacent and gaudy—imposed at the top of the Avenue de l'Opéra. It is precisely this quality of looking 'imposed' that characterizes so many of what the French call their 'monuments'.* In French, a *monument* may be a statue, a church or a public building, and in any Paris guide book you will find the word used for the Arc de Triomphe, the obelisk in the Place de la Concorde and Notre Dame.

The use of the word is not without significance. Monuments these constructions certainly are. Monuments to an official, autocratic attempt from an Olympian *above* to impose a formal, bureaucratic-inspired ideal of beauty and grandeur upon an ancient, largely medieval and still rebellious city that just *grew*. They are monuments representative of the same spirit that inspired Louis XIV's architects when they imposed their formal designs and rigid schemes upon the gardens of Versailles and transformed a charming hunting lodge into a huge architectural yawn.

To stroll in the gardens of the Tuileries or to sit upon a bench among the parterres of the Louvre and the scattering of Maillol's sculptures of nudes between the two outflung arms of the museum is to invite quick depression. Everything is so formal, so planned, so rigid and so very unimaginative. All this stiffness of architectural

---

* Revealing, how often this word *imposed* is used in French! In how many histories of French art, civilization, culture, etc., do we find it in such sentences as 'pendant le 18e siècle, le style français *s'impose* . . .', 'la mode de Paris *s'impose*', 'le goût Louis Quinze *s'impose*'! Imposed and imposing—France conquers and is dominant.

rigor mortis is as boring as that monotonous sheet of water that passes for a lake at Versailles, as hollow as that funereal nineteenth-century church of Saint-Augustin on the Boulevard Malesherbes, as inimical to the imagination as that long view down the Champs-Elysées to the Arc de Triomphe, as artificial as the Sacré-Cœur, as dispiriting as a walk down some of those residential boulevards which give an air of dreamy uniformity to so many parts of the city, and as imbued with that tyrannical idea of formality and measured grandeur as the alexandrines of Corneille or the patently false endings to even the most trivial business letter in which you beg the recipient to believe in your distinguished sentiments . . .

These 'rectilinear' streets which Rémy de Gourmont rightly wished to bend according to his whim are another monument. They monumentalize the nineteenth-century bourgeoisie triumphant. As every French schoolboy is supposed to know, they were partly inspired by military considerations since they made it much easier for the military to quell insurrections. As such they may still be useful, but if you look carefully at the buildings that line them you will see that they are the symbol of bourgeois solidity and solidarity. Few, if any, of the boulevards can be accounted beautiful or charming. Most of the buildings date from between the 1860's and the 1930's and in style they range from the tolerably unassuming to the overbearing. It is easy to recognize a pre-Haussmann building or an avenue or boulevard. The doorway will be simple and unadorned, the façade is flat and the windows, with their wooden shutters neatly folded back, are beautifully spaced and proportioned. They have the same simplicity of line and unpretentious, classic elegance as a row of English Georgian houses. You may still see them all over Paris, particularly in such districts as those to the north of the Boulevard Haussmann where quiet, early nineteenth-century streets have survived untouched.

Their successors were built to a uniform height but simplicity went and all the worst tricks of the later nineteenth-century architects are distressingly in evidence. To walk the full length of one of the longer, more residential boulevards is a cheerless undertaking. Assuming that you are a lover of plain elegance, your eyes will soon tire of the never-ending series of ornate doorways, pseudo-caryatids, heavy, over-sculpted cornices and balconies, rhetorical flourishes and occasional eczema-like excrescences with which builders saw fit to bedeck the façades. You may be yearning to see houses—real houses—which are a rarity since Paris is predominantly a city of flats and rooms. Those private houses you do see are mostly wealthy men's mansions or small town palaces which are called *hôtels particulier*. Paris has many fine *hôtels* of great historic and architectural interest but they are certainly not town houses in the English sense of the term. With their high walls and huge doorways they have an exclusive undemocratic air as though their owners resented being set down in the midst of the ordinary workaday people. They are also very big. For smaller, humbler houses and simple, graceful early nineteenth-century blocks of flats you must go to one of the poorer districts, the Faubourg Saint-Antoine, the working-class districts behind Montparnasse or, better still, to the heights of Belleville where the air is the cleanest and freshest in Paris, or to a few streets in Montmartre where the atmosphere of a country village still clings to a few streets.

This is the 'popular' Paris of René Clair's pre-war films and Jacques Prévert's songs, but now most of it is doomed. The little artisans' dwellings and workers' cottages with their occasional, English-looking patch of front garden are coming down and the skyscraper tenements have long since started their inexorable march across the Buttes-Chaumont and the back of Montparnasse. Soon, they will be legion. The Paris of the future, the city of the planners, is being built for the year 2000 and there is no longer any time for sentiment.

There is a feeling in Paris of loss, especially of that more intimate part of Paris belonging to the people of a far older city. The most literate, knowledgeable, privileged connoisseurs and lovers of the city will tell you that much of the essential, secret charm of Paris is being lost for ever for such is the price of progress...

Paris is overburdened by its historicity, it is too dependent on its odd corners, its old stones and its little streets, its sudden surprises and oases. It has remained unchanged for too long, its appeal has become too closely dependent on its medieval charm and secret alley-ways and it is now paying the price in too short a time.

The new Paris that is beginning to emerge is unsentimental but if you *are* sentimental and know your Paris as the city demands to be known, then you cannot help feeling that the magic is going. A very short time ago, the Paris-lover for whom the city of René Clair, Prévert and Piaf was the *real* Paris had only to walk across Belleville, through its little winding streets with their low houses and tiny shops, and cross into Ménilmontant, a poorer district which now and again resembled the old and equally doomed East End of London. There, he would find his way to the intersection of the Rue de Transvaal and the Rue des Couronnes. He would see a newish housing estate—no uglier and no less brutal than others of its kind—towering above a wasteland and nearby, close to a flight of steep steps leading down into lower Ménilmontant, one of the oddest-looking hotels in Paris, the Hôtel de Transvaal, empty and waiting for the demolition squad. The view over Paris was superb. He could look across the roof-tops of working-class Paris, the Paris of the 11th *arrondissement*, the still-medieval or sixteenth-century Paris of the Marais, a dark, grey Paris stretching out below and beyond the new block of flats and the wasteland, and the steep sinuous streets of old Ménilmontant, with its crumbling houses, its sightless windows blocked up with cement as though to conceal some ghastly secret, its sad pavements with dim shop-fronts and dusty cafés and sinister dark corridors and alley-ways. To walk down from the Butte was a disturbing and melancholy experience. You passed old men shuffling listlessly to the wine shop or *bistrot*, children playing in the streets, housewives with strained faces carrying shopping bags and now and again, in their midst, unseen and unseeing, the haunted face of an Algerian. To walk down such streets was to be conscious of an air of impending death and dissolution; the whole district seemed to be holding its breath as though waiting for the first fall of the pickaxe on all that remained of this desolate survival of an archetypal Paris that was poor and unhygienic but profoundly 'Parisian' in its bitter-sweet picturesqueness.

Now, with a few demolitions here and there, a few housing projects, a few squares and green lawns, how evanescent this poetic aspect of Paris is proving to be! It was here that the true Paris-lover, the sentimentalist and poet, the indefatigable walker and explorer of the city, could still look down at the old Paris of Hugo and Zola, of *Sous les Toits de Paris*, the Paris of the Commune which ended in blood and despair not so very far away, of a song by Piaf who was born in the Rue de Belleville and whose voice, as the plaque on the house in front of which she was born states, 'overwhelmed the world' just as the myth of Paris overwhelmed and stirred the hearts and minds of men the world over. Now a cold wind is blowing over the Butte, and if you look hard towards the south of the city you will see the vast housing slabs rising above Montparnasse, half as high, it would seem, as the Eiffel Tower, once a glorious symbol of a 'new' France now called the *belle Epoque*.

This part of Paris illustrates an aspect of the city that strikingly contradicts the mythical *Ville Lumière*: the tragic. In many ways Paris is a dramatically tragic city, to an extent unparallelled in any other great Western city. Parts of Paris which survived Haussmann's planning have a melancholy grandeur commensurate with that of its thousand years of history, and it is hard to spend any length of time in the city without becoming aware of the fact. To see an old city die is always a moving experience, and much of that old Paris which is dying has a fascination and magic that goes far beyond the tritely picturesque and superficially charming. Far closer to this *old* Paris than any banal postcard painting are the dark and powerful etchings of Méryon who so well caught the grotesque, sinister and dark aspect of what is still one of the most extraordinary surviving examples of a medieval rabbit-warren city—a city that has little place in the modern world.

Much of Paris is a kind of gigantic Potemkin village: the great boulevards and straight thoroughfares have created two cities. Behind the bourgeois façades of the Second Empire and *belle époque*, there still lives the Paris of Balzac and Victor Hugo but it is now in serious danger and its lovers are already mourning its passing.

This most physical of cities is also one of the most ensnaring: to love Paris means to know it and how to know it is to be bound to it by an almost visceral attachment. No wonder that the emotions it has aroused—and can still arouse—are correspondingly strong and profound! But if those secret recesses and intimate villages which make up the heart of Paris are lost, what will remain but that official beauty which, we may have seen, was mostly *imposed* and verges on the vulgar and banal? A modern capital city with a theatrical, stage-set, monumental architecture scrubbed clean? A shop window of a city?

After having stood still for a hundred years and decayed gracefully or dramatically, as the case might be, Paris is changing again and part of it is dying in the process. The heart is already doomed. The Halles district is decaying and the market has gone. It was not 'beautiful' but it was 'picturesque' and above all it was alive. Parisians will tell you that by destroying Les Halles, more than a market was destroyed. A whole 'quarter' was sentenced to death with it. To many Parisians and tourists, the Halles district was the *real* Paris, the Paris between the Boulevards and 'monuments', the Paris that Haussmann spared and time forgot like parts of the Latin Quarter and the Marais. It is still working class and 'red light' Paris with its shabby, disreputable streets (and what names they have: Rue de la Grande Truanderie, Rue des Mauvais-Garçons!), its small, cheap restaurants, its bars with zinc-lined counters, its great tourist-pulling restaurants, where porters could drink a large glass of *vin ordinaire* at the counter, its sordid hotels, brothels, prostitutes and *clochards*. It was very much the Paris of the myth—the Paris of Henry Miller and James Baldwin (who catches the tragic atmosphere with astonishing precision and sensitivity in *Giovanni's Room*) and the poor artist or student from abroad for whom the sensuous beauty of Paris was the smell of fresh fruit, meat and bread, the taste of *Gauloise* cigarettes, the half-loaf lying on the paper tablecloth next to his *bifteck-frites*, and the glass of Sancerre drunk standing at the zinc bar.

All this is part of the Paris that has been taken for granted and that poets and writers have been praising for generations. Walk along the Seine and try to forget the traffic rushing past you and look at Notre Dame in the golden haze of a summer's evening and you feel that Paris is beautiful from the viewpoint of a tourist—one essentially uninvolved in the drama of the city. What has brought you to Paris is still myth, the idea of a way of life and a compelling compound of other peoples' memories and nostalgia. You are looking for the embodiment of the myth, a stage Paris, and when you find its semblance you are reassured, but it is a superficial beauty that only lightly touches the soul. Paris is a city that must be learned and the best teachers are those who love their city. Your Parisian guide will lead you on sentimental pilgrimages through little streets and into old-fashioned shops, bars and restaurants. The beauty of Paris *is* old-fashioned and Parisians are much more sentimental about the past than Londoners—if they can afford the time. The connoisseur of the city will point at the painted ceramics and tiles of an old baker's shop or *bistrot* and invite you to admire them: 'there aren't many bread-shops like that now! Look at the lettering over the front—genuine *art nouveau*!' He may offer you a drink in a dusty, cavernous old *bistrot* with a marble counter and a perpetual air of desolation: 'what atmosphere! It's completely nineteenth-century!' This 'picturesque' Paris is being lovingly recorded for its enthusiasts in anticipation of the time when it will have gone. The book-shops are full of picture books of Paris past and present (especially past), with sentimental or erudite forewords and commentaries by well-known writers and artists. The Paris of the *belle époque* is all the rage. There has been a craze for *art nouveau* antiques and *bric-à-brac* for years. There is a Nineteen-twenties craze and far-sighted dealers have prepared for a Nineteen-thirties craze. At this rate, there will soon be a Nineteen-fifties and -sixties craze.

All this frantic collecting activity and these oceans of nostalgic prose being poured into print are part of a clinging-on to a dead and dying Paris. Nowhere, perhaps, is this tragic and dying aspect more apparent than in those quarters peripheral to the Halles, and particularly in the district to the north of the market place and to the south of the great boulevards, the Poissonière, the Bonne Nouvelle, and the Saint-Denis. To walk—especially at night—along the Rue Montorgeuil, the Rue Saint-Denis and the narrow streets intersecting them is to take a journey back into the past. All those doorways, those festering façades, those gloomy courtyards, that old and lavish ironwork, those roughly cobbled and narrow, streets and *impasses*, those intimate but dingy little cafés speak of a tragic and rich past, of a city with many secrets. They arouse a sense of history which is often stifling and overwhelming. They are all part of the city's heart which, as it is opened up and modernized, will lose much of that fiercer quality which contributes as much as the more facilely picturesque aspect to the fascination of Paris.

The history of Paris has often been ferocious and bloody. To understand, or at least to sense, the near-physical influence that the city has had on the moulding of its inhabitants, we must know something of its past. This part of Paris has seen too much suffering, too much horror and cruelty, too much civil strife, not to have affected its people from generation to generation. It is not a happy city. In the remnants of the Jewish ghetto, adjacent to the Marais, the Gestapo and their French colleagues hunted the Jews along the labyrinthine corridors and alley-ways, the Communards fought and were shot down by the Versaillais in 1871, and nearby the Revolution exploded. Centuries earlier, Parisians fought with Burgundians, a king of France was stabbed by a mad monk and condemned men were torn to death, all a few hundred yards from the river and the spires of Notre Dame. The poverty and squalor were immeasurable and have still remained in many side streets. Old Paris has a dramatic atmosphere and even when you reach the quaysides facing the sinister towers of the Conciergerie, the feeling of a violent past is still omnipresent. On one of those evenings when the sky of Paris is like a lurid backcloth to the city and its grey river, you can imagine the surge of great crowds along the banks, down the Rue Saint-Antoine, towards the open squares, the Place de la Grève and the Concorde, where the guillotine raised its arms to the sky and the mob roared at the sight of yet more blood being spilt on those stones which have seen so much blood in the last few centuries. The violent past is very near, and a violent future is always a possibility . . .

*

Paris is not only tragic: it is a sad city. That peculiarly French quality of sadness that is to be found throughout France, in small towns in the provinces, in isolated villages, in schools, in families, in the faces of old women in the métro at seven in the morning, in French love songs and even in the depressing aspect of an official document with its grey-blue paper and old-fashioned type, is to be found in Paris in heightened, quintessential form. You can sense it as you walk down the melancholy canyons of the residential streets of the 16th *arrondissement*, unrelieved by cafés or strollers, or as you walk in the hush of a Saturday or Sunday afternoon along the quiet streets around the Bourse, the Bibliothèque Nationale and the Marais—particularly the last.

Not only is the Marais one of the most historic districts of the city with its wealth of seventeenth- and eighteenth-century houses and palaces, it is also one of the gloomiest. Once again, historicity and sadness go hand in hand. The greys of the buildings, the little quiet squares, the funereal quality of the main show-pieces, the mausoleum-like churches all conspire to depress your spirits. Sometimes you can walk down an empty street, past the old houses and squalid courtyards and, if you are poetically-minded or sensitive, feel crushed by the deadness of the atmosphere. You might be a figure in a painting by Chirico, intruding into some architectural stage-setting, into a world not of the present, where people live like ghosts behind their shuttered windows—waiting for what? . . .

The sadness of Paris is to be seen in the faces of its people so often revealing of the tensions and anxieties assailing the major part of the population. Not for them is Paris beautiful. Paris is a hard city to live and work in—you can see it in their expressions. It is a place where you must struggle, where to *se débrouiller*, to 'get along', is essential, where the housing is some of the worst and most insanitary in

Europe, where prices are continually rising, where nothing is certain in the future and where your fellow beings are more often a nuisance than companions, and where you are all too well aware of the worst of human nature from bitter experience, and, if you are old enough, from having lived through the dark and terrible days of a not so distant past.

There are more beggars than in London. You meet more lonely old people talking to themselves, more tramps weaving their alcoholic way towards you, glaring from bloodshot eyes, clutching their litre bottles of bad wine, more bad-tempered people in a hurry, more human wrecks, more exasperated mothers pulling their whining children after them ... You live in Paris for a length of time and you collect so many images of Paris *tristesse* in your mind, like snapshots, each illustrating an aspect of Paris melancholy, or Paris tragic: the mournful old lady who for no apparent reason suddenly decided on the métro platform to make you a party to her resentments, 'Now they give all the work to the foreigners, the Portuguese, the Spaniards ... *Monsieur, je vous demande* ...'; the pathetic little concierge from the Auvergne whose bony hands would flutter and tremble when she handed you the mail; the little old women who seem to be perpetually rummaging and poking in dust-bins in back courtyards, soliloquizing as they conduct their furtive explorations; old men creeping past you on ancient wooden staircases, to vanish behind their battered doors like so many mice; again, a concierge and her family glimpsed through the window of their one-room *loge*, huddled around the dining table, the old father picking at his plate with rheumatic hands; the appalling gloom of so many Paris churches (the deadening sombreness of Saint-Denis-du-Sacré-Cœur in the sad Marais; a concourse of tiny old ladies, all in black, hearing mass in a side-chapel in Saint-Etienne-du-Mont and then shuffling out into the light like a flock of crows); the parterres of the Louvre and the Luxembourg on a grey afternoon; those long, terrifyingly dark corridors and stair-wells in old houses; the faces of so many school-children trotting off to school at seven-thirty in the morning, or being marshalled by their *surveillants*, their hunched backs, narrow shoulders and pale, bespectacled faces bearing witness to the academic strain imposed upon them in anticipation of their *baccalauréat*, in the interests of what myth, what ideal, what greater glory of French civilization? ...

*

The tension in the air, the nervousness of the people and especially their rudeness—that notorious Parisian rudeness—are famous. Once again it is Paris that seems to magnify and crystallize that rudeness, jumpiness, lack of patience and constant readiness to show vexation which are attributed to the French people as a whole. Official recognition of French rudeness came a few years ago. As the first parties of English school-children began to straggle around the Louvre and the Invalides, a politeness-campaign was launched under the name of *opération courtoisie*. Motorists began to decorate their car windows with slogans saying 'Priority for smiles' and 'Don't let's get cross' and the authorities began to turn their attention to the tourist. The French were rude, they frightened the tourist! There was a great cry of official alarm. Rather than brave the general lack of interest and surliness of their irritable hosts, and the cantankerousness of ticket-sellers, café waiters, shopkeepers and passers-by, would-be tourists would hunch over their maps, their time-tables and steering-wheels and grimly race through France to sunnier and friendlier climes.

The official remedy came from the Ministry of Tourism who launched a French National Campaign for Welcome and Friendship. French *courtoisie* was to be the rule—not the exception. Roses were handed out at airports to foreign visitors as they landed, customs posts were gaily decorated with flowers, postal workers and museum attendants were instructed to bear kindly with the fumbling, inarticulate foreigner, and—the most original feature of the campaign —tourists were given wads of 'smile cheques' (*chèques-sourire*) to distribute as they thought fit to natives whose outstanding politeness thus entitled them to take part in a kind of lottery with prizes including cars and trips to Tahiti.

The car stickers have remained. The cars have increased. Even more than the 'absurd buildings', one of the first aspects likely to impress the visitor is the number and ferocity of the cars in the city. In no other capital of Western Europe—except Rome—does the motor-car seem to have become so invading, so destructive and so spiteful. As we know, Parisians are rude enough in public—with their own special brand of bad temper—but when they are in cars they are terrifying. When you cross a road at the lights and see the cars lined up on your left or your right, it is hard not to feel that they are positively itching to leap forward and crush you as soon as the lights change—sooner if only it were possible. French cars are about the ugliest in the world and to see a thickset, bullet-headed Parisian crouching over the wheel in his hideous, tinny Panhard or Renault a mere eighteen inches away from you is to become aware of an ill-concealed ferocity, a bad temper, and a capacity for explosive hatred and contempt for the fellow species, that you may have the good fortune to avoid on the pavement, in the shops or cafés, but which you will surely encounter every time you start to step into a road.

There is something insane about Paris's traffic. What the guide books call 'the most beautiful square in the world', the Place de la Concorde, has become a seething mass of metal for most of the day. The roads along the Seine are a race track and you can hardly walk through the narrow streets of the Left Bank and Latin Quarter and look in shop windows because passers-by will probably shoulder you off the pavement into the endless stream of cars. Most of the wider boulevards, particularly those with a central strip of pavement, have become car parks and you can hardly stroll under the trees without the slithering monsters nosing and nudging past you as though resentful of the fact that your means of locomotion are still natural. They are even right-wing in their sympathies: when De Gaulle came to power, when Pompidou was returned to power, hooting cars tore up and down the Champs-Elysées, klaxoning a paean of mindless exultation.

Paris's last Prefect of Police, Maurice Grimaud, has mentioned, with regard to traffic problems, the 'electric atmosphere' in Paris's streets. He was quite right. After the dreamy, placid cosiness of London, the atmosphere of the Paris streets is bracing, sharp and nervous. It crackles with bad temper, impatience and a frustrated desire for speediness. People snarl or seem about to snarl if you step across their paths or in any way impede their progress.

And yet, this verbal or hinted violence which is so common a feature of public life in Paris is rarely followed by physical violence and may well act as a safety valve. The exception is that now well established, peculiarly Parisian crime: the fight (which has even ended in death) between two motorists after a collision at a street crossing when there is a dispute over priority. But by and large, despite all the violence that the capital has seen, that readiness to punch that can be seen quite frequently in English pub-brawls for instance, is rare in heated public interchanges. The violence remains one of words and gestures.

Reasons for this rudeness and irritability which, for so many people, have been among the main defects of the Parisian, may not only be found in the excitability of the French temperament but in that discomfort that is so great a feature of Parisian life. Not only is the overcrowding in the city notorious, not only are many wages scandalously low, and not only do prices continue to soar, but the Gallic genius for discomfort is to be found in its most heightened form.

At its most elegant, Paris discomfort may be seen in certain living rooms where everything seems to be for display only and where there is nowhere comfortable to sit, no cosy English armchairs, no inviting sofas, only creaking floors and rickety hard chairs and stools; at its most sordid, it may be seen in the eternally atrocious toilets in so many cafés, in the hideous hole-in-corner recesses where you are expected to telephone in many *bistrots*, in those dreadful métro carriage doors which you have to force open, in the hard seats of buses and, all over France, those torturing green seats in second-class train carriages where you can never quite sit at your ease, and in so many converted flats with their grotesque juxtapositions of hip-bath and toilet basin, lavatory and kitchen combined, kitchen and shower, etc., where everything is cramped and domestic life is a perpetual squeezing into confined and ridiculously placed spaces and a constant fear of banging one's arms and head on jutting cupboard doors and shelves, awkward taps and curiously placed washbasins. It may also be seen in those lift-less buildings with their flats on the seventh or eighth floor, those endless treks with dustbins down dark stairs, those disgusting communal lavatories in passages, those dripping taps, and the cardboard-thin walls of *chambres de bonne* which are so eagerly sought after by young students and workers, the indigent and the old and rootless.

No matter how *chic* the district, how elegant, how imposing the main entrance, with its heavy glass and wrought-iron door, its carpeted foyer and clean, carpeted staircase, there are always other, steeper flights of stairs just beyond, other, murky courtyards, sometimes with a creaking iron lift of unutterable age and suspicious design, to take you up to uncarpeted corridors in the domain of the *chambres de bonne* where you may hear the heavy breathing of some asthmatic old man, the wail of a child, or the droning of a student's record-player behind the shabby, ill-fitting doors while, only a few yards away in the same building, couples and single people inhabit magnificently spacious high-ceilinged flats crammed with real or fake Louis Quinze furniture which they have inherited from their families and grandparents.

Paris may be a beautiful lady but she has some filthy underclothes. Various official bodies, institutes and the World Health Organisation have published the statistics of the overcrowding and lack of sanitary conveniences in Paris and they are appalling despite the new Parises which are being built at such a rate outside the walls of the city.

In such a city which still has so much discomfort and dirt; in which it is almost impossible to park your car; in which there are so few parks and public gardens where children can play; in which it is taken for granted that your concierge and her entire family live in one, or at the most, two rooms while you inhabit a four- or six-room flat left to you by your parents and for which you pay a derisory rent; in which even single rooms are a desirable property, to be bought for speculation or as an investment; in which every street seems to have its estate agency advertising flats at huge prices which remain empty for years and in which horsemeat shops are as frequent as fish and chip shops in the working-class districts of an English town because, expensive as horse flesh is it is still less expensive than beef or lamb, is it surprising that so many people should be tense and jumpy and quick to show their irritation?

*

Modern Paris is mostly confined to the suburbs. There is a singular lack of new post-war buildings of any distinction. A new Science Faculty has been built on the site of the former Halle aux Vins by the Seine, and vast projects are nearing completion at the Rond-Point de la Défense outside Paris proper. There is the Maison de la Radio on the city's outskirts in Passy, an unassuming Hilton Hotel near the Champ de Mars and an ugly Faculty of Law in the Rue d'Assas near the Luxembourg, and there is the UNESCO building, but there are few gracefully modern buildings to give a new style to any part of the city.

It is in the area to the rear of the old and now vanished railway station at Montparnasse that the greatest building is in progress. A district of small dwellings, lively little streets, workmen's *bistrots*, horsemeat shops and artists' studios, is being torn down to be replaced by gaunt, monolithic blocks and complexes which will tower over the city's southern skyline. The first great blocks over the new station are already completed. They are huge, ruthless, terrifying and crushing. They are so ludicrously out of proportion to everything around them that you cannot quite believe in them. They are a chilling reminder that *somewhere* there is a determination to impose a new city on the old just as Haussmann's Paris was brutally forced upon a predominantly medieval capital.

Although the transformation is beginning on the outskirts it threatens to affect the heart of the capital at Les Halles. Meanwhile, another subtler, more insidious change has been taking place in parts of the city that *are* Paris both to many foreigners and to so many Parisians alike.

Something else that is disappearing from Paris is its 'Parisianity' and that 'good taste' for which it has long been reputed the centre.

Part of the myth of Parisians and the French in general is that they are an innately distrustful, cynical, individualistic and conservative race. They are suspicious of change and modernity. They are the least 'Americanized' people in Europe. They are impervious to high-powered publicity and refuse to be stampeded into new, commercially fabricated mass enthusiasms. They like their antiquated buses, their well-worn but comfortable restaurants, their somewhat shabby but venerated cafés. The businessman with his office in the Champs-Elysées likes nothing better than to get back to the countryside and drink the cider and local wines he knew as a boy and to stop after work at the *bistrot* of his choice which has remained virtually unchanged since before the war. Almost every Parisian has some roots—somewhere—in the provinces, and like the provincial, holds fast to tradition. But now it seems that Parisians like their new drugstores, their 'quick-snack' lunches, their 'English pubs' and their Wimpy Bars—in short all that is least Parisian and most foreign. Nowhere is the evidence of the new fashions and changes in taste more striking than in the district of Saint-Germain-des-Prés which gave France so much of its intellectual and artistic life since the war.

Cocteau once said 'everything that has a value today was born at Saint-Germain-des-Prés'. Now the Saint-Germain of Sartre, Juliette Greco and the spiritual heirs of Guillaume Apollinaire has gone 'pop'. It is still full of art galleries, publishers and bookshops. The street market in the Rue de Buci is as colourful and attractive as ever. The narrow streets are full of curio shops, modest and friendly restaurants, a few genuine *bistrots* and clubs in cellars, but the artists, writers, critics, journalists, night-birds and old-established habitués have seen their kingdom invaded by teenagers and become a kind of fun-palace for the monied young from the bourgeois Paris symbolized by the *seizième arrondissement*. As evidence of the decline of Saint-Germain-des-Prés they will point accusingly at the boutiques that have mushroomed everywhere in the last few years and at that super-boutique, the *Drugstore Saint-Germain*. The district has become Carnaby Street and Mary Quant territory, with the drugstore as its symbol, and is likely to remain so long after Carnaby Street has receded into myth and the pages of social histories.

'*Le Drug*' was built on the site of the former Royal Saint-Germain, a noble café-brasserie with oysters, shrimps and clams displayed outside to tempt the passer-by and delight the eye. It disappeared to make room for a riot of bad taste. Its walls are decorated inside with large brown plaster casts of eyes and mouths of famous film stars—Brigitte Bardot, Jeanne Moreau, Belmondo—magnified many times larger than life. Brassy poles soar up from the floor and end in monstrous seven-fingered hands pressing up at the ceiling. The entire place is a nightmare and a maze of glass, chrome, formica, mirrors, brass glitter and unconvincing pastiches of *art-nouveau* decoration. Echoes of a film set for a Western saloon bar fade into weary exercises in Daliesque surrealism. There is no one, recognizably distinct style and it is all highly undignified although useful since you can buy books, papers, watches, cigarettes, cameras, crocodile-skin ties and handbags, tinned food and sausages, cosmetics and English 'novelties' until late at night. It is a magnet for young smart Parisians with English-inspired shirts, ties and dresses. When it was first opened, the *tout-Paris* and the *tout-Saint-Germain* came crowding into it for one of the biggest and best publicized parties ever seen in the district and it does a roaring business. It is all outrageously 'novel' and like so much that is novel, it will soon degenerate into banality. How long will the monster last? Will the plaster casts of Bardot's eyes and Belmondo's lips be replaced in time by other lips and other eyes of more up-to-date idols? Will it be torn down to make way for a cafeteria in the form of a Chinese pagoda, a spaceship or a drive-in motel? Or will it remain as a monument to one of Paris's short-lived fads?

The first drugstore on the Champs-Elysées was born some years earlier. It is comparatively inoffensive and exactly what you would expect on that now unbeautiful avenue, but the drugstore disease has spread. Another opened on the Boulevard des Italiens with décor inspired by American Westerns. So contagious did the disease seem to be that not long ago it was rumoured that another drugstore was to make its appearance in Montparnasse—perhaps even on the sight of the old Coupole. And why not? Even the famous Brasserie Lipp was rumoured to have been the object of an offer from Courrèges who wanted to turn it into a dress shop . . .

A few yards away from Lipp, the old Chope Saint-Germain has been vandalized. It was once one of the nicest restaurants in the district, a quiet, solid, comfortable place with friendly waitresses, flowered tiles on the walls, and green upholstered seats. You could eat and drink there until midnight for eminently reasonable prices. Then it was renamed the Port Saint-Germain and the style of decoration became pseudo-Saint Tropez. The cafés Flore and Deux Magots have survived but further along the boulevard other new cafés have opened. Like so many other new or redecorated cafés in France, they are places of multi-coloured plastic furnishings, harsh lighting and nasty little square tables which seem to get up and jab at you with their sharp corners as you leave your seat. Judging by them it would seem that the French had become possessed by some urge to destroy all the traditional, comfortable qualities that made the café such an inviting second home.

There is a café in the Place Saint-Sulpice which used to be 'traditional' with its heavy brown tables, its few mirrors and its wicker chairs outside. Then it too became another victim of the new craze for angular formica shapes. Upon enquiry, the owner confessed that he thought it had been vastly improved since he had 'modernized' it. But he had not modernized it: he had made it anonymous. The idea that the café had lost its character and become indistinguishable from a hundred other such cafés seems never to have crossed the owner's mind. To what compulsion did he surrender when he spent so much money on its transformation? Why should the Chope Saint-Germain lose its genuine *fin de siècle* decorations while the Drugstore adapted and bastardized the style?

To find a truly 'French' café has become increasingly difficult in Paris. Even in such 'popular' districts as that of the Rue de la Gaieté there is a newish small café made hideous with multi-coloured bits of glass and glaring yellow lights and in the Latin Quarter cafés you cannot hear yourself speak for the din of the pinball machines but *they*, at least, have been there for years and have become almost an institution, just like the astonishing number of 'English' pubs that have been turning parts of Left Bank Paris into an English Toytown. At least the 'pubs' offer more comfort and gentler surroundings than the average café, which is a sad reflection on French design.

*

We take it for granted that Paris is the feminine city *par excellence*. Her patron saint—Sainte Geneviève—is a woman. The symbol of the Republic is female; when Delacroix painted Liberty storming the barricades, he painted her as a woman; the Terror of the Revolution is remembered for its women, the *tricoteuses*, who sat around the guillotine known as the 'Widow'. Even the topography of the city, with its softly meandering river, its graceful bridges, the weeping willows on the Ile de la Cité, its garlands of lights at night, the grace and elegance of classic buildings and the delicate tracery of the Eiffel Tower are all feminine.

The politics of Paris have been feminine with their jealousies, their plots, quarrels and alliances and their stories of intriguing ministers' wives and mistresses. Even the blanket of dullness and provincial puritanism that was widely believed to have fallen over the city during the Gaullist period was symbolized by 'Tante Yvonne', the President's wife. French foreign policy is feminine: France turns away from the boorish Anglo-Saxon to flirt with the fascinating, virile Russian and Eastern European, only to draw back and recommence the coquettish game. The Paris risings of 1830 and 1848 were like feminine outbursts. Paris was bored and wanted a change! The instability of emotions in the city are feminine: after the passions and riots of May 1968, came apathy and thoughts of summer holidays...

The great *salons* of Paris were run by ladies and even the cafés were feminine unlike the masculine bars and pubs of the Anglo-Saxon world. They were for *parisiennes* to sit and be admired, to gossip and critically examine the dresses of their rivals and, perhaps, to embark upon erotic adventures after a happy encounter there.

The myth of Parisian eroticism is still strong. Lovers and honeymooners from abroad will still go to Paris for the thrill of making love in the city reputed to give primacy to women's passions, whims and attire. Until not so very long ago there remained the contagious myth of Paris as the 'naughtiest' of capital cities where every erotic daydream could find both fulfilment and toleration, where the heart and the flesh ruled over the head. Even the homosexuals on the Left Bank look more feminine than in other cities, more graceful, languid and wickedly alluring.

The elegant *midinette* still survives in guide books and sends writers into ecstasies as they perpetuate the myth of the shop girl or underpaid secretary who knows how to give herself that incomparable Paris *chic* with a scarf and a blouse bought for a few francs and worn with such flair. Yet how hard it has become to see pretty young girls in the streets, cafés or métro! They seem to be found only in certain restaurants, night-clubs and homes. When other young *parisiennes* are not dressing depressingly, their attire is simply uninspired. Nice girls from 'good' families seem determined to go on wearing a uniform of short pony-tail hairdos with bows, tweeds, silk scarves and chunky shoes until the next Deluge. Shop girls wear the darkest colours and whenever one of those sudden crazes to which Paris is prone afflicts the city there is little sign of individuality to be seen among the phalanxes of students trotting down the Boulevard Saint-Michel whether they be wearing split skirts, *jupes-culottes* ending well below the knee, pastel-coloured woollens, or whatever other accessories such as chain belts or enormous spectacles the mode has been decreeing for months on end.

There are pretty clothes in shops and the department stores—many of Anglo-Saxon inspiration—but they are expensive. How is the shop-girl, post-office clerk or typist to pay for them out of her wages, with prices as high as they are in France? For traditional elegance and that expensive *chic* foreigners have heard so much about, you must look at well-off older women and those fascinating, witty Paris ladies of a more interesting age who alone seem to maintain Paris's traditions of female panache. No wonder there is such an erotic myth of the 'older woman' in France! And no wonder that Parisians have been so fascinated by the pretty and already half-mythical English girl, with her well-kept hair, her leggy, mini-skirted charm and that complexion that so few *parisiennes* can ever hope to acquire or keep!

Young elegance in Paris appears to have become a man's monopoly. Even the advertisements and posters in Paris lack pretty girls. The most audacious poster model in recent times was a languidly beautiful male youth photographed in the nude (almost) by the advertising firm of Publicis to promote the sale of a make of men's briefs. A sign, perhaps, of a conspiracy to keep feminine beauty in eclipse? Perhaps it is another sign of the conspiracy responsible for the aggressive, mannish appearance of so many models who posed for the more avant-garde dress designers, with their knee-length stockings, their Bermuda shorts and their science-fiction inspired apparel ranging from the asexual geometric severities of Courrèges to the plastic and metal concoctions of Paco Rabanne?

But in one aspect, at least, the traditional Paris Feminine has survived: the prostitute of the streets, almost unchanged in appearance since Atget took his famous photographs of her more than a generation ago. She is still to be seen in certain streets near Les Halles and the Bastille—bosomy and huge, astonishingly old-fashioned with her gash of blood-red lipstick, her ridiculously high-heeled shoes and her tight skirt. She is raucous, challenging and earthy and as much a part of that older Paris of much-vaunted immorality as the narrow streets of the 'belly' of Paris that once stank of fresh meat and uncomplicated lust.

*

In spite of eccentricities, scars, changes, crazes and disconcerting lapses of 'French good taste', Paris holds fast to her reputation as the Mother of Arts. Not only the administrative centre of the country, it is its cultural despot. French literature, drama and art are mainly a Parisian activity. In spite of all the *maisons de culture* that have been planned and occasionally built for the rest of France, there is no doubt that everything still ends and begins in the capital.

The raw material of French culture may be found elsewhere, in the provinces and their towns, but it must flow towards Paris. There it will be sorted, tested, rejected or accepted. It will eventually be 'Parisianized' before being delivered to the rest of the country or for export abroad, with each successive product bearing the unmistakable label: 'Made in Paris.'

To succeed in France means to succeed in Paris. The city will then dictate your success in the provinces. But first, you must come to terms with the dictator. Mere ability and talent are not enough—especially outside Paris. According to myth and tradition, only Paris can give the French cultural product that vital, unique quality of 'Frenchness' which is none other than the magical quality of the capital.

THE CAPITAL OF THE SPIRIT

If we wish to make even the briefest and most selective survey of the state of French literature and artistic activity we have no choice but to begin in Paris. We may even be in danger of remaining there and forgetting to move beyond its limits. Like so many other of the nation's activities, painting and publishing, theatrical creation and literary fashions are centralized in this city which has arrogated to itself such a towering position of dominance towards the rest of France that the adjective 'provincial' is almost an insult, suggesting banality, lack of inspiration and complete inability either to understand or to innovate. And as for being a 'provincial', is not one of the definitions of this word, given in the Littré dictionary of the French language, 'someone who is from the provinces and who ignores the things of the capital or of the court'?

Paris has been said to be vital to the culture of the rest of the world. In France, it is essential to the rest of the country. It can consecrate, condemn or create. You do not argue with the dictator. Instead you go to his court.

*

To spend any time in Paris and to take an interest in its arts is soon to become aware of the compactness and visibility of its small but very lively literary-artistic world. We have seen that the city can still attract many foreigners who are far from agreeing with cynical journalists and disillusioned former residents of the city that Paris has fallen to the rank of a minor centre, having long since been dethroned by its more vigorous and freshly creative rivals in America, England or Germany. Indeed, during the whole Gaullist period, there seemed little immediate evidence that Paris was in the cultural doldrums as had been so maliciously suggested abroad.

The expatriate artist, intellectual or writer and the ardent lover of French culture for whom a pilgrimage at least once a year to Paris is a necessity for his mental and emotional well-being, can still point at the flood of new books that pours into the windows and stands of the Left Bank bookshops, at the lectures, debates and forums that are always being held, at the new reviews, the number of literary periodicals, art galleries, exhibitions, new films, private viewings, cocktail parties, dinner parties, tea parties, the celebrities so easily accessible in the few but famous cafés where 'everybody can meet everybody', the passionate political positions taken by well-known writers and critics, the little experimental theatre groups that spring up now and again, and Paris's avid interest in anything new, bold, out-of-the-way and *avant-garde*.

Should you try to argue that it is surprising that so little of all this exciting new activity has been reflected in French cultural and artistic exports abroad, that such or such a book greeted as a masterpiece in Paris should have been a flop outside France, and that the number of contemporary French works that have been sold in any great numbers in England or America is minute, you may well be reproached for being uncivilized, insular, and unappreciative. After all, how can you—unimaginative, stolid Anglo-Saxon that you are—really appreciate the charm, wit and specifically French (or Parisian) sophistication of this or that novel, play or collection of thought-provoking essays? It was all your public could do to appreciate Impressionism in the end! As for really understanding the best of modern French culture, you have to be a Parisian in spirit and to be Parisian, as a most Parisian friend once told this writer, you must 'share a certain complicity'.

A hostile critic might state that this Parisian 'complicity' is 'provincial' and too cut off from the rest of the world, absorbed as it is in its own image and complacent in a sense of rightful superiority, strengthened by awareness of its rich past. The ardent defender of Paris who would rather read one *nouveau roman* than three novels written by provincial writers in his own country and who is convinced that in France, as in no other country, to be a writer or artist is a title that automatically will earn you the respect of everybody from the street-sweeper to the business tycoon, will retort that what you call provincial is the natural tendency of all that is creative and intelligent to converge and cross-fertilize in a centre. Look at Athens in the age of Pericles! And what about Florence during the Renaissance? Provincial indeed—you simply don't understand! And what about all those great names who have won honour and respect in France: Borges, Octavio Paz, Asturias, Ungaretti, that astonishing Egyptian painter whom England and America have so lamentably failed to recognize, and that revolutionary author of 'concrete poems' from Sardinia whose name is only to be found in the most esoteric of little magazines in English, who has just had his new volume hailed by the critics and who wrote a catalogue-preface for that brilliantly attended private viewing of the latest work of that most 'moving' of Paris's semi-abstract, erotico-surrealistic painters who is still so unaccountably ignored by American museums and Bond Street art galleries?

And how can you call a city 'provincial' when it is undeniably so open to the talent of those writers and artists who come unknown to offer, to receive and finally to make their name?

If you have decided to make your name or at least to participate in the cultural life of Paris, which in effect means meeting and knowing the people who have already made their name and who have participated in this life, then there is no doubt that Paris is a very pleasant city. You need some money—that is only natural. And you need at least one good introduction to someone who can do something for you. To this you cannot possibly object: it is the way of the world and after all, you will not go to a foreign country without taking something with you, if only an address in a pocket diary, and some financial resource, or the promise of an employment.

The system of moving from one person of interest to you to another is very well developed in France. In cultural as in less creative social life, you still tend to make acquaintances and eventual friends by the process of social escalation: a telephone call will be followed by an agreement to meet at a café. Conversation over a coffee or a beer may then be followed by an invitation to after-dinner drinks. You may then meet again for a meal in company with others. Eventually, you may be invited home for dinner and to a party. By then you will have really made your entry into the world of your choice. As you make your way from one person to another, following up those telephone numbers you have been given and always announcing yourself with the ritual *c'est de la part d'un tel* . . . (I have the honour to ring at the suggestion of Monsieur—who suggested . . .) you will nearly always meet with politeness and a willingness to help you become a part of *that* Paris. Your welcome may be formal but it is nonetheless a welcome.

The great prerequisite is that you have something to offer. You must be interesting—even sexually. Paris still has its mythical women-who-count and it is not uncommon to be told that if, by one of those charming hazards of Paris, you should attract the eye of such and such a lady then it will be both worth while and pleasant to follow up your initial advantage. Like this not altogether mythical lady, Paris is eager to be seduced and charmed. Hence this agreeable impression of cosmopolitanism and lack of any kind of xenophobia or chauvinism which the newcomer from abroad might have expected. School text-books, articles by French Academicians and the sonorous speeches of politicians inaugurating exhibitions of French art and literature might suggest an overwhelming sense of national superiority in the field, but everywhere around you in that restricted Parisian world which 'creates' and 'appreciates' there would seem to be an agreeable spirit of cultural internationalism.

A characteristic of Parisian cultural life is the apparent many-sidedness of so many writers, painters and critics. Often, all three activities may be combined by one person. The foreign resident who feels himself the spiritual citizen of this cultural Paris will point out to you the number of writers, who, not content with merely producing their novels or plays or poems, will also readily write reviews for literary papers, or the columns of newspapers, besides taking part in various political or artistic debates. They seem to do *so much*: you will find such and such an eminent writer at all the first nights of plays, or new films, or attending the private viewing of some painter whom he not only knows personally but for whom he has campaigned actively in his critical articles. A literary journalist is not only a writer of his own books and his opinions on other peoples' books for he will suddenly make his appearance as a dramatic critic in one paper, only to reappear later as a film critic before taking time off from Paris to attend some festival of *avant-garde* music and sculpture in Italy or Jugoslavia. A critic of the cinema will become a film-maker himself and the literary critic of one review will have his novel reviewed in another journal by yet another well-known novelist turned critic. In short there would appear to be no barrier between the various activities and although you may detest painting entirely you will be distressingly un-Parisian and uncultivated if you do not show some interest when invited to join literary friends and mentors at a cocktail party in some smart new gallery.

This constant surface activity and air of excitement about personalities and events has its lure for the foreigner. Something is always happening, there is so much to see, so much to do . . . Whether the heady world of Paris 'culture' is beneficial to the artist or writer is another matter. You will meet expatriates and temporary immigrants who have been swallowed up in the life of this Paris, who will have succumbed to the same enthusiasms that will have affected their French friends, who will have adopted the same cults, moved in the same atmosphere that has shaped their attitudes, styles and judgements of fellow artists or writers and have met the same people who 'must be met'. Such immigrants are that earnest and charming American/English/Irish/Australian painter/poet/novelist who is to be seen at all the important private picture-viewings in and around the Rue de Seine, at cocktail parties, and who is engaged in the elaboration of a very 'difficult' and 'experimental' novel of which an extract has been published in the *Paris Review* perhaps, or that Brazilian/Egyptian/Swiss poet and playwright who takes his inspiration from Raymond Roussel and Roger Vitrac, collaborates on some little magazine, campaigns on behalf of some other foreign writer or poet and painter, and who receives the flattering accolades of his Parisian patrons and well-wishers who welcome him as one of their company and who will tell you that he is 'such a charming boy' whom you must meet at all costs.

Such is the air of sophistication and we-understand-and-welcome-the-exciting-the-new-and-the-avant-garde that the fear of being (or being thought) bourgeois or conservative is worse than elsewhere. If you say that you are a writer, it is automatically accepted that you are a 'serious' writer. An 'experimental' novel? Perversely erotic? So much the better! Why not show a few pages to X? Say you are a friend of Y's! But to distract you from your main task, there are so many drinks to go to, so many people to be met, so many friends to meet in your favourite café, so many supper parties or nice little dinners in that charming little restaurant 'we all go to', and always so many things to see!

This feeling that cultural life in Paris is so alive and in such a constant, pleasant state of excitement is reinforced by the newspapers with their accounts of the doings, witticisms, opinions and quarrels of literary personalities and famous artists. Quarrels in this world are widely publicized for a large and fascinated public. They sometimes attain a virulence verging on the ludicrous as when Roger Peyrefitte riposted to a typically wailing protestation on behalf of morality by François Mauriac with a viciousness and a wealth of salacious innuendo that a smutty-minded but literate schoolboy might envy.*

In this feverish atmosphere, personalities in the arts loom large in the public eye and move in a dimension somewhat different from that of their craft. Certain names will always appear in papers and

* Over a proposal to film Peyrefitte's novel of young homosexuality, *Les amitiés particulières*.

magazines and even though their owners may not be 'personalities' as such, with all the word implies in English, they make their presence felt and maintain it in the gossip art columns with a regularity and emphasis only rivalled by film stars and television idols in England. There is no question but that most of the best-known French writers live their semi-public lives in Paris. A few recluses or grand old men of literature and art may reside in the provinces but most of the writers who 'count' seem to live in Paris as though their literary successes depended on it. There is of course one literary 'establishment', if not several, but its members are not only powers in their own domain but also public performers. You just cannot miss them.

The peculiar atmosphere of literary Paris has been beautifully and succinctly expressed by Julien Gracq, himself an important writer. It is well worth quoting for although it was written in 1949 it is relevant today:

> ... in France literature is written and criticized against a noisy background that is to be found nowhere else, and from which it is doubtless inseparable: the clamour of an unstable and over-excited crowd, the feverish murmur of a perpetual Stock Exchange. And in fact—its exact volume and size are unimportant—this volatile public (Paris has always had its salons or its literary districts), like the members of the Stock Exchange, has the strange peculiarity of being almost constantly in a state of excitement: there is the same snatching up of news, which is absorbed everywhere simultaneously like water sinking into sand, amplified into rumour, coined into echoes, into the gossip of the corridors—the same edginess, even the same feminine instability in one's reactions—the same need to have one's state of excitation continually stimulated by the *new*—the same lightheaded frenzy to interpret whatever turns up: not a single book or a single author is thrown as fodder to this crowd, but it is worked upon by a kind of leaven, computed, dissected, interpreted, sounded, prolonged already into an imaginary future, evaluated from every possible point of view. Contact with this over-stimulated and over-stimulating public, whose pulse beats slightly above normal—a contact that is not easily forgotten—does not leave the writer unaffected. (43)

Nor does it leave the foreigner unaffected—whether he has come to Paris simply to drink at the sources of French culture or to find a stimulus necessary to his creativity which the myth tells him is to be found in Paris. The prominence given to France's (which is virtually to say: Paris's) writers in the press and on the radio, the number of literary periodicals—*Figaro littéraire, Lettres Nouvelles, Lettres Françaises, Quinzaine littéraire*—and the space given to reviews—in *Le Monde, Le Nouvel Observateur, Les Temps Modernes* —the articulate and partisan way in which writers are discussed, their varied cultural interventions outside their own principal domains, their polemics and attitudes towards the questions of the moment, all suggest a country in which the arts are taken with the utmost seriousness and respect.

By some kind of mental osmosis, by contact with his French friends and by what he hears and sees, the foreigner will feel that he is in the very heart of a living, highly aware, very open civilization which continues to give primacy to things of the spirit. How stimulating Paris is! How adventurous, how cosmopolitan, how welcoming and how infectious is the atmosphere of this city in which a new book is a public event and a new *ism* of world-shaking importance! There is something in Paris which will mould his judgement, give new awareness, shift emphasis and produce enthusiasms which he may carry away with him back to his homeland but which he will find difficult to communicate and which will fail to arouse the same keen responses in others.

The foreign worshipper of Paris's cultural life may even become a figure of fun. You will know him by his passionate espousal of certain French cults, his scorn for the unreceptive climate of his native land, his utter disbelief that such and such a book cannot arouse the same interest outside France ('If there is one book which should be translated now it is ——; it is a shame and a disgrace that so-and-so is so little known . . . But what do you expect, people just haven't got the same respect for literature here . . .'). And, of course, the distressing thing is that so many of these French books which *should* be translated and French painters who *should* be known and honoured in all the world's museums and galleries seem unable to survive the process of export. Can this be due to the fact that other people simply are behind the French as far as taste, discernment and interest go, or—awful thought—to some fatal defect of incommunicability in these works which have so much power to charm and impress inside France yet which lose their quality to excite and to stimulate once removed to an alien climate?

Let us take the example of a play: Romain Weingarten's *L'Eté* which so delighted and charmed Paris during its immensely long run. It is a beautifully written fantasy of two adolescents on the threshold of maturity in a country cottage inhabited by two ironic and yet sentimental cats who comment on the play, and the gradual awareness of love that comes to the young people. In French, how witty, how graceful, how cruel yet enchanting! French wit and intelligence allied to the spirit of a Lewis Carroll: how could it fail to succeed? And yet, translated into English and beautifully acted, it flopped after only a few days in London. Why? Its magic worked in Paris—why not in London? Do the English not have a taste for fantasy and poetry—after all, look at their poetry and humour! What mysterious process of alchemy in reverse is this which can turn gold and quicksilver into base metal so that nothing is left but thin whimsey, tritely expressed and, without the covering of the French language, shabbily clothed? Why did it appear gold in France? Was it due to some subtle magic of the French language, its resonances, its intimate illusions, a peculiarly French sensibility, either acquired or innate, and that Parisian spirit of complicity of which we should try to analyse the nature and the secret?

Can it be that the Parisian is really the most provincial of Frenchmen as far as his culture and manner of appreciating it are concerned? So much in the city seems to say that the Parisian spirit is open to the whole world. Paris has long been famous as a queen of cosmopolitan cities. But could not this cosmopolitanism be simply another name for a taste for the exotic and foreign—both to be appreciated from an exclusively Parisian viewpoint? The term refers to a way of life, of thinking and of feeling resulting from constant contact with the arts, attitudes and ways of peoples from the four corners of the earth. It relates to a system of fruitful relationships with the foreigner, with cultural and social imports which help to open the national spirit to other ways of thinking, seeing and behaving. But in Paris it becomes snobbery and French society's persistent mania for English clothes, tea, decorations and other *bric-à-brac* is only a sign of a taste for the exotic and for collecting status symbols. It is also noticeable that the popular image of England that has persisted is an aristocratic one with great snob appeal: the impeccably well dressed Englishman with his cool, lofty demeanour, his bowler hat, neatly furled umbrella and cavalry coat, always living against a background of country houses, elegant London squares, and his eternal club. As for French interest in American civilization, what is it but a vogue for films, detective novels, gadgets, and all the folk-lore elements of a way of life which still remains profoundly misunderstood when not simply ignored?

Similarly, the very fierceness with which some expatriates proclaim their Parisian enthusiasms and assume that they are beyond the comprehension of their fellow countrymen at home is the reverse of cosmopolitanism and the sign of a mentality which, through contagion, has become not merely provincial but parochial. Even a provincial may appreciate foreign imports but this does not make him a producer of goods for export.

*

For all the outward liveliness of artistic life in Paris during the 1960's, there has been a remarkable amount of nostalgia accompanied by a revival of enthusiasm for English culture with many Paris critics convinced that the new renaissance in painting, drama, music, literature and even the art of living was to be found on the other side of the channel.

The myth of London as the 'swinging city' was firmly believed in Paris. The London of Carnaby Street, Soho, the Beatles, a new 'permissiveness', a new classlessness and a new democracy in the arts was contrasted with the dullness of a Paris suffering from several years of Gaullist respectability and boredom. But, of course, not everybody in Paris could appreciate this new, much-praised creativity and sophistication of *la bonne vieille Angleterre*. The Beatles were not a particularly great success when they came to Paris ('their wit and sophistication were above the level of appreciation of our audiences' was what one French writer reprovingly told his readers in a magazine) and Christiane Rochefort's valiant attempt to translate *John Lennon in his own Write* was a disastrous failure in the bookshops; but more and more French pop singers made English-style sounds and grew their hair long, and much pop music broadcast on Radio Luxembourg and Radio Monte Carlo came from the land of the 'Liverpool beat'.

Film and theatre critics became almost embarrassingly effusive about things English. Films like *Tom Jones*, the James Bond sagas, *The Knack*, the thrillers of John le Carré were praised to the skies and indicated as examples of a new, free, uninhibited, unconventional England that breathed the spirit of its new youth—so stimulating and delightful after the puritanical, sterile fog that seemed to have descended upon the French spirit under the Gaullist régime which was making France materially richer but spiritually poorer.

Intellectualizing film critics produced verbose exegeses of English 'off-beat' comedies while women queued up at the Bazar de l'Hôtel de Ville to buy 'James-Bond-Goldfinger' gold-coloured underwear that some enterprising manufacturer had launched on the market to coincide with the film. Young, sophisticated Paris went to hear and dance to English-style 'beat' music at the Bus Palladium hall in Pigalle. A journalist wrote articles praising London for its youthfulness and dynamism, its shops ('some of the most surprising and secret shops in the world') and its stimulus for artists. English plays invaded the Paris stage. Joan Littlewood received the rapturous acclaim in Paris that had been denied her in London. Years later, the stream of English plays was still showing no signs of drying up. James Saunders' *Next time I'll sing to you* was hailed by the Paris critics and dubbed a 'feast of intelligence'—words which, you would have thought, would once have been applied only to a French play. Similarly, the vogue of Americana had already shown itself in Paris's 'drug-stores', the craze for 'westerns' (often made in Italy), American thrillers, old Raoul Walsh and Humphrey Bogart films, and gadgetry. The one mania that did not seem to have been inspired by the Anglo-Saxon world was the collecting of key-rings.

Coincident with this passion for Anglo-American imports was a nostalgia for a livelier, friendlier, more stimulating Paris—a nostalgia frequently expressed by the older Parisians for whom the city had been first and foremost a giver of intellectual, artistic and bodily pleasure.

While humbler Parisians have been content to earn more money, acquire more cars, television sets, modern flats and better plumbing, the descendants of the Parisians of the boulevards, cafés and salons have been lamenting a decline in the quality of *their* Paris life. If you happen to go to Paris now, or if you lived there in the last few years, how often did you hear your Parisian friend regret that you didn't know Paris some five, six or ten years ago? It was such an exciting city in the past. In spite of the Algerian war, the police raids and brutalities, the *O.A.S.*, and the plastic bomb attacks, Paris was livelier, friendlier, more self-confident, and exciting, more intellectually stimulating, more charming . . .

Paris was naughtier. You were shown such and such a club and told that it was once the most amusing, daring *boîte* in Paris: you went in couples only and left your clothes in the cloakroom before dancing . . . The *chansonniers* were wittier and crueller . . . There was more good-natured vice, more prostitutes to enliven the Paris street scene, more scandals, more impromptu parties, better jazz, more truly Parisian personalities who reigned over a gayer, more brilliant, adoring *tout Paris*. Even the gossip-writers and foreign journalists told you that the big spenders, international celebrities and eccentrics had been gradually deserting the city.

Like a hypochondriac always taking his own temperature, Parisians in love with their city's recent past have been eagerly looking for the least sign of a renewal in the quality of Paris's life. When the riots in the Latin Quarter broke out in May 1968 and the students seemed to be ruling the Left Bank, many Parisians felt that they were living in a new renaissance and that the city had regained all its former charm and vitality. But a few weeks later, this apparent transformation of a previously dulled city had shown itself to be ephemeral. Apathy and reaction were the aftermath. The inhabitants turned from thoughts of politics to thoughts of summer holidays and began to desert a Paris which was left to dream again of its one-time splendour, to take comfort in its myths and continue worshipping its idols of the past.

5

The Idols

THE LAST great mythical 'golden age' of Paris was centred around the district of Saint-Germain-des-Prés. In the first few years after the last war, it seemed that everything was possible for those with the talent, the vigour and the courage. Cultural life was richly creative and exportable abroad where it could be sure of both sympathy and intelligent appreciation. Paris was once more the giver, not only to France but to a Europe and a world that badly needed brightening. It was the time of Paris's cellars and 'existentialism', meetings at the Flore or the Deux Magots cafés, wonderful jazz, passionate left-wing optimism and a complete break from the bourgeoisie who had collaborated or simply accepted France's sad condition during the Occupation. The memories of those heroic days and nights of parties, music, all-night discussions and impromptu creativity are part of a legendary history. The myth has still attracted a newer generation who come to the district that *was* Paris in search of more than its present gaudy attractions. Meanwhile, the survivors of these glorious days mourn for the vanishing of a certain spirit of Paris.

This regret for a legendary age, combined with a widespread tendency to feed upon myths of past creative achievements and to content itself with a continuation of the old rather than the elaboration of the new have been some of the main characteristics of Paris's recent cultural life. They give the cultural climate its tone and its anachronistic quality. They are represented by certain great idols and myths which we shall now examine in some detail. They represent segments, not the totality, of the literary-artistic scene in Paris today but they are important since they so well illustrate, more than anything else, the city's apparent inability to contribute anything fresh in the arts or to radiate any more of that spirit and state of mind which is called Parisian, which is so easy to recognize and so hard to define.

Great myths have their heroes. One of the greatest of the age of

THE IDOLS

Saint-Germain-des-Prés was Boris Vian. In the last few years he has been rediscovered and become idolized by a new, young public who never knew the age he typified. He strikingly incarnated a spirit of Paris which was turned outwards. It may not have radiated very far abroad but when we come to examine his personality and his works, they still shed a glow of what is most civilized and admirable in the Parisian spirit, compounded of sadness, affection, wit, and cynicism and a detestation of cant, hypocrisy, vulgarity, and inhumanity. The quality reflected by his works and personality is the antithesis of that expressed by another prominent aspect of Paris's cultural life. This, as we shall see, is one that is essentially turned inwards, marked by narcissicism and an anaemic inability to move in any other direction than that of the past and the 'exotic'.

*

No one was better fitted to represent the spirit of Saint-Germain-des-Prés than the singular and charming engineer-poet-singer-composer-jazz-trumpeter-jester-novelist-playwright Boris Vian. For several years, he was one of the leading personalities who alternately charmed and scandalized a city eager for amusement and originality.

His life was brief, like the era he incarnated. He never lost his youth since he died at the age of thirty-nine of a diseased heart, in 1959, years after he had withdrawn from the Saint-Germain that had already outlived its great period.

He was born at Ville d'Avray, near Paris, on March 10, 1920, into a prosperous middle-class family and seems to have spent a very happy childhood. He had two brothers and a younger sister, a jovial, indulgent father and an affectionate mother, and led a protected, comfortable existence in what must have been the very nicest kind of French bourgeois family atmosphere. Unfortunately, a fever he caught at the age of twelve led to the heart trouble that was to menace him for the rest of his life: a 'valvular insufficiency of the aorta'. But despite this setback to his health, young Vian did well at school, and eventually took an engineer's diploma at the Ecole Centrale in Paris during the Occupation. His main interests were already becoming apparent: he had begun to write, had fallen in love with jazz after hearing Duke Ellington play in Paris in 1938, and started to learn the trumpet and organize impromptu jam-sessions with his friends. His life during the Occupation was comparatively peaceful. He married and had a son, met Claude Abadie, a clarinettist and band-leader, played jazz frequently, gave parties and worked as an engineer for an organization called the *Association Française de Normalisation*. He began to write his first novel, *Vercoquin et le Plancton*, a high-spirited tale of youthful parties, high jinks, lovemaking and practical jokes, full of word play and anarchic humour, mainly to amuse his friends. It was read by Raymond Queneau who gave the book his qualified approval and it was published in 1946 by the distinguished firm of Gallimard, when Vian was already a member of the Saint-Germain 'set' and engaged in writing his second novel, with several short stories already to his credit.

In the small, highly centralized but welcoming ambience of the Left Bank, he began to make his name as a jazz player and also as a 'personality' with a markedly original humour and verbal dexterity and his own brand of hedonistic anarchy. He met Simone de Beauvoir and Sartre and collaborated for a time on the *Temps Modernes*, Sartre's monthly review which published some extracts of his second novel, *L'Ecume des jours*. Simone de Beauvoir's early impressions of him are revealing: at a first meeting she thought that Vian 'listened to himself too much and that he was inclined to cultivate paradoxes for their own sake'. But later, in the course of a long *tête-à-tête* at a party he gave, she 'no longer found anything affected in that long pale, smooth face, but instead great kindliness and a sort of stubborn candour. Vian was as vehement about hating what he called "*les affreux*" as he was about liking what he liked'. Much of his literary production was to be informed by his 'great kindliness and stubborn candour' and his constant hatred and contempt for various institutions and those who serve them.

But in the meantime, as he moved in the literary-bohemian world of Saint-Germain-des-Prés with its 'existentialism', all-night parties, drinking bouts and underground jazz, he was singled out by the Paris press as a perfect symbol of that 'irresponsible' way of life supposedly inspired by a philosophy of which only the most superficial aspects reached the public. He became known as the 'Prince of Saint-Germain', a tireless jester, a charming companion and party-giver and a talented jazz player, but the image of himself that he projected was certainly not one of a 'serious' writer.

But whether he thought of himself as 'serious' or not, he was writing steadily. *L'Ecume des jours* was published and flopped. It was followed by another, even odder novel, *L'Automne à Pekin* which left the reading public equally indifferent. Vian was by now far more successful as a jazz reporter and correspondent for the newspaper *Combat* and the French jazz review, *Jazz Hot*. By one of those paradoxes in which he seemed to take such delight, fame or rather notoriety came to him after he had published a pseudo-American thriller written under the name of 'Vernon Sullivan' and entitled *J'irai cracher sur vos tombes* (I'll spit on your tombs). According to the playwright François Billetdoux, after hearing that a Paris publisher was looking for a thriller to rival the success of James Hadley Chase's *No Orchids for Miss Blandish*, Vian spontaneously offered to write one for him in a fortnight. The result was a short, violent hotch-potch of sex, booze and sadism. Despite the fact that the publisher proudly compared the book (which 'could not be published in the United States') with the novels of Caldwell, Faulkner and James Cain, and printed the name of Vian as 'translator', critics had their doubts concerning the existence of Mr. Sullivan. The book sold well, attracted great publicity and much condemnation. It was followed by three other novels under the same name, always with the same 'translator', and the publisher, printer and Vian were eventually fined 100,000 old francs in 1948 when the secret of 'Sullivan's' true identity was already out and a prosecution was brought for obscenity. A stage version of *J'irai cracher . . .* was prepared; public advertisements for the play were forbidden in the métro and it was a failure.

A year later Vian had given up his profession as an engineer. He devoted himself entirely to jazz, Bohemian life, and writing. As a celebrity he was one of the main attractions in clubs like the Tabou in the Rue Dauphine, and Le Trou in the Rue Saint-Benoît. It was a tiring life: a doctor had warned him that if he did not give up the trumpet and lead a quieter life he would not have more than ten years to live but Vian was by now too much a part of Saint-Germain life and the jazz he loved. He continued writing about jazz as well as playing it, he translated books to earn much-needed money, published a selection of short stories, *Les fourmis*, in 1949, staged a play he had written four years before, *L'Equarrissage pour tous*, in 1950, and saw it fail, and in the same year published another novel (under his own name this time) *L'Herbe rouge* which also flopped, and a limited edition of ten poems with illustrations by a little-known artist. He was also to have published a 'hand-book of Saint-Germain' but it never saw the light. He had fallen in love with a Swiss girl and set up house with her, marrying her in 1954, two years after obtaining a divorce from his first wife.

His health was worsening and money problems became more pressing. He began to withdraw from Saint-Germain-des-Prés, which was losing its magic in the early 1950's, and had to give much of his time to translating, although he had also begun to write songs and advise a record company as artistic director. His last novel, *L'Arrache-Cœur*, appeared in 1953 and failed to attract attention, although his *Automne à Pekin* was recognized by the important firm of Editions de Minuit who republished it in 1956. His range as a translator was varied, to say the least: in a few months he translated General Omar Bradley's *A Soldier's Story*, a monumental work of well over 500 pages, and went on to a mixed bag that included science-fiction, a novel by Nelson Algren, Brendan Behan's *Quare Fellow* and even some Strindberg with the help of a Swedish collaborator. His musical activity as a player decreased in favour of journalism, song-writing, composing and even singing in clubs and cabarets.

In 1953, Vian moved to Montmartre, almost as though to symbolize his break with Saint-Germain-des-Prés. He had become a member of an eccentric neo-Dadaist institution that ridiculed other institutions, the Collège of Pataphysics, whose 'science of imaginary solutions' inspired by Alfred Jarry in a posthumous work, the *Life and Opinions of Dr. Faustroll*, appealed to his taste for verbal play, satire and general hatred of 'establishments' and authority. He was made a 'satrap' of the College and was later honoured by the extraordinary title of *Promoteur Insigne de l'Ordre de la Grand Gidouille*. An active member of the 'College', Vian contributed a series of highly personal letters to its publications, one being a witty expression of his attitude to war and all things military ('we don't get the wars we pay for . . . the day when nobody comes back from a war it will be because the war has at last been properly organized . . .'). After the Algerian war had started to poison France and cast its shadow over life in Paris, Vian again came into conflict with the authorities. He had composed and sung a song, *Le Déserteur*, in which he explained to *Monsieur le Président* his reluctance to take part in any organized killing and his intention to desert. After being launched in January 1955, it was a *succès de scandale* only to be forbidden on the radio after several singers had sung it to millions of Frenchmen.

The state of Vian's health had become desperate. He was seriously ill in the summer of 1956; a year later he confessed that it was an extreme effort even for him to hold a pen; he lived on medicine and his abnormally swollen heart could be heard across a room. He had the satisfaction of seeing one of his plays, *The Empire Builders*, published by the College of Pataphysics, and the film rights of *J'irai cracher sur vos tombes* were taken up by a producer. On June 23, 1959, he went with a friend to see the preview of the film and died of a stroke ten minutes after the projection had started. A few years before, he had told his wife, Ursula, that he would never live to see forty.

*

Real literary success came to Vian posthumously. This was largely due to his devoted friends and admirers. He had an immense capacity for inspiring affection and for those who remembered and mourned him, his spirit was enshrined in the few novels, poems, songs and plays he had left. Critics discovered him; former friends and collaborators wrote prefaces to his novels and stories which were again republished; his verbal tricks and audacities and the allusions which fill his novels provided ample material for exegetists; an exhibition was held in his honour in a book-shop on the Boulevard Saint-Germain; a short life and study of Vian was written by a sympathetic American university teacher. (44) It has now become possible to buy nearly everything he wrote without difficulty, two of his novels in paperback have sold in tens of thousands to a public largely composed of young people who were barely children at the time of his reign in Saint-Germain, and his plays have been performed and even translated into English. In short, Vian has become very much a part of the French culture of the Sixties.

His friends were right. Almost everything that Vian wrote was pure Vian. There is certainly nobody at all like him in French literature and he is certainly one of the few French writers who seem capable of inspiring affection—especially among the young in France.

Why? Although at least two of his novels have been translated into the English language, this very 'Parisian' writer is difficult to translate and the peculiar quality of his 'charm' is not one that can easily survive transposition into another language and culture. To some English critics, a book like *L'Ecume des jours* seemed little more than an exercise in French whimsey and verbal acrobatics in the manner of Raymond Queneau who, as has been noted, admired Vian. Indeed, it is difficult to imagine that an Anglo-Saxon public would become enthusiastic over such a 'difficult' Vian novel as *L'Automne à Pekin*, a strange and elaborate fantasy set in the imaginary country of Exopotamia in which various characters meet to act out their intrigues and take part in a futile railway-building venture. Nor does Vian's comparatively simple first novel, *Vercoquin et le Plancton*, with its celebration of the high-living of young and irresponsible people have much to convey to a non-French public.

All Vian's last four novels—that is, those written under his own name and not the pseudo-American thrillers—are set in some surrealistic fairy-tale land of his imagination and are nourished by his own experiences, prejudices and passions. They contain many of his private jokes, people he knew are brought in thinly disguised, and various events in his own life such as his disappointing failure to win the literary prize, the Prix de la Pléiade, provide material for satire and incidents in *L'Automne à Pekin*, for instance. Vian might be accused of putting too many 'in-jokes' and private references into his novels and his bizarreries are susceptible of interpretation as evidence of affectation and a love of mystification for its own sake. Our suspicions that he is really an ivory-tower writer or cult figure seem to be confirmed when we learn that many parts of his novels were directly written to amuse his friends and his Saint-Germain-des-Prés set, and to an unsympathetic reader brought to these books by the passionately voiced admiration that Vian has aroused among his French friends, much of his writing may even seem affected and over-whimsical.

Two of Vian's novels, *L'Ecume des jours* and *L'Herbe rouge*, are generally considered by his admirers to be his masterpieces. At first sight, they would seem to deserve those accusations of preciosity and over-elaboration that have been levelled at much French literature in the last two decades. *L'Ecume des jours*, which Raymond Queneau has called 'the most poignant of contemporary love stories', is the story of two young couples, whose marriages come to a tragic end. Colin, a pleasant young man of means, falls in love with Chloe. He marries her at the same time as his friend Chick marries Alise. Chloe falls ill and dies, Chick is killed by the police, Colin and Alise are left alone and bereft of everything. The novel, which is written as a kind of fairy-tale with an unhappy ending, is rich in examples of Vian's word-play and fantastic imagery. He used every verbal trick in his repertory to produce a sad little tale with patches of black humour and an underlying sense of the tragedy in life from which none of us is ever safe. What message or 'philosophy' there is in *L'Ecume des jours* is mostly to be found in what the characters say. They have the simplicity and directness of children or the heroes of fairy-tales. When a doctor in the book asks Colin what he does in life the answer is 'I learn things. And I love Chloe'. The young couples live to enjoy themselves. Work is a bore or a degradation and love is the most important thing of all. Happiness is menaced by employers, authorities and official institutions, the church and human ailments. When love has gone life is empty. Religion is useless as a consoler. Like work, it cannot make men happy. Youth is soon gone and is to be enjoyed as much as possible. If such is the theme of Vian's novel it is not very original. But what is remarkable about the book is not its fantasmagorical detail, its verbal jests and its off-beat humour as much as the intensity of Vian's anguish and tragic vision. Despite the eccentricities of Vian's form and style, it is his enormous sincerity and the simplicity of his vision that give *L'Ecume des jours* the power to touch the emotions and to linger in the memory after the bizarre framework of the story has been forgotten.

If the sunshine which at first predominates in *L'Ecume des jours* is eventually clouded by tragedy, the atmosphere of *L'Herbe rouge* is almost wholly one of despair. It is the darkest of Vian's novels and the most disturbing. Once again we are in Vian-land, in a strange world in another dimension in which words are made to play clever tricks and which is peopled by flora and fauna of the writer's own invention. Again the protagonists are two doomed couples.

The setting is a weird landscape where the grass grows red and sinister and a mysterious science-fictional machine is operated by two men, Wolf and Saphir Lazuli. Wolf has a beautiful blonde wife, Lil, and Lazuli has a tender girl-friend, Folavril, whom he seems afraid to love. From the very beginning, Vian introduces his strange living creations: a dog called Senator Dupont who can talk and who is mercilessly teased by Wolf who finally makes it happy by finding it an odd little animal called *ouapiti*. As at the beginning of *L'Ecume des jours*, there is a party and dancing, but it is very soon clear that the two couples have none of the joyfulness or thoughtless hedonism of Colin and Chick and their wives. Both the men are oppressed by undefined anxieties. Something is holding Lazuli apart from Folavril; Wolf awakens from an uneasy sleep and tries to calm his nerves by drawing with coloured chalks on a piece of parchment, like a child in search of distraction, but the chalks crumble into dust...

The machine turns out to be some kind of Wellsian time-machine in which Wolf travels back in search of his own past and his memories and is interrogated by a succession of authoritarian personages. Meanwhile, each time that Lazuli draws close to Folavril, he is shocked by the disturbing apparition of a pale-faced man in a dark costume who stares at them both. In what might have been a tender love scene, Lazuli is reduced to impotence by the repeated apparition of the mysterious stranger. He kills him with a knife only to see another, identical man appear. He strikes them in turn and then falls dead to the ground, wounded by his own knife blows. The corpses disappear and even Lazuli's apartment in the house he shares with Wolf and Lil vanishes. Wolf continues his quest in search of himself and his past in the machine which can annihilate memories, and finally kills himself in despair. The two girls leave the house and the novel comes to an end with the cinematographic image of Wolf's naked corpse with empty eye-sockets, lying in the red landscape not far from the time-machine which is beginning to disintegrate.

It is a very subjective novel, and displays Vian's anguish at its most intense and irrevocable. The scenes in which Wolf is interrogated during his time-journey contain many of Vian's own attitudes. He is questioned by a priest who gives him a photograph of 'God' who turns out to be his old school-chum. Another of his inquisitors tells Wolf that the important point of their interview is to define in what way his studies contributed to his disgust with life and in what way they formed him.

Sixteen years of school, Wolf remembers:

> Sixteen years of boredom—and what remains? Isolated, minute images ... the smell of new books on the first of October, the leaves one drew, the disgusting belly of the frog dissected in practical studies with its smell of formaldehyde, and the last days of the year when you see that the teachers are human because they are about to go off on holiday and that there's fewer of you. And all those great fears of which you no longer know the cause on the eve of examinations ... a regularity of habits ... it had come to that ... but do you know, Monsieur Brul, that it is ignoble to impose a regularity of habits that lasts for sixteen years on children? Time is faked, Monsieur Brul. Real time is not mechanical and divided

into hours which are all equal . . . Real time is subjective . . . you bear it within you . . . Get up at seven every morning . . . Lunch at noon, go to bed at nine . . . and never will you have a night to yourself . . . They've robbed me of sixteen years of night, Monsieur Brul. They made me believe, in *sixième*, that to pass into *cinquième* should be my only progress . . . in *première*, I had to have the *bachot* . . . and then, a diploma . . . Yes, I thought that I had a goal, Monsieur Brul . . . and I had nothing . . . I was going forward in a corridor without beginning and without end in the tow of imbeciles, preceding other imbeciles. Dressed in asses' skins they cheat life. Just as they put bitter powders into tablets to make you swallow them without trouble . . . but, you see, Monsieur Brul, I know now that I would have liked the true taste of life.

Such an apparently autobiographical and deeply felt outburst is rare in Vian's novels. A few lines later, Wolf makes his feelings even clearer. After his interrogator has spoken a few reassuring words to him, telling him that he finished his studies and attained an honourable position. Wolf declares: 'It wore me away, Monsieur Brul, I hate those years for wearing me away and I hate wearing away.'

But we are all wearing ourselves away, Brul objects. Yes, replies Wolf, but 'not quite in this way. We defoliate ourselves . . . our wearing-away comes from the centre. It's less ugly.'

'Wearing away is not a defect,' said Monsieur Brul.
'Yes it is,' replied Wolf. 'One should be ashamed of wearing oneself away.'
'But,' objected Monsieur Brul, 'everybody is in the same state.'
'What does that matter,' said Wolf, 'if you have lived. But to begin with, that's what I'm against. Look, Monsieur Brul, my point of view is a simple one: as long as there is a place where there is air, sun and grass, one should be sorry not to be there. Especially when you're young.'
'Let's get back to our subject,' said Monsieur Brul.
'We're in the thick of it,' said Wolf.

This is surely the voice of the man who was never slow to make his deepest prejudices and enthusiasms known, and who hated every moment in which he 'wore himself away' in not following his deepest inclinations, knowing that one is only young once, and that he was not to live long. His was a personal tragedy, but he expressed it in a way that aroused responses among many of his readers. No market research organization has attempted to assess the exact proportion of young French people of high school and university age who have 'rediscovered' Vian and made something of a literary hero of him. But if he has become so popular and so idolized as a literary figure in the years since his death, part of the reason must be that he was 'on their wavelength'. His anguished awareness of the ever-present if latent hostility of the powers-that-be in a world where the freshness and enthusiasm is too often stifled before youth has ended and his preoccupation with the *quality* of life have a new resonance and topicality. In a country in which many enthusiastic students who called for radical changes in an authority-dominated way of life were bludgeoned, tear-gassed and humiliated by a brutal police force representing authority, Vian's vision was relevant. His message might have been simple—naive and unrealistic even, but so are most messages of revolt and cries that all is not right with the world. It is easy for a foreign reader to smile condescendingly when Wolf says in *L'Herbe rouge*: 'It would be better to learn to make love properly than to sweat oneself stupid over a history book.' But in that 'student revolution' of the Sorbonne and other French universities during the early summer of 1968, what do we find among the slogans that were scribbled on the walls of faculties or printed on the posters that blossomed on the walls of Paris:

> 'Why work yourself silly for three years for a life of boredom afterwards?'
> 'The more I make revolution, the more I want to make love.'
> 'Forget everything you have learnt; begin by dreaming.'

It is not enough to say that neither such slogans nor Vian's apparent philosophy are 'constructive'. If we may speak of such a thing as a 'climate' of life and culture at a certain time in a country's history, we must conclude that Vian contributed to it with his sincere, individual, and courageous voice. By idolizing this attractive personality, his admirers have also been paying homage to the memory or the legend of a brief period in which there was to be found a compassion, an enthusiasm, a sense of fraternity and adventure which are too often absent from other, more grandiose monuments in France's recent cultural landscape.

*

The extent to which Vian has influenced part of French youth in its revolt is open to debate. But there is no doubt that another, far older idol has been exerting its fascination and attraction among Paris's artistic and literary circles for a long time.

In 1959, a well-known and influential French art and literary critic, Alain Jouffroy, took part in a ceremony to commemorate the 145th anniversary of the death of the Marquis de Sade. It was held in the Parisian apartments of Joyce Mansour, a newcomer to the original Surrealist group ruled by André Breton. The ceremony had been arranged and staged by a young French-Canadian painter Jean Benoît. This is how Jouffroy described it:

> We were a hundred guests. When the doors of the great white room in which the ceremony was to be held opened, there resounded a great noise like a kind of menacing cry bursting out of the depths of a volcano. We were standing shoulder to shoulder, staring at the closed double-doors facing us, in the empty half of the room.
> Among the numerous painters, poets or critics, there were André Breton, André Pieyre de Mandiargues and his wife Bona, Julien Gracq, Victor Brauner, Octavio Paz, Edgar Morin, Matta, Robert Lebel. No one was talking. Certain looks betrayed an indescribable sentiment of curiosity and embarrassment. The deafening noise then ceased. A loud-speaker broadcast the famous 'fifthly' of the Marquis de Sade's will in which he asked that his grave be dug in a 'covered thicket' and that 'acorns be strewn upon it so that when the ground over the grave will have grown again and the coppice be thicketed as it was before, the traces of my grave will disappear from the face of the earth as I flatter myself that my memory will be erased from the minds of men'.
> The voice that slowly, solemnly read this fragment of the will was that of André Breton.
> Motionless, in the space that had been left empty in the room, at the furthest left end, opposite that which was still to be opened, a young man was standing stiff and motionless behind the conductor's rostrum on which a few loose pages had been laid. After the silence which followed the reading of the will, the door opened, making way for a fabulous monster. The ceremonial of the execution of the Marquis de Sade's testament, by Jean Benoît, was beginning. The entrance of the monster into the room became strangely painful and vehement. From two klaxons, concealed in its high boots, there burst out noises that were both strident and dull in turn.
> Bent over as though crushed by the weight of a mask of four superimposed heads, a veritable totem of anonymity, the monster advanced on sumptuously decorated crutches, pushing its enormous egg-shaped belly before it, its right boot dragging behind it a little carriage of the same colour as the costume, the wings, the mask and crutches: silver-grey or reddish-brown and night-blue punctuated with reds; a fiery glow beneath the cinders.
> When it had painfully made its way to the centre of the empty space and come to a halt, the hundred silent spectators watching it found themselves curiously 'out of their natural element' in this apartment in which they had been talking so much at their ease only a few minutes earlier. The embarrassment was quite overwhelming: everyone did their best to hide their own behind a screen of remarks. The ceremony of the methodical disrobing of the monster then began, explained by a text which the

man at the rostrum read in an even, neuter, fairly implacable voice, without either grandiloquence or familiarity.

A blonde young woman in a black dress, her hair drawn back, proceeded to disrobe the monster, piece by piece. Each of the elements she detached was then hung on the wall, gradually disintegrating into an analytical panoply, the totem-being yielding obediently and almost mechanically to the rotating movements it was made to accomplish by the young woman, in order to display the different sides of the costume to the spectators.

She took off the mask. There appeared another amazed, astonished mask. Then the face, painted black with the eyelids and inside of the ears the colour of blood. Then the body painted entirely in black but on which the same arrows as those on the costume had been drawn. Finally, the sexual organ, concealed under an enormous phallus of black wood, decorated with straw.

At that moment I heard someone near me murmuring: 'That's the heart of the matter.' Jean Benoît, his body tensed by this slow ceremony, each second of which he had ordered and meditated upon, then lifted the phallus to simulate erection, by fastening the thread attached to it on a ring on his right hand. Underneath the phallus, one could distinguish two mirrors in the form of an hour glass, one in the shape of a man, the other, of a woman. The young blonde woman lit a fire in a receptacle by her feet and plunged an iron with a phallic handle into it. The flames were reflected for a few seconds in the mirrors of the hour-glass. The phallus fell down again.

As abruptly as everything had passed slowly before, Jean Benoît tore away the red cloth star that had been over his heart, threw it into the fire, seized the iron with the phallic handle and burned—to the third degree—the letters SADE on his skin, where the star had been. His eyes, which his make-up had made more intensely blue and sharp, seemed to me to be as piercing as a suddenly unsheathed knife-blade. Then, brandishing the iron with the letters SADE with which he had just burned himself, he cried out to the audience in a strong voice 'FOR WHOM DOES THE IRON HAVE CONVICTION?' and then eclipsed himself through a little door after having thrown the iron back in the fire.

There was a moment of confusion. During the entire ceremony, not a single word had been spoken aloud apart from the implacable words of the explanatory text, accompanied by quotations, that the narrator had read.

Then threading his way through the persons surrounding him, after avidly watching the last part of the ceremony, Matta went into the space that had been left clear in the room, unfastened his tie, unbuttoned his shirt collar and placed the iron on his skin. Someone wanted to imitate him but was stopped by a woman. The ceremony had apparently finished.

According to Jean Benoît who had imagined and made the costume, the whole apparel symbolized 'the symbolical transference of the tomb of D. A. F. de Sade' and its colour was 'specially designed to take on all its intensity in the warm light of the setting sun'. All the arrows decorating it were vertical or slanting, or curved, none were horizontal. Thus, each of the details had its symbolic key. Together they were all an invitation to a resurrection of mythical life. Everything was absolutely faithful to a traditional sign-language: you have only to visit an exhibition of masks in the Musée Guimet to gauge the sum of the inventivity of the rites and significances that Jean Benoît had achieved with this costume.

The act itself, which consists in burning oneself with the letters of Sade in a society as talkative and as little inclined to gestures as that in which artists live at this moment in Paris, is visibly a defiance. A defiance of conformisms, a defiance of laziness, a defiance of sleep, a defiance of all forms of inertia, in life as in thought. It is quite evident that such a ceremony, in absolute contradiction to the vulgarity peculiar to our time, can only be an object of derision in the conversations of our supposed intellectuals. It is, however, a recall to the essential. I mean, to that mysterious axis around which the human being revolves and which the Hindu Tantrics call *kundalini*—the energy that the sexual act liberates and which permits the bolted doors of our condition to be broken open for a few seconds. (45)

*

This interesting description of an unusual act of literary homage is revealing on several accounts. In the first place, it would seem to show the lengths to which certain members of the Parisian artistic and literary world would go to proclaim their passionate admiration of the Marquis de Sade and his works. That Jean Benoît should scar himself with a branding-iron bearing the letters of Sade's name might seem extravagant, foolish or dangerous, but such gestures are a part of Paris life and in the tradition of many avant-garde groups and movements proclaiming their various defiances of the existing order of things. Precisely what useful purpose this far from public gesture (the whole ceremony suggests a case of preaching to the converted) was intended to serve is not very clear but, nonetheless, Jouffroy and his fellow spectators seem to have taken it very seriously, unaware, perhaps, that the whole ritual had a rather old-fashioned air.

However much feminine instability Julien Gracq—himself an onlooker—may have detected in the reactions of the Paris public, there is no sign yet that the attachment of a certain French public to the vogue of the Marquis de Sade is in any danger of declining, nor that the trappings, at least, of Surrealism are ceasing to fascinate.

The event described above took place in 1959. Seven years earlier, Edmund Wilson had already turned his attention to the phenomenon of the Sade-cult and to the fact that the last war had brought him to 'the fore of the French literary consciousness'. He mentioned Sade's faithful biographer—not to say hagiographer—Gilbert Lely, whose studies of the Marquis can hardly be regarded as models of objectivity since, as Wilson noted, he wrote 'tender little poems' to Sade and even coined the slogan *Tout ce que signe Sade est Amour* ('all that Sade put his name to is love'), and who has made such a potent contribution to the cult ever since he discovered Sade in a kind of ecstatic revelation. He also mentioned how initial impetus was given to the let's-worship-Sade movement in France by Guillaume Apollinaire and Maurice Heine, and how Sade was then taken up by André Breton and his Surrealist group who made him a central figure in their Pantheon.

Since then, studies of Sade have continued to appear, often written by writers specializing in the erotic such as Pierre Klossowski and Georges Bataille. Sade has been treated both as a philosopher whose importance has been unjustifiably neglected and as an idol and constant source of inspiration, to such an extent that almost any surrealizing French artist today is bound to make his bow to the 'Divine Marquis' known in one way or another. In recent years his less obscene books have appeared in French paper-back editions, and in M. Patrick Waldberg's history of Surrealism we may see a photograph of André Breton, the 'pope' of the movement, posing with unabashed theatricality in front of a stone carving in the grounds of the Marquis's château at Lacoste in the South of France. Sade's influence, inspiration and popularity have continued to be present in French art, literature and even the cinema where Roger Vadim 'adapted' him in his characteristically shallow fashion in the film *Vice and Virtue*. In short, Sade is still one of the great monuments looming over the French cultural scene and when French writers have not been writing about him with a deathly, ponderous gravity which would seem rather to belong to some pedantic Teutonic professor of a caricature than to a nation whose writing has been esteemed for grace, concision and a sense of measure, he has been fervently worshipped by disciples of Surrealism and artists as though he were some kind of magic totem-pole.

Since Apollinaire put Sade on his special pedestal, French literary attitudes to him have not only been conspicuous for their lack of restraint and objectivity, but for their total and depressing absence of humour. There is as little awareness of the absurd or artificial in

Alain Jouffroy's account as in some fake black mass ceremony practised by eccentric old ladies in some quiet English village, or in the manifestoes of André Breton.

Concurrent with this Sade-mania, which has also spread abroad,* the last few years in France have witnessed a remarkable increase in the public taste for books, magazines and films of 'sadistic' inspiration. 'Horror' films are certainly popular enough in other countries, but in Paris where highly successful seasons of horror films have been held in some of the most 'in' Left Bank cinemas under the title of 'Sadistically yours', the cult has taken on intellectual undertones even among the very young who enthusiastically discuss the latest products of Hammer films and the Italian cinema with devotion and pedantry. When the film *King Kong* was reissued in Paris in 1965, Michel Cournot, a critic who often expressed himself in the columns of the *Nouvel Observateur* with an arrogance and a prolixity that are unhappily frequent in so much critical writing about films, wrote ecstatically:

> Let us all go and see *King Kong*, let us all go and see the force of love, the triumph of art, the beauty of Evil. Enter into the dream and see how one used to dream at a time when the laurels of darkness had not yet been cut. Great emotions must be paid for: you will leave *King Kong* full of despair. But, as André Breton said: 'Despair is of no importance, it is a drudgery [*corvée*] of trees that will still make a forest, it is a drudgery of stars which will still make one day less, it is a drudgery of days which will still make my life.'

Note the reference to the 'beauty of evil', implying that like every other good Surrealist follower, Cournot is a worshipper of Lautréamont's *Chants de Maldoror* and Baudelaire, and again, the submissive references to André Breton, the Mao-Tse-Tung of Surrealist thought and the final arbiter of taste in an important French cultural domain.

Sade, Lautréamont, the Gothic novel, Lewis Carroll, Baudelaire, Gérard de Nerval, Frankenstein, *King Kong*—what a Pantheon! They dominate various film magazines; Sade casts his shadow over the Theatre of Cruelty and almost any excursion into the imaginary, not to speak of various erotic and much talked-about novels like *Histoire d'O* (to be discussed later). Similarly, minor 'Sades' like Gilles de Retz continue to find a ready audience in books, with many

---

* In September 1965, an opera by the Italian avant-garde composer, Silvano Bussoti, *Passion of the Marquis de Sade*, was first performed during a festival at Palermo.

of Paris's main literary figures giving the lead. Whether it be 'old hat' or not, there is every likelihood that the vogue for Sade will continue to flourish in France for a long time to come, given the enduring enthusiasm for the modishly exotic.

The ceremony described by Jouffroy is also revealing in the way it continues the Surrealist posturing of the Thirties. The presence of André Breton who read the fragment of Sade's will is to be noted, as is that of André Pieyre de Mandiargues, a comparative newcomer to the Breton group, although he always remained slightly outside it, and the artists Matta and Brauner. In its use of masks, grotesque costumes, and giant phalluses, the ceremony has such an old-fashioned air! It is quite easy to imagine that Jouffroy's account was written in 1930. Heaven knows that there have been enough artists who have succeeded in defying conformism and inertia in a more modern manner, without having to resort to such archaic flummeries. And observe the shrill tone of the article with the writer's assertion that such 'a ceremony is in absolute contradiction to the vulgarity peculiar to our time' and his sneering reference to 'our supposed intellectuals': such a spirit would not have been out of place in a Futurist manifesto of 1913, let alone the pronouncements of the Dadaists and Surrealists of the Thirties.

It may be objected that the author is giving too much emphasis to this particular aspect of Paris cultural life. After all, the ceremony was a private affair. Such enthusiasm for Surrealist manifestations, Sade 'happenings', the unusual, shocking and bizarre are certainly not confined to Paris alone. That a group of literary men and their favourite artists should meet and proclaim their common enthusiasms is surely not extraordinary? But the difference in Paris is that, to a large extent, it is *these* people who have been in power, and the very extent of their influence is a striking sign of the most noticeable tendencies in French art and writing since the late Forties—a flight away from life towards a superior plane of imaginary freedom in a city where the *cult* and the *hermetic* are high fashion.

A careful look at the bookshops and art galleries of Left Bank Paris would seem to suggest that Surrealism and its interest in all forms of the bizarre and fantastic was the last great movement to have left its mark on the city. One of the most successful books to have been published in France in the last fifteen years has been *Le Matin des Magiciens* by Louis Pauwels and Jacques Bergier, and it is sub-titled 'An introduction to fantastic realism'. Roger Caillois and other authors have been producing a steady stream of books on the fantastic in art, the erotic in Surrealism, the surreal and the sadists in cinema, etc., and an avid public have bought picture books on the grotesque, the *insolite* (the unusual, out-of-the-way), and the sensational. The taste of the Surrealist few has become successfully commercialized. 'The unusual sells well', commented one French magazine in an article dealing with the phenomenon of the 'bizarre'. It does indeed.

Until his death, Breton continued to confer his influential approval on books and painters who seemed to fit into the category of the surreal, and such was the colossal vanity of the man whose manifestoes are not only distinguished by keen perception and intellectual rigour but by humourlessness, intolerance, querulous dogmatism and a Stalinist hatred of dissent, that a case can still be made today in Paris for saying that Surrealism is even now one of the most potent influences on modern painting, poetry, sculpture, fiction and theatre. In his way, Breton has been responsible for creating a new bourgeois taste in France. What had been an ideal to Breton has become a case of 'Oh, how amusing!' to the new and affluent buyers of picture books to be left on the coffee table between the television programmes and the latest glossy magazine.

In art, some of the best publicized and smartest exhibitions have been those displaying works that can be loosely labelled as Surrealist. Breton himself attacked the retrospective exhibition of Surrealist art held at the Galerie Charpentier in 1965 as being a watered-down display for popular consumption. Some of the most elegant, pretentious and snobbish gatherings have been those at the private view of galleries exhibiting the works of such ancient monuments of Surrealism as Max Ernst, Magritte, Léonor Fini—a painter whose art has declined from the crystalline-precious to the languidly-precious and effetely-'camp'—and Victor Brauner: artists who had lost the fire of their early inspiration but who still went through the motions of creation before an admiring crowd who would be more at home in Maxim's or Castel's night-club, who may be avid for sensation and novelty but who are fed by the rehashed exotica of the Thirties.

Take the case of that undeniably talented and unusual artist, Clovis Trouille, a 'Sunday painter' whose profession is making plaster manikins for shop windows and the Musée Grevin waxworks show. As we might expect, he received the all-important accolade from André Breton who told him that 'you paint with glowing coals'. What do we find in his brightly coloured, slightly 'pop' paintings? Monks with evilly glowing eyes, lascivious nuns pulling up their silk stockings as they reveal their thighs and puff cigarettes in cloisters, naked ladies posing amid coffins in cemeteries, still more slobberingly lecherous ecclesiastics investigating a witch's mark on the bottom of a pretty half-naked pin-up girl, and, of course, the appearance of the Divine Marquis himself, complete with cat-o'-nine-tails in his hand—all the erotico-anti-clerical, sacrilegious *bric-à-brac* of 1930-vintage Surrealism with the same monotonous emphasis on whip, leather and boot-fetishes as can be found in the works of a dozen other minor specialists in the 'unusual' and in the obsession-ridden films of Luis Bunuel whose popularity continues to be immense in Paris. To the most vociferous and 'engaged' of French critics all these antique trappings represent the 'powerful affirmation of an inner liberty'. To other, less indulgent, less fanatically backward-looking critics and observers, what can they be but the signs of infantilism and refusal to grow up that have bedevilled so much of French art since the war?

The kind of erotico-sadist, surrealizing vein that runs through the art of other painters and draughtsmen in Paris today like the German Bellmer and the Parisian Balthus has been diffused on a more popular level. It is for consumption by the 'new rich', young executives, and the public that is avid for magazines which cater for a new 'sophisticated' public, ever ready to be titillated by the French equivalent of the *Playboy* magazine 'philosophy' and the prospect of joining the community of those-who-know-what-life-is-all-about-and-who-have-shed-their-bourgeois-prejudices. A perfect example of the way the Surrealism and exalted eroticism of the few have been made into marketable products for the many is the magazine *Plexus*, a companion periodical to *Planète*. 'Read Plexus and de-complex yourself' says the advertisements for the magazine which offers a heady cocktail consisting of reproductions of paintings by established artists like Labisse and Magritte, 'philosophic-sociological' investigations on the 'sexual revolution in the world', interviews with actresses and pop-singers, short stories by Sade, photographs of 'happenings', advice on how to have a good time in Sweden, how to find your way about the brothel quarter of Hamburg, Tokyo or Barcelona, articles on sex mainly culled from the American or Scandinavian or British press, comic strips, 'daring' drawings and photographs and personal confessions with such titles as 'eroticism and I'...

To return to the art world, although the precise significance of the term 'school of Paris' may now be open to debate when it is used, it is to be noted that works displayed in a good many galleries still continue to make use of masks, literary references, dolls, monsters, and sexual symbolism of one sort or another. Thus, in the catalogue to an exhibition of sculptures by Hiquily held at the Galerie Claude Bernard in 1964, we may read:

> Hiquily's work is the reincarnation of Eros . . . this consciousness of totality as erotic reality, this will to pan-erotic simplification which is peculiar to him has been superbly expressed in *Sun* in which the 'stings' are both the rays [of the sun] and the phalluses of copulators. To each sting its hole. We can imagine nothing more subtle and less anthropomorphic.

Niki de Saint-Phalle's unusual methods of pictorial composition may now be old-fashioned, but there is no reluctance to draw upon the heritage of a certain vein of bizarre-obsessed Surrealism on the part of younger painters and sculptors. Paris needs to be amused . . . Paris needs novelty . . . If the bourgeois can no longer be shocked (they've seen it all before) at least the gallery public (who have also seen it all before and revel in it) can still be stimulated and titillated. Such stalwart partisans of the Surrealist tradition as Nelly Kaplan, author of books full of elaborate puns, eroticism, elements of science-fiction, monsters and vampires (*Géometrie dans les Spasmes, Le Réservoir des Sens*), Joyce Mansour, Marie-Laure de Noailles, Pieyre de Mandiargues, Pierre Klossowski and a band of professional critics have been dominating this domain of French art. They are to be seen at all the 'right' private views, taking a hand in the composition of the catalogue texts, presenting certain painters and generally officiating at exhibitions with all the gravity to be expected from people whose influence is so important in this richly coloured but airless world. They all speak the same language: the style of the critics is distressingly similar with monotonous insistence on words like 'oneirism', 'delirium' and 'a will to affirm interior liberty' and well spiced with such expressions as 'a work that goes beyond the bounds of the everyday world', 'an ardent eroticism' and 'a baroque feast of the liberated imagination'. Writing about the swirling-cloud-like, Turneresque works of a young and fashionable Corsican painter, Graziani (himself afflicted with the Surrealist taste for dolls and unusual junk), leading Paris art critics have written of his 'wonderland' and how his painting 'spreads around itself its sensual abnormality, like a debauch'. To another critic the paintings illustrate 'the irreality of dreamed representations . . . mixed and macerated in the laboratories of night'. To the well-known critic, Gérald Gassiot-Talbot, the artist was 'one of the five or six painters . . . who have succeeded in adding to the Surrealist approaches of oneiric worlds . . . means of expression which completely escape the conventions of objective reality and the ineluctability of awakening'. The literary approach to other works of the same tendency is always the same: so-and-so's paintings are like 'a voyage of exploration into the uncharted seas of the imaginary' but, all too often, such voyages are made by works that have the weight of paper boats and the uncharted seas are like a muddy pond in some village green.

Outside this neo-Surrealistic domain, one would think that the two most important artistic events in the last few years had been the discovery of *art nouveau* by the general public and an interior-decoration-conscious middle class with intellectual aspirations (as opposed to that for whom the only styles are Louis XIV, XV and XVI), and that of the comic strip by intellectuals. A new interest in *art nouveau* is certainly not confined to France but in no other country has it been so self-consciously adopted for interior decoration schemes and a certain style of architecture of which the Saint-Germain Drugstore is the most conspicuous example. Perhaps *art nouveau* owes its phenomenal new popularity in France to the fact that there is nothing as yet to represent a truly modern French style in building and interiors. In any case, do not the French call it 'the modern style'?

Nothing could be more revealing in this respect than the enormous success of one of France's most fashionable decorators of cafés, restaurants and 'drugstores': the legendary Slavik, a new version of a Des Esseintes become 'pop', with his impeccable English suits, his interesting 'aesthetic' appearance, his mania for exotic curios and his habit of driving around Paris in incense-perfumed limousines. This three-quarters Russian, one-quarter German expatriate has designed the Pub Renault in Paris, the restaurant of the Maison de la Suède, a Russian-Jewish restaurant, the Saint-Germain drugstore, another in the Elysée II housing estate near Paris, and the Bistrot de Paris.

Slavik, as he called himself (his real name being Viatcheslav

Vassiliev), has expressed his aims to make new places—distinct from the generally hideous modern café—in which a public can circulate with ease, relax in warm, enfolding surroundings, escape from loneliness, alienation and the harsh world outside, and generally enjoy themselves while watching others do the same in a kind of theatrical make-belief land.

His materials are the antithesis of plastic and neon. Wood, leather, brass and plush upholstery are his favoured materials. His inspiration is almost exclusively derived from the nineteenth century, being a pastiche of Imperial Russian, *art nouveau*, Second Empire and industrial nineteenth-century *à la Jules Verne* styles. He has defined it as 'certain poetic tenderness added to a satisfaction of real needs'. But he is not only under the spell of his own vision of the last century. Slavik, too, shows the mark of neo-Surrealism in his style, with the seven-fingered hands of the Drugstore in Saint-Germain, in his own home where he keeps the windows curtained against the daylight, collects curios and junk, oddities and huge horns and every painting of a fire that he can lay his hands upon ('I like fire'), and in declarations to the press: 'I am a bat. I like night, greyness, black, the mirrors of the witch in which the image becomes concentrated, horns which perforate and give death.' (46) At this rate, some neo-Surrealist critic may soon be writing glowing articles of praise for Slavik's fidelity to the spirit of Baudelaire, Huysmans and Lautréamont and—Sade.

As for the comic strip, anyone curious as to the nature of the cult it has provoked among French intellectuals need only consult a periodical with the curious name of *Giff-Wiff* published by Jean-Jacques Pauvert in Paris. The magazine is the official organ of an association called *Centre d'Etudes des Littératures d'Expression Graphique* (centre for studies of literature employing graphic expression). The *C.E.L.E.G.* includes a member of the French Academy and is headed by a Monsieur Lacassin who is not only an enthusiast for a kind of Gothic cinematic culture beloved by Surrealists and their followers, but a man convinced that the comic strip has meanings quite as profound as those to be found in the writings of Joyce, Hegel or Marx and for whom 'there are more than mere affinities to be found between the paintings and sculptures of Michelangelo and the Tarzan drawn by Hogarth [*not* the Hogarth of *Rake's Progress*]'. During a conference of the *C.E.L.E.G.* at Bordighera in February 1965, M. Lacassin and his followers made a profound study of 'Rooseveltian Utopianism in Mickey Mouse', 'angst symbolism in Donald Duck' and various other equally erudite themes, and asked a number of comic-strip authors specially brought over for the occasion to explain the profound sense and motivations of their works.

I do not know whether the use of comic strip by the American painters like Lichtenstein was discussed but it is a fact that when Pop Art triumphed at the Venice Biennale in 1964, and Robert Rauschenberg won the Grand Prix for painting in the American Pavilion, the attitude taken by many French critics and journalists was one of outrage and dismay—shrilly voiced amid a mass of articles devoted to the 'crisis' in French painting. The fact that the American artists were using the comic strip directly in their painting while Italian and French intellectuals were using them as subjects for profoundly pretentious exegeses was apparently considered vulgar and unrefined: further evidence, if evidence were needed, of the Anglo-Saxon menace to European—which is to say French— art. A typical diatribe against the new tendency was launched by the critic André Ferrier in the *Nouvel Observateur* and in the weekly magazine *Arts et loisirs*. For M. Ferrier, 'Pop art is an ugly animal issued forth out of the encounter between psychoanalysis and puritanical democracy, a sort of asexual minotaur to be fed each day with his ration of old tyres, old socks, comic strips, torn posters and other refuse of urban over-production.' (47) At the same time that American art was showing its vitality (a vitality shared in Britain by a distinguished band of younger painters including Peter Blake, Hockney, and Alan Davie), one of Paris's leading galleries, the Galerie Daniel Cordier, was closing down because of the critical state of the modern art market in France. After expressing sympathy with M. Cordier in his article, Ferrier revealingly praised him for having been so successful in 'making the *bizarre* [this author's italics] fashionable on the Right Bank and even, perhaps, on the Faubourg Saint-Honoré'. And who, according to Ferrier, was the greatest talent to be found in Paris that year? Ségui—an artist who only too clearly belonged to that school of the 'bizarre' with Brauner, Matta, etc.!

Whatever objections might have been raised against 'Anglo-Saxon' Pop Art, one fact was clear enough: it took its material from life— particularly the urban, highly mechanized life of a modern civilization surrounding the city-dwelling artist. What it did with this material was another matter—the spirit was modern and resolutely unesoteric: both characteristics strikingly absent from most modern French painting. For art allegedly inspired by reality in France, the public was invited to the annual exhibitions of French painting held in the mausoleum-like Musée Galliera by the Municipality of Paris. There, all the works displayed were painted to a single theme. One year (1964) it was 'Bread and Wine', the following year, 'The French'—paintings of a desperate banality far exceeding in triteness anything to be offered by the Royal Academy summer shows—only a few steps away from two of the least well provided museums of 'Modern Art' in Western Europe . . .

Simplicity, discipline and directness were the most unusual qualities to be discovered in a world of art which still continued to set a premium on the unusual and the 'gimmick'. In London, the purity of a Bridget Riley—in Paris, a painting that is either programmatic, esoteric, or one of *escape* and *dreams* . . . And for the wider public, Bernard Buffet and Mathieu, both artists of the 'school' of Maxim's and the fashionable night-clubs! Of the two, Mathieu is perhaps the most significant for with his emblematic, heraldic, and flashily calligraphic style, he was certainly the perfect artist to decorate one of the *maisons de culture* opened by André Malraux since he reflected the ex-minister's grandiloquent style so well.

*

In the Paris theatre, the same vein of Surrealist nostalgia lingers on. M. Romain Weingarten has admitted that his play *L'Eté* owed a debt of inspiration to Lewis Carroll who was canonized by some Surrealists and their former adherents, of whom the late Jacques Brunius was the foremost exegetist and admirer of the creator of Alice. But far more spectacular has been the enormous rise to popularity of the plays of Arrabal. That he is a Spaniard is of no account— he has become 'Parisianized'. Living in the city, it is Paris that has made his success and it is there that he has flourished even to the extent of having three of his plays performed simultaneously during a recent season. His dramatic work ranges from short Dadaistic pieces and interludes to lengthy excursions into a highly-coloured and fantastic world of violence and obscenity with Surrealist touches ('little elephants swim in the waters gushing out of your behind', etc. (48), in such plays as *Le Grand Cérémonial* and *The Architect and the Emperor of Assyria*. His plays are what older audiences might consider 'shocking' and their stage effects are quite as important as dialogue, as English critics and an astonished public found out when they saw Arrabal's *Théâtre Panique* present their production of *The Labyrinth* in the spring of 1968.

Arrabal's favourite means of expression are sado-masochism, fetishism, obscenity, sacrilege, violence, death, copulation and ritual. Echoes of Bellmer the artist and Buñuel the film-maker abound in *Le Grand Cérémonial*. A beautiful girl is seduced and then made to strip by a hunchback after he has told her that he has murdered his own mother who wanted him to remain a virgin and who would only allow him to make love with life-size dolls . . . In *The Architect and the Emperor of Assyria*, we see such scenes as a man dressing up as a woman and being flagellated prior to a dialogue with a crucifix surmounted with a skull . . Any suspicions we may have that Arrabal may be cleverly exploiting the traditional baggage of Surrealism would seem confirmed when we see his collection of paintings executed in a near-Dali style by artists working to his orders, all reproducing him in various unusual and apotheotic situations (being carried by angels over a valley of tombs, etc.), and know that he keeps a bicycle in his drawing-room and a plaster of Paris bust of himself featuring a monstrous penis. All these elements are reflected in his plays in which there is never a *real person* present and in which the exotic *object*, the sensational *effect* and the tired *symbol* remain predominant. There is far more of the genuine 'fantastic' in a play by Harold Pinter because it deals with real people whose behaviour, quirks and manners of speech will always be more bizarre, unexpected and surprising than any amount of gaudy junk and fancy dress in the Portobello Road of Arrabal's theatrical imagination. As for any 'messages' that a message-hunter would care to detect in Arrabal's works such as the absurdity and cruelty of the police state, bureaucracy, society and so on, they can hardly be considered original. But at least it must be conceded that the popularity of Arrabal's plays is perfectly representative of a current, widely diffused Paris taste—a taste that is both sensation-avid and complacent. Nothing would be more mistaken than to think that this so-called *avant-garde* theatre, this spreading fascination of the unusual object, the remnants and pastiches of Surrealism, are signs of any great public shift in attitudes and cultural demands. The Paris public may be ahead of that in the provinces in its tendency to succumb to crazes and expect the novel and seemingly outrageous.

But its taste is still scarcely different from the prosperous and deeply conservative provincial Frenchman's liking for multi-coloured marble eggs, pieces of crystal with insects or watch parts embedded in them, and quaint bits and pieces such as beautifully mounted bird skeletons which are all so fashionable, and which he will buy as 'novelties' because they are amusing and will place among his antique furniture. Originally, Surrealism and all its manifestations had revolutionary and creative aims. Now it diverts and has become a popular consumer good. It is worth remembering that at the same time as it was becoming so modish, the two stage spectacles that provoked the greatest public indignation and degree of shock were Jean Genet's *Les Paravents*, which produced a fine display of right-wing hooliganism among the audience, and a mildly anti-Gaullist little song *La Campagne*, which led that veteran worshipper of De Gaulle, François Mauriac, to jeer and boo at its singer, Mademoiselle Suzanne Gabriello, in January 1967 at the Olympia music hall, for daring to make mock of an idol of a different nature.

6

The Byzantines

MANY OF the tendencies just outlined would seem to converge and meet in the person of one of France's most famous and admired writers of the 1960's—André Pieyre de Mandiargues, a Prix Goncourt winner and best known to the Anglo-American public for his erotic fantasy, *Girl on a Motorcycle*. In view of the long-enduring taste for the exotic and the flight from reality which we have noticed, it is no surprise that he should have come to hold his present high place in contemporary French literature. Just as Vian may be seen as one of the personalities most representative of the Left Bank Parisian spirit in the immediate post-war years, so Pieyre de Mandiargues may be seen as a representative of the new, politically and socially anaesthetized culture of Gaullist France.

Even before he was awarded the Prix Goncourt in 1967, for his novel *La Marge*, thus being suddenly assured of a wide public, Mandiargues was esteemed by many critics to be one of the most refined French stylists today, and one of France's most subtle and imaginative story-tellers. In brief, he is one of those authors in France whose every book is an 'event' when published. But another quality of his writing that has been less emphasized is its tendency towards the *precious*—a tendency apparent in the works of several other contemporary writers as well as painters.

Apart from his style, one of the first things to be noticed about Pieyre de Mandiargues is that he is so very 'Parisian'. Not only was he born in Paris in 1909, but by his many activities in journalism and the world of art, he is a perfect example of that type of professional French writer who is also a highly active member of a French literary-artistic 'set'. He is a well-known critic, an assiduous visitor to art exhibitions, the champion of various painters, and last but certainly not least, a sympathizer with Surrealism. As we have seen, he was present at that ceremony described by Alain Jouffroy, and together with other figures such as Marie Laure de Noailles, Nelly

Kaplan, Maurice Nadeau, Léonor Fini and Pierre Klossowski, is an influential member of that group which proclaimed its allegiance or kinship to André Breton. How great is Pieyre de Mandiargues' attachment to Breton may be seen by this following statement of his (49): 'Surrealism can only be defined in relation to André Breton ... perhaps, if we were real Surrealists, we would no longer write or publish anything, since the only person for whom these books were destined is dead.' Naturally, such an avowal should be taken with a pinch of salt, but it is still revealing of that *hermetic* spirit at work in much French writing today which seems designed more for a group than for a public.

Like all good Surrealists, from his youth Pieyre de Mandiargues was influenced and inspired by the German Romantics, the poetry of Coleridge, the Elizabethan drama and Lautréamont's strange and sadistic poetic fantasy, *The Songs of Maldoror*. He began his literary career as a poet and the first book he published, in Monaco during the Occupation, was entitled *Dans les années sordides* and appeared with a title page and two drawings by one of the author's favourite artists, Léonor Fini, between whose highly wrought pictorial style and that of Mandiargues' prose critics might care to find affinities.

This was a collection of prose poems and bizarre short tales and it was followed two years later by a long poem of more marked Surrealist inspiration: *Hedera, or the persistence of love during a rêverie*. Shortly after the war, he began to take part in the activities of the Surrealist group. Although spiritually he was greatly drawn toward them, he remained rather on their fringe, retaining his artistic autonomy and always following his own path in his writing. His first important book was a collection of fantastic tales, *Le Musée Noir*, which has now sold great numbers in a French paper-back edition, but which was ill-received by the critics when it was published in 1947. This was the period of 'engaged literature', dominated by the figures of Sartre, Camus and Simone de Beauvoir. Such baroque tales and poetic fantasies in exquisitely mannered prose were too precious and esoteric for the time. One might say they were too luxurious and escapist for a literary public drawn into involvement with the dramatic issues facing society and the world at large.

Le Musée Noir was followed by other books in the same vein—mostly collections of stories such as *Soleil des Loups*, *Le Belvédère*, *Feu de Braise*, *Porte Dévergondée*, and his two successful novels, *La Motocyclette* and *La Marge*. Besides these prose works he continued to publish poetry, and various studies such as a book with photographs on the strange carvings of monsters in the gardens of Bomarzo in Italy, and another on the 'masks of Léonor Fini'. An ardent lover of Italy and connoisseur of the 'curious' with a specialized but intense erudition like that of José Borges, Pieyre de Mandiargues has taken a great interest in various artists with Surrealist tendencies—Baj, Gail Singer, Marie-Laure—and has written commentaries for many exhibitions of paintings as well as critical articles for various periodicals.

Both his short stories and his poems show his predilection for the strange and extraordinary. A collection of poems like *Astynax* (1956) is full of themes and images of blood, eroticism, death and such visual jokes as an assembly of bishops in a swimming bath. A tale like 'The Diamond' in *Feu de Braise* will suffice as a typical example of Mandiargues' baroque imagination: an old Jewish diamond dealer, Moses, lives alone with his daughter Sarah in a beautiful old house. Sarah is a virgin who apparently has never had the least interest in men and, according to her father, her state of maidenhood makes her eminently suitable to judge the quality of a fine diamond. Every night, before such an inspection, it is Sarah's custom to fast and spend some time in solitary meditation before examining the precious stones. On this occasion, she wakes up in the middle of the night and drawn by the fascination of the latest diamond her father has bought, tip-toes upstairs to see it, after first bathing and undressing as is her ritual before such inspections. As she scrutinizes the magnificent stone which she has taken out of its bag and placed on a table before her, she suddenly faints.

By some process of magic, the girl then finds herself in the centre of the mysterious diamond, imprisoned and reduced to microscopic proportions. After a while, a ray of burning light invades the centre of her curious prison and she finds herself facing a naked, red-skinned man with a lion's mane and an erect penis who informs her that he had come into the stone to be united with her since a union between a virgin belonging to the race of prophets and a man with a lion's mane issued out of a ray of sunshine would produce an offspring with a 'sovereign spirit' by whom the 'persecuted race' would be illumined and made to dominate the world. The strange apparition then deflowers Sarah. After her father has visited the room and inspected the diamond himself, Sarah loses consciousness a second time and awakes to find herself back in the normal world, restored to her usual size. The story ends with her wearing the diamond in a ring on her finger while she feels the strangely conceived living being who is to illumine the world growing in her womb...

In its concentration on the microscopic and the detailed, its emphasis on ritual, its use of the theme of an 'other' world beyond that of everyday normality, and its suggestion of unearthly eroticism, the 'Diamond' is typical of Mandiargues' poetic imagination and of his precise but cold style. He does not sympathize: he *observes* with the eye and the mind of some collector of rare but beautiful tropical insects or flowers (indeed, insects and flowers are frequently used in his stories). There is nothing warm or even very human in his writing. Eroticism, death and more than a hint of sadism are all so many elements to be arranged with the precise aim of securing the best aesthetic effect. It is the material detail, not the living being, that counts. Like the title of his first collection, Mandiargues' stories are all a 'museum', crammed with bizarre or striking objects to be selected and pored over. He is a writer of *things* and it is in this, as well as in his withdrawal from real life, that he represents an important tendency in French writing today. Alain Jouffroy has said, 'It is *against* diurnal reality that Mandiargues has taken his stand. All his poems are the products of a fight against consciousness, to foil reason and its authority.' Another less enthusiastic critic has pointed out that 'what is here related to us is less important than the manner' and that because of the absence of *living persons* 'there is no one here ... [the stories] are nothing but poems, delicately wrought'.

Now of course there is no earthly reason why Mandiargues, like any other imaginative writer, should not write as he likes, in any manner that suits him, and to pick him out and present him as proof of French literary 'decadence', 'escapism' or 'withdrawal from contemporary issues' would be as unfair as it would be absurd. But what is significant is his present enormous popularity in France and his position as one of the main figures in a small but tightly-knit French literary and artistic group who are to no small extent contemporary arbiters and makers of taste in the Paris-based world of French art and literature. In almost any kind of literary gathering you are likely to hear his name mentioned. His opinions, tastes and influence *count* and he has played no small part in spreading that taste for the unreal and exotic that has been growing under the banner of a modish after-Surrealism and which has been encouraged by an important part of the book-buying public (even more of a minority in France than in Germany, the United States or Great Britain) for whom he is certainly more readable than most of the so-called 'new novelists'.

Pieyre de Mandiargues is an archaic writer. With his aesthetic tastes, his exquisitely composed French prose style, his sympathies for an old culture, centred around the Mediterranean, he might be a contemporary of Théophile Gautier, Huysmans or Villiers de L'Isle Adam. In a cultural world renowned for its love of the new and the experimental, to find that one of the most reputed and read French writers today is practically the spiritual contemporary of the *fin de siècle* aesthetes and 'decadents' would seem to indicate that French literary taste is resolutely directed backwards.

But before we label Mandiargues as a literary anachronism, two of his latest novels, *La Motocyclette* and *La Marge*, call for further remarks. The first, known to an English reading public as *Girl on a Motorcycle* and as a film starring Marianne Faithfull, is contemporary inasmuch as it makes use of topical elements of modern folk-lore: black leather, powerful motor-bikes, an amazon for a heroine and eroticism at a hundred miles an hour all described with relentless detail, utter coldness and absolute humourlessness. The second novel, which won for him the prestige-charged Prix Goncourt, continues the microscopic-detail technique. The story as such is simple: the hero (if we can call him this) of *La Marge* is Sigismond Pons who has come to Barcelona to replace his cousin who is a travelling representative for French apéritifs and liqueurs. He is married to a young, witty woman with a penchant for mockery, has a son and lives in an old farmhouse in the South of France. In order to collect the letter he expects from his wife, he goes to the *poste restante* in the central Barcelona post office but is given a letter by the old family servant instead. Opening the envelope he first sees the end of the letter and reads the lines 'she ran to the tower of the winds. She went up the winding staircase. She threw herself down from the top. She died at once'. Instead of reading the rest of the letter at once, from the beginning, Sigismond begins a three-day tour of the city after making up his mind to delay reading the whole letter and to live in a kind of 'bubble' withdrawn from the reality of his existence, in the 'margin' of life. Most of the novel then becomes a painstaking description of the city, supposedly seen through Sigismond's eyes, but in which the author's own microscopic observation remains dominant. The following passage is perfectly indicative of the style of the novel: we are back in the middle of *thing*-country:

> Now his eyes are drawn to another statue perched on a column, to the left, on a raised strip in which little red flowers mingle with oily plants. Once there, an inscription on the pedestal tells him that the man is Antonio Lopez, marquis of Comillas, founder of the Spanish Translantic Company, and he remembers that while he was briefing himself for the trip he recently read something about this businessman who, in the first years of the century, commissioned the architect Gaudi for several works, mostly religious. In his overcoat, with a scroll of paper in his hand, the fellow is the very image of those statues which are the focal points of the paintings of Giorgio de Chirico in the so-called metaphysical period. But instead of an empty space having been made around him in a square or in an arcaded street where he would have been a stone phantom almost on ground level, he was set up at a height of nearly thirty metres. In no other town are statues placed as high as in Barcelona, as though people had been afraid of leaving them within reach of men.

And so on ... In the course of his marginal existence, Sigismond thoroughly explores the seedy but picturesque 'red light' area of the sea-port, paying special attention to the prostitutes' district, and fornicates with a pretty tart, while always leaving the fatal letter under a bottle on a table in his hotel room. When it is finally time for him to break his 'bubble', Sigismond reads that his only son had drowned accidentally and that his wife had committed suicide in despair as a consequence. He drives out of the city and shoots himself in a quarry.

Thus summarized, the novel sounds straightforward enough, uncluttered by any secondary considerations. With Sigismond's determination to live a withdrawn if temporary existence, on the 'margin', it may be seen as a brilliant though unintended symbol for so many French novelists' isolation from their world and their society as they enclose themselves in their 'bubbles' of the imagination or literary theory. But the novel also shows the intrusion of Pieyre de Mandiargues' own political sympathies and evidence of that nostalgia and romanticism of the Left which are so marked in France today and which seem to grow in inverse proportion as the real political effectiveness of the opposition declines.

In an interview given to the periodical *Nouvel Observateur* for which he frequently writes as a critic, Mandiargues stated that 'Sigismond Pons ... conceives a great love for the Catalan people as victims of oppression. As he moves towards his own destruction, his love for them grows all the time as does his indignation at the régime'. (50) Furthermore, it appears that Sigismond envisages his suicide as a kind of magical operation which, by virtue of his own disappearance, will entail that of Franco and thus lead to the liberation of the people of Catalonia. One example will suffice to give the reader an idea of Sigismond's political behaviour: after watching some workmen taking their Sunday walk and being moved by 'seeing in them the brothers of the proud men whose wrath and whose laughter was the unforgettable reply to the Church and the barracks, etc.', Sigismond comes to the torn remnants of one of the posters that the Franco régime put up all over Spain to celebrate 'Twenty-five years of peace', twenty-five years after the end of the Civil War. After various anti-Franco reflections, Sigismond sees an old man standing beside him, in front of the poster, ostentatiously spitting in the direction of a small group of *guardias civiles* going down the street. With similar ostentation, Sigismond then spits after the guards, and then again at the remains of the poster. After a quick look round, the old man repeats the gesture, at the poster, scoring a bull's-eye in the loop of the letter P for '*paz*' which sends him into a rapture of delight and encourages him to sing an old Catalan Republican song. However, let us conclude this affecting scene in a literal translation of Mandiargue's own words:

> Without his corporeal covering having become changed, loaded with years and dirt as it is, he has become prodigiously younger inwardly and this return of fire in the old rebel has a beauty that might frighten some people. Two sailors from the *Altair* [an American ship in the port] in white as though making their first communion, look at him and listen to him with the air of idiot children.
>
> Assuredly, this was one of those proud men of whom Sigismond was thinking; one of those who were free more than twenty-five years ago. Both men had understood each other. No need to shake hands nor to talk; even less to make use of the facile gesture of offering a cigarette and giving a light, since this is a rite suited to the brothel and inseparable from prison and army life. They smiled at each other, they looked at each other like brothers, and then the old man went off along the sun-filled pavement in the direction taken by the troop of civil guards the last of whose cocked hats could be seen shining in the distance.

Similarly, at the very end of the book, Sigismond's last thought before shooting himself is of the 'Catalan people with whom he feels himself to be linked by friendship as much as solidarity' and the wish that they may be delivered from dictatorship. Now, it is obvious that Sigismond is a stranger discovering Barcelona for the first time (or if not, why the 200 pages of description in a novel of 250 pages?) and in view of the fact that he has learned that his wife is dead, it is surprising, to say the least, that his self-imposed wanderings among the beggars and tarts of the sea-port area of Barcelona should have roused in him such a great love for the Catalan people. Furthermore, after learning that his son is also dead, it is odd that his last thoughts before dying should be for Spain rather than his lost family, but this is how the author would have it and this is how the reader must take it.

It would be ridiculous to question the sincerity of Pieyre de Mandiargues' political convictions which, from such evidence, would appear to be wholly admirable. It is simply worth pointing out that in a novel of such a nature they serve no essential purpose and have every sign of being *grafted* on to the main body of the story. Whether this is the result of some twitch of political conscience at choosing one of the main cities in Franco's Spain as the setting for this story (Barcelona being a city that has long fascinated the writer) is of no importance here. What is interesting is that such rhetorical-sentimental-aesthetic devices perfectly reflect the traditional style of a certain language of the 'cultured' Left in France—a Left only too prone to poetic romanticism (a 'new spirit' in France during the student riots; a wonderful 'awakening' of the French people; forget everything—begin by dreaming again, etc., etc.). Note the imagery: the old man, body bowed but spirit unbroken, the gleam of defiance in his eyes, Sigismond's sympathy for the Spanish workers, the sudden complicity between him and the old man ('no need to shake hands . . . they looked at each other like brothers'); we are back in the literary climate of early Malraux-ism, Saint Exupéry-ism, the Left Book Club, Aragon's '*lendemains qui chantent*', the poetics of a film like Rossif's *Mourir pour Madrid* or almost any French film on Vietnam with its pictures of noble old peasants, fresh young peasant girls, or defiant, noble-faced young students scanning the skies with a spade in one hand, a rifle in the other. It is a remarkable fact that many Frenchmen who accepted the official banalities, the semi-democracy and complacencies of the Gaullist régime and the brutalities of its police force will be affected by the fact that Spain, Portugal or Greece are living under a repressive authoritarian régime, unlike that of the 'mother of liberty', and proceed to wax lyrical about their fellow-men—as long as they are not French or

Arabs. You can meet such Frenchmen almost everywhere on holiday, like a minor executive this writer once encountered in Madrid who lamented the fact that it was hard to pick up a girl in Spain and proceeded to tell two Spanish students of the blessings of French Liberty ('You see, in Paris if you want to pick up a pretty woman, you can go up to her in the street and talk to her. If she wants to come with you, she will, if not, nobody's offended. We're free in France!'); not to speak of a certain kind of young French intellectual of the Left who has carefully mapped out his ideological position and collects records from specialized shops with such titles as 'Revolutionary songs of Chilean peasants and workers' or 'Homage to the Portuguese Resistance' while blandly ignoring the fact that his concierge and family are huddled together in a single smelly and insanitary room.

However, even the above examples of political romanticism pale by comparison with the poem that Pieyre de Mandiargues composed to adorn one of the posters designed for the 'French Revolution' of May–June 1968. Here it is quoted in its entirety:

> Quand l'extraordinaire devient quotidien
> C'est qu'il y a une Révolution!
>
> La splendeur de ces mots de Fidel Castro
> que nous avions lus à la Havane
> Les étudiants et le peuple de Paris
> L'ont fait refleurir pour notre joie
> De la grande République jusqu'au Lion de Denfert
> Sous le soleil d'un 13 mai réconcilié.
>
> Que s'ouvre donc et que s'épanouisse
> Une rose rouge tellement démésurée
> Qu'elle recouvre la France entière,
> Nous lui vouons notre plus grand amour
> Mais nous garderons en mémoire
> que le cœur de l'ardente églantine
> Est inséparable du Quartier Latin.*

* Poster with design by the poet's wife Bona reproduced in *Affiches de la Revolution de mai*, Editions Tchou, Paris 1968. Literally translated, the poem is as follows:
    When the extraordinary becomes everyday/it is because there is a Revolution!/The splendour of these words of Fidel Castro/which we read in Havana/the students and the people of Paris/made reblossom for our joy/from the great Republic (i.e. the Paris square) to the Lion of Denfert (i.e. the Place Denfert-Rochereau with its leonine monument)/ under the sun of a May the 13th reconciled/May there open then and blossom/ a red rose so measureless/that it will cover France entirely/We vow it our greatest love/ but we shall remember always/that the heart of the burning eglantine/is inseparable from the Latin Quarter.

At least it must be conceded that the majority of the posters produced by those events were refreshingly modern in design—no mean achievement in a country in which poster art never seems to have got beyond the Twenties and Thirties.

Nourished with bad poetry and sustained by the sight of such ancient monuments as Aragon and Elsa Triolet at the head of a political procession (full of unpoetical workers more concerned with the minimum wage than with joining student barricades), it only remained for the romantic-minded Left to make another political charge of the Light Brigade. *Ce n'est pas la Révolution—mais c'est magnifique!*

Still, if the style of the literary Left in Paris tended to be that of Victor Hugo or early Aragon, that of power in France remained that of Corneille. As Jean-François Revel pointed out (51), with De Gaulle and Malraux France went back to a period of great 'stylists'—in the prose of politics as in that of literature. But aesthetic considerations do not deter the stylists-in-power from giving those out-of-power a resounding crack over the head with a policeman's truncheon when the occasion arises . . .

*

Another essential element in a literary culture largely living off the corpse of Surrealism is, of course, eroticism.

Part of the myth of France is that she is the natural home of Eros. Chauvinism has even invaded the French bedroom. Whatever the Ancients may protest up on Olympus, Eros is French. The conviction remains strongly entrenched on various levels from that of the French student who proudly tells you that, on his recent holiday to Sweden, the local girls were practically besieging him or queueing up for the pleasure of 'being made love to properly—by a Frenchman!' to that of the erudite academician poring over the history of 'the erotic tradition in the *chanson de geste*'. Rare is the Frenchman who will not assure you that in matters of love and sex (not a French division) the French have nothing to learn from and much to teach less privileged races and that Anglo-Saxon reticence is alien to the French temperament. Be that as it may and granted that the French have been refreshingly unhypocritical in their approach to sexual matters, on the most superficial, visual level there is little to suggest these days that Paris is a particularly emancipated or 'naughty' city.

There has been a good deal of talk of the 'new wave of puritanism' in France. It began shortly after the Liberation when the Loi Marthe Richard officially closed France's brothels. Since that time and especially since De Gaulle came to power in 1958, the 'dirty' or 'daring' book market has all but been killed. Today, London, New York, Copenhagen and Amsterdam are the new Babylons. Provincial Frenchmen on a spree must go to Hamburg, not Pigalle for a 'good time'. As for less pornographic and more literary 'erotic' works, they have had to suffer from the arbitrary, highly undemocratic mis-application of censorship laws which were happily slackened in 1967 after being tightened up in 1958. When an amendment made to a law of July 16, 1949, which had been aimed at protecting children and minors from corrupting publications, decreed that it was 'forbidden to propose, to give or to sell to minors under eighteen, publications of any kind presenting a danger to youth by reason of their licentious or pornographic nature or because of the place given to crime. It is forbidden furthermore, to expose these publications to public view in any place whatever, and notably on the exterior or in the interior of shops and kiosks, or to give any publicity to them in any form whatsoever', this meant, in fact, that it became an offence to review a book deemed 'a danger to youth' in any paper or periodical, to list it in a catalogue, to mention it inside the jacket of another book, or even to keep it inside a locked case in a bookshop.

One instigator of such draconian measures has been widely believed to be Madame de Gaulle. The truth of this statement will probably never be known. But the mere fact that such a theory could be so widely and readily accepted was eloquent comment on the state of French 'democracy'. It was, moreover, pointed out with glee that André Malraux, until recently Minister of Culture and one-time student of erotica, kept silent during this repressive legislative period even though he had once written an introduction to a French edition of *Lady Chatterley's Lover* in which he had condemned English stupidity in condemning the book . . .

The law regarding censorship was modified in January 1967 after a debate among eighteen members of parliament—a proportion of the National Assembly's 460-odd deputies probably corresponding to that of France's population interested in her present-day literature. It has now become easier again to learn something of recent French achievements in erotic literature. The first fact worth noting is that there *is* an erotic literature in France, unlike England or America where erotica means either *Fanny Hill*, a book of 'bawdy bedroom ballads' or *My Secret Life*, or a flood of cheap paperbacks with titles like *I Was a Nymphomaniac*. It is also a highly cerebral, intensely intellectualized and hermetic literature. Like that literature of the *aesthetic object* so well represented by Pieyre de Mandiargues, most recent French erotic books are characterized by their exclusion if not disdain of recognizably human, living *persons*. This is, of course, a defect that applies to most erotic and sub-erotic or pornographic literature. The people in them are automatons or puppets, made to copulate in a variety of ingenious or unusual ways either with or without a garnish of theory or philosophy, as the case may be.

The most famous French erotic book since the war has undoubtedly been the *Story of O* by a mysterious person called Pauline Réage, whose real identity has yet to be revealed. It was published in 1954, created a typically Parisian literary stir, and was said at various times to have been written by such eminent figures as Malraux, Raymond Queneau or Pieyre de Mandiargues. It has sold well in translation in Germany and the United States and escaped total banning in France. It is written in crystal-clear French; there is little dialogue, not a grain of humour, and certainly not much attempt at characterization. Lucid as the style undoubtedly is, the whole book has a deadpan tone that becomes suffocatingly monotonous as the story progresses. And yet, an adjective that is frequently applied to the *Story of O* by French critics, intellectuals and 'cultured' readers (by which is meant those who keep up to date with literary events and production) is that of 'beautiful'. The book has also been called 'mystical'. One critic (52) stated that being far more than a licentious work, 'the *Story of O* comes close to certain legends and certain poems dedicated to the glory of *l'amour fou*, to the *Song of Songs*, or *Romance of Tristan and Yseult*'; to another enthusiastic and well-known admirer, Pieyre de Mandiargues (who even dedicated one of his short stories to Madame Réage), the novel shows a process of 'complete spiritual transformation' and the mysterious author is 'about to enter that small circle of blessed and accursed creatures which constitutes the only aristocracy which one can consider today with any degree of respect' (53).

Similarly, nothing could be more glowing than the preface that Jean Paulhan, a member of the Académie Française and the sometimes presumed author of the book, wrote for the original edition. For Paulhan, the *Story of O* is 'one of those books which marks the reader, which leaves him not quite, or not at all, the same as he was before he read it'. The one word that comes to his mind when he thinks of *O* is *decency*. The book is the fiercest love letter that a man has ever received and contains a great truth at a time when perhaps 'it is more difficult than ever to understand what boys and girls are saying in the streets'.

The theme is that of happiness in slavery. O is a woman who is carted off by her lover to a château in which she is abominably treated and progressively transformed into an object for the delectation of her lover, his friend who is a mysterious Englishman, and practically anyone else who happens to be around. All the elements of the sado-masochistic, pornographic novel are present: chains, beatings, leather, sodomy, fellatio, rape, Lesbianism, bondage, humiliation and even infibulation, described with clinical precision and detachment. Unlike the characters in Sade's novels, the men who ill-use their slave do not seem to derive any pleasure from their treatment of O who, at least, ends up by becoming happy in slavery. There is something of a dream-like quality in the novel and it may be taken as an allegory if not as an uncompromising exploration of a deep and generally unavowed female urge, but despite the various theories it has inspired the *Story of O* is generally admitted to be completely outside the category of pornographic books written for sensation's own sake.

But to return to the adjective 'beautiful' in connection with the book: it is significant that the first appeal of the novel was to a French literary intelligentsia. It was written for *intellectuals* and for intellectual reasons and certainly not for a more prosaic- and unmetaphysical-minded public whose first reaction would doubtless be to express amazement at O's submission to such thoroughly unpleasant men as her lover and her friends. The book is animated by ideas and it is the idea that your French intellectual friend really has in mind when he solemnly shows you the book on his shelves, asks you if you have read it and proceeds to inform you how beautiful it is. Despite his flowery appraisal of *O*, Jean Paulhan was on the right track when he wrote that 'it sometimes seems to me that it is an idea, or a complex of ideas, an opinion rather than a young woman we see being subjected to these tortures'.

This conviction that *O* is 'beautiful' is part of an attitude that has become profoundly entrenched in French modern literary culture. The intellectual and the aesthetic appeal of a situation or an idea takes predominance over any kind of sympathy or empathy with the personages involved in them. Indeed there are no personages in the *Story of O*, only shadows and a fictional piece of long-suffering, much-abused flesh. The beauty to be found in it is one projected into the minds of the beholders by a process of pre-conditioned intellectual reflex, and for these minds to be thus charmed, a certain literary, social education and conditioning has been necessary.

O is a *Parisian* book for a restricted public conditioned by their experience of Surrealism, their own fads, fashions, intellectual vogue for Sade, approach to literature and use of language—in short, by their own *state of complicity*. Hence the reason why so many books, novels, stories and *belles lettres* often seem so incomprehensible and even ridiculous to the foreigner: he is outside the dimension in which they have their appeal and justification. When a Frenchman of undoubted culture exclaims 'but you cannot understand!' after you have protested that you can see nothing in such or such a book which can never be translated successfully and reach a foreign audience (because it is so 'precious', 'rarefied', 'high-flown', 'metaphysical', etc.), he is not being chauvinistic. He is quite right. Your mind and your critical faculties, your ability to appreciate have not been formed in the same climate and dimension. You do not share the same system of aesthetics. What to the Frenchman is something on a high intellectual or aesthetic plane may be for you only ridiculous or banal.

In 1966, a novel by a writer called Charles Estienne was published. Its title was *O et M* and it was inspired by both the *Story of O* and Charles Mathurin's famous 'Gothic' novel *Melmoth the Wanderer* which had recently been republished in France in a new translation with a preface by André Breton (who else?) and which had been glowingly reviewed by Pieyre de Mandiargues.* Charles Estienne stated that the reason for this literary offspring of two such (apparently) dissimilar books was that 'since I first read it I was haunted even in my nights and my dreams by the moral personage and the physical person of O. And when I had read the re-publication of *Melmoth* a few years ago, there was slowly and silently born in me the idea of making O and the wandering Man meet, with the secret desire of knowing just how far the most naked wedding of the

---

* I am sorry to give the impression of relentlessly persecuting this writer. If I mention him again it is only to show how interlocking and intimate is this small literary world of Paris. Again and again, the same few names recur...

physical and the mental could go in this encounter' (54). Ridiculous? Sheer literary mannerism? A typically Parisian literary phenomenon? This much is certain: no literary climate is more favourable than that of Paris for this kind of literary exercise. It almost has the spirit of a Baccalauréat essay: 'Réage's O meets Mathurin's Melmoth. Discuss the implications of such a meeting. Imagine their dialogue.'

Pretentiously intellectual or not as the *Story of O* may have been, there is no doubting the high seriousness of the erotic novels of two other French writers who have been becoming increasingly prominent in the last few years. They are Georges Bataille and Pierre Klossowski and, of the two, it is the first who has rapidly been becoming the more widely fashionable.

The intellectual guns carried by Bataille's erotic vessels are very big indeed, so much so that they almost end by capsizing them. Georges Bataille was a high priest of French eroticism and the author of a study simply called *l'Erotisme* as well as a highly reflective, metaphysical essay, *l'Expérience intérieure*, a study of evil in literature (including Sade of course), an essay on Gilles de Retz, and a lengthy and involved introduction to Sade's *Hundred and Twenty Days of Sodom*. Thanks to the recent relaxing of the censorship laws it has been possible to publish his clandestine works and for them to be reviewed at length in the press. He is now one of the latest intellectual idols of the younger French book-reading generation.

At first sight he is an extremely puzzling writer. A visitor from abroad who might be led to buy a book by Bataille such as *Madame Edwarda* or *Ma Mère* will find chapters or sections preceded by such proclamations as: MON ANGOISSE EST ENFIN L'ABSOLUE SOUVERAINE. MA SOUVERAINTÉ MORTE EST A LA RUE. INSAISISSABLE—AUTOUR D'ELLE UN SILENCE DE TOMBE—TAPIE DANS L'ATTENTE D'UN TERRIBLE—ET POURTANT SA TRISTESSE SE RIT DE TOUT.*

OT LA VIEILLESSE RENOUVELLE LA TERREUR À L'INFINI. ELLE RAMÈNE L'ÊTRE SANS FINIR AU COMMENCEMENT. LE COMMENCEMENT QU'AU BORD DE LA TOMBE J'ENTREVOIS EST LE 'PORC' QU'EN MOI LA MORT NI L'INSULTE NE PEUVENT TUER.†

---

* *Madame Edwarda*, Paris 1967, Editions Jean-Jacques Pauvert. 'My anguish is at last the sovereign absolute. My dead sovereignty is a vagrant. Unseizable—around it the silence of the tomb—crouching in wait for the terrible—and yet its sadness scorns at everything.'

† *Ma Mère*, Paris 1967, Editions Jean-Jacques Pauvert. 'Old age renews terror to the infinite. Endlessly it brings the being back to the beginning. The beginning I glimpse while at the edge of the tomb is the 'pig' in me that neither death nor insults may kill.'

The opening pages of *Madame Edwarda* are equally cryptic: the narrator is at a street corner, seized by anguish and the need to undress himself or the girl he desires. After drinking a Pernod he continues to wander in the streets, drunkenly. He takes his trousers off and carries them over his arm . . . After visiting a brothel he leaves it with one of the inmates, Edwarda, still in a state of mortal anguish. Edwarda is similarly afflicted and falls in a fit to the ground. Eventually, they enter a taxi and Edwarda seduces the taxi-driver in the car. She goes to sleep at the back of the car. The narrator is the first to awake, ill. 'The rest is irony, long waiting for death . . .' An extraordinary story told in a hesitating, complex, tortured manner: 'Let me explain: it is useless to bring in irony when I say of Madame Edwarda that she is GOD. But that GOD should be a prostitute in a brothel and a madwoman has no sense in reason. At the most, I am happy that people have to laugh at my sadness: only he hears me whose heart is wounded with an incurable wound, such as that none ever wished to heal . . .' Admittedly it may be both dangerous and unfair to quote out of context in a work like this, but even so we may see that any reader hoping for anything titillating or pleasurably erotic in the manner of *Fanny Hill* or a traditional 'naughty French novel' is doomed to disappointment. What manner of man was this strange writer who pursued the obscene to its utmost limits and who died in 1962?

Georges Bataille was educated at one of the leading schools in Paris, the Ecole des Chartes and then went on to take up a career as a highly esteemed and erudite librarian—first at the Bibliothèque Nationale and then, after moving for reasons of health, at the provincial libraries at Carpentras and Orléans. From indications in his books, his childhood was a very strange and perturbed one, filled with sexual obsessions, and he had become a Catholic convert at the age of sixteen although he relinquished his faith after the First World War. At first he was drawn towards the Surrealist movement but found it too cerebral and was even attacked for his 'morbidity' in André Breton's second Manifesto. He became preoccupied with politics, sociology, anthropology and primitive art, was a friend of Michel Leiris the anthropologist and André Masson the artist, founded a *College of sacred sociology* with Leiris and another well-known anthropologist, Roger Caillois, was reconciled with Breton, became an intellectual rebel obsessed with death, eroticism and the spiritual value of 'excess', was co-founder of a review called *Critique* and laboriously pursued his theories in various books and novels, many of which had to appear clandestinely under a *nom de plume* because of their scabrous and scandalous content.

Bataille was not really interested in writing novels as such and used writing as a means for experimenting in his quest for the 'impossible' and the 'absolute'—a quest which would ineluctably end in death and oblivion. With such aims in mind, his 'erotic' novels are above all the expression of *ideas* and need to be read with their prefaces and his philosophical writings which are often very hard going indeed. Far from being written with hedonistic intent or to give pleasure to the reader, or in celebration of the joys of sexual activity, Bataille's books are so many steps forward on a spiritual quest. Erotic experience could never be divorced, for Bataille, from spiritual activity. The most exaggerated obscenities were all means to his ends. In his *Le Mort*, a young woman undresses by the bedside of her dying husband or lover and then goes to a nearby inn and indulges in a long orgiastic series of every sexual perversion imaginable until morning when she returns home to die and join her lover in the tomb. In *Histoire de l'Oeil*, Bataille relates a series of sexual memories, obscenities and sacrileges that would appear ridiculous if it were not that we know that the author was a passionate theoretician obsessed with the idea of transcendence, through sexuality, horror and obscenity, and a necessarily vain attempt to break through the barrier of the possible into the impossible-possible.

This virtual monopolization of the erotic and the pornographic in modern French fiction by the intellectuals has been continued by Pierre Klossowski, a writer more in the midst of the literary 'swim' in Paris than was the retiring Bataille, and the brother of the Surrealist-approved painter Balthus. His books, *Roberte ce soir*, *La Révocation de l'Edit de Nantes* and *Le Souffleur*, are much harder to read than anything Bataille wrote unless the reader is interested in being drawn into highly complex speculations on eroticism as a means to knowledge and attainment of the Absolute. Theology and long disquisitions on the soul invade Klossowski's books together with a residue of Surrealist devilry in all three novels which are centred on the character of Roberte, a woman in search of complete freedom of soul to be attained through unflinching exploration of sexual perversion and excess.

Like Bataille, Klossowski has become one of the high priests of a recent literary erotic tendency, imposing the tyranny of the idea and the theoretical speculation upon the form of the novel to such an extent that his books are practically incomprehensible to any but a specialized audience with the requisite intellectual baggage. But like other high-aspiring, over-cerebral writers and thinkers, Klossowski is not free from the risk of falling off his intellectual perch. When he does so the result is hilarious or pitiful—at least it would be outside this mode-obsessed society in which what would be futile or affectedly esoteric to anyone with a sense of humour and proportion becomes invested with an aura of intellectual respectability by the ruling mandarins.

One of those artistic-literary events so dear to Parisian 'cultured' society took place in June 1967 when a collection of drawings by Klossowski was exhibited in the Galerie du Cadran du Solaire in the Rue Saint-Jacques. They were drawn as illustrations to the three novels, featured Roberte in various odd situations and were said to have been created in the course of the same complex quest that had been pursued in words. By any standards, it must be admitted that the drawings were bad—very bad. Also they were completely unnecessary since their very badness could cast ridicule over the written work. To find anything admirable or worthwhile in drawings so pitifully executed took an awe-inspiring amount of complacency and affectation—and they were not lacking. The pictorial themes included Roberte (a singular unprepossessing female with hips and legs drawn gigantically out of proportion sitting on a lavatory seat with a vague male form looming behind her; Roberte wearing a New Look dress down to her ankles and apparently dancing, or struggling, with a naked man and putting one hand over his mouth while he lifts her skirts over her thighs . . .). A review by another writer, Pierre Bourgeade, reaches further heights or depths of pretentious silliness: 'the drawings of Pierre Klossowski are, for all those whom women intrigue and, in the first place for women themselves, a lightning-like revelation. The exemplary calvary of Roberte, in some twenty episodes, life-size, is splendidly described in them. Roberte is not alone. Other women surround her, anonymous or not, and as pure, or impure as her. Among them Juliette and a few innocent sleepers. The evident spirituality of these angelic figures throws a cruel light on their essential eroticism. Never, perhaps, has the ambiguity of this objective being, woman, been so clearly represented. Ambiguity of her body. Ambiguity of her gestures . . .' (55)

'Ambiguity': in other words, a woman who seems to invite yet repel advances at the same time! An awesome and original revelation!

It sometimes takes an eroticist to appreciate another eroticist. Pierre Bourgeade represents 'smart' as opposed to 'cerebral' eroticism. The author of a short collection of *récits*, halfway between prose poems and short stories, he was one of those writers who were 'talked about' in the year (1967) that it was published and his book had a decidedly fashionable success. The book is about 'women'. The review that appeared in the *Nouvel Observateur* is no less revealing: 'All the women whose silhouette Pierre Bourgeade sketches in *Les Immortelles* have a common trait: they emerge intact from the adventures in which the writer had them live. And this subtle blend of eroticism and somnambulism allies them to that Juliette who emerges almost immortal and innocent from the tortures invented by Sade.' But then, the writer points out: 'there are shapes in this book but no persons.' 'No persons'—haven't we heard this before somewhere?

From producing an 'intellectual' and a 'society' eroticism, Paris has gone on to create a comic-strip eroticism. For the general public, eroticism was not the novels of Bataille or Klossowski, a novel like *Aux pieds d'Omphale* by Henri Raynal (praised by Breton) and various other productions all of a high literary tone, but the films of Roger Vadim with their flashy glamour, their Sagan-like concentration on a rich world of beautiful women, parties, whisky galore, fast cars and seduction in elegant settings. For a richer public, always on the look-out for some new craze, the smart thing was to buy the new-style 'erotic' comic-book. Examples of these not so serious erotica were *Barbarella* and *Jodelle*, two heroines somewhat in the tradition of permanent half-undress made famous in England by the much lamented 'Jane' in the *Daily Mirror*, all in colour and bound between hard covers, selling like hot cakes at £5 or £6 a volume* and eminently suitable for giggling over with

---

* *Barbarella* by Jean-Claude Forrest, Paris 1965. A comic-strip adventure featuring a sexy heroine who undergoes a number of sensational and alarming experiences in a science-fantasy world. When it first appeared, the book had a certain amount of trouble with the authorities, even being subjected to the law of *interdiction à l'affichage*. Even though it was priced at 53 francs (then about £3 16s. od.) it sold more than five and a half thousand copies in the first few days after publication. It has been made into a film by Roger Vadim, which is no surprise.

Jodelle, by Guy Pellaert and Pierre Bartier, Paris 1966, was published at 60 francs, and was similarly successful and told the story of a nubile female spy in ancient Rome with a generous ration of sex and sadism. It has been followed by other 'daring' comic-books for the delight of a prosperous public and people like François Lacassin.

friends between glasses of whisky. A fashion, in short—like the constant use of the word *érotisme* in the catalogues for so many art exhibitions when none but the strictest and coldest abstract painter seemed able to dispense with the vital word . . .

But if the surrealizing novelists like Mandiargues and Pierre Bourgeade seem to have succeeded in expelling any semblance of life and real persons from their books, the so-called 'new novelists' seem to have been even more fanatically bent on making sure that not even life of the most fantastic or exotic type should remain in their works. Practically all the French writers of the last ten years who have attained prominence (among critics, university professors and students of national literature—not any large public) abroad, as representative of the latest tendencies in French literature—Robbe-Grillet, Nathalie Sarraute, Le Clézio, etc.—also have as their first and most striking characteristic their intense *intellectualism*.

In the course of this take-over of the novel by the intellectuals, the death of the traditional novel was proclaimed, its grave was danced upon and the 'unhappy general public' or 'average reader' was scorned as was any intention to please, amuse or enthrall. The new novelists produced almost as many theories as they did novels and new dogmas were proclaimed with arrogance and pomposity. As we move along the literary spectrum from the surrealizing but narrative novel to the more cerebral novels of the new 'school', the absence of life remains constant. If not the *object*, the *idea* remains sovereign. After being dominated by naturalism or symbolism, the French novel that is 'talked about' and taken abroad as most representative of contemporary cultural activity in France is mainly one fed by ideas, or to be more precise, ideas on ideas, in a continuing flight from life in which the apparent 'intellectualism' of the writer is more an expression of his interest in interpretations of existing ideas than in any strong desire to achieve creativity in the realm of thought. To the Francophile obsessed with the idea of French cultural superiority ('in France they really care about things of the mind', etc., etc.) such a tendency has been taken as a sign of a promising interdependence of the arts and sciences. Thus, Christine Brooke-Rose has written in the *Times Saturday Review* of March 2, 1968, 'it is this interdisciplinary all-inclusiveness which has made the French literary scene—with all its faults—so exciting during the last decade or more. Writers are influenced by and passionately interested in contemporary philosophers and scientists and vice versa. They are not all cut off from each other, as we are here' (note the apologetic tone taken with regard to English literature).

But for whom is this literary scene 'exciting', considering that the sales of these French novelists have remained so tiny abroad and that the general reading public obstinately continues to prefer the works of Sartre, Camus or Simenon when buying anything that has come from France? The new French writers may not be cut off from each other but they are certainly well on the other side of a gulf separating them from anything large enough to be called a 'public'. Lévy-Strauss's 'structuralism' which has become so intellectually fashionable (more fashionable than understood in all probability) may have inspired a 'structuralist' novel by Pierre Rottenberg, in which the central 'character' is called 'La Structure', and Robbe-Grillet may have been an agronomist and a statistician, and some other writer an engineer or a beekeeper, but their books have still to attract more than the few readers who have so far been willing to make the effort to read them.

Academics may welcome them, particularly in America where the amount of critical work done on the new novelists has reached staggering proportions, but to less partisan readers, the main characteristic of most of the new writers must be boredom and alienation. We know that many French novelists have declared that it is no longer possible to write a 'traditional novel' whatever that may mean. Such anti-novels, or non-novels which they can bear to produce have been largely distinguished by their austerity, dryness and an overwhelming feeling of futility and despair. The reader has been scorned: everything that might have involved him, such as character or humanity, has been ignored or rejected in favour of what can only seem to be an obsessive determination to be esoteric and 'experimental'. There is no such thing as the 'impossibility' of writing a 'novel'—there is only a state of mind. And what a state of mind it is too! What recognizable human characters there are, like Le Clézio's, seem to be cut off from the rest of the human race, trapped in their own obsessions and their ghastly closed world of self-questioning, doubt, and indifference. Language itself to many of the 'new' novelists is a subject for speculation and doubt—certainly not an instrument for communication and emotion. Nothingness, impossibility, futility, these are a few of the cheerless, predominant themes of books produced by writers who seem to be earnestly saying (if you care to listen—they don't care very much anyway) that the very thought of writing reduces them to a state of semi-paralysis or mental confusion; who wheel round and round in their endless, verbal convolutions, dropping a word here, a scrap of dialogue there, a few pages of description further on with the weary casualness of a bored sultan tossing coins to his uninteresting subjects; and who dwell on their own frustrations with the repetitiveness and sterile energy of a dog chasing its own tail.

Even when the occasional novel of this sort has displayed the presence of a questing mind and a grim determination to achieve something new (however unsatisfactory to the public) the product is about as absorbing to the reader as the sight of a crossword puzzle being solved by an addict is to a non-addict. An obsession with the difficulty and even the futility of putting words on to paper is rarely absent. Typical of this attitude is Phillipe Sollers' *Drame* in which the author revolves around the theme of the impossibility of a story ever becoming a story, draws away from his work, gazes dourly at it and concludes that the whole thing is no use anyway. With this, and similar avowals of literary impotence, in a literary climate clouded by convictions that the novel is in a state of crisis and with what novels there are being reduced to the status of illustrations or appendices to manifestoes and critical theories, it is not surprising that so few readers are reached since all links with them have been sundered or abandoned as worthless.

To a foreign public largely composed of university teachers, students with the inevitable thesis to be written at the back of their minds, critics, journalists and our earnest friend, the worshipper of French culture, the recent literary life of France has been largely represented by the novels of Butor, Robbe-Grillet, Sarraute, Le Faye, Sollers and Le Clézio. But the gap between a wider public willing to read new books and such academically respectable literature has never been greater than now.

A minority literature by a few theoreticians and self-conscious experimentalists, dominated by ideas on ideas for one small minority; the literature of a writer like Mandiargues, dominated by the picturesque object, or an erotic genre characterized by metaphysical preoccupations for a somewhat larger minority; and endless war or historical romances such as Lartéguy's paratroop sagas, the 'Angélique' novels, translations of American block-buster romances by Frank Slaughter, or a flood of thrillers and endless paperback reprints of Saint-Exupéry, Camus, Sartre, Zola and Dumas for the largest reading minority in a country revelling in the myth of its own literacy and culture—such has been the overall picture of literary France in recent years.

But where are the novels inspired by life and where are the new novelists who can reach to a wide public with something that is new without being either experimental to the point of esotericism or intellectualized beyond endurance? The so-called 'new' novelists may have their appeal for a few but their expenditure of effort and their anxieties are out of all proportion to their creative achievements and their ability to communicate on any wide scale. It is all very well for someone to write five hundred pages on the 'crisis of the novel from Balzac to Gide' or to issue a manifesto declaring that the 'novel is in an impasse. A revolution is needed', but where are the books that *live*? Intellectual they may be, but the novelists of the 'new' genre have been apparently divorced from history, moral or political problems, awareness of society and its ferments, and even from a mere interest in people as *people*. But at least it must be admitted that esotericism, withdrawal and escapism have been a largely truthful reflection of the state of the French people living in a semi- or pseudo-democracy in which culture was either 'the glory of France's monuments' to be extolled by ministers and local civil servants or the privilege of a self-conscious Parisian minority who would no more dream of writing a book that appealed to a wide public than of going to dig in the fields.

If such has been the culture of Paris, what of that traditional culture of France that every local dignitary may be expected to praise on official occasions and which even the most philistine Frenchman will hold to be his heritage and pride? What has the cultural court of Paris given to its provincial subjects? Monuments of past glories or participation in a living culture? Or simply an invitation to come to the capital and there lose all provincialism, just as peasants in Byzantium might hope to become courtiers after submitting to emasculation?

PART THREE
FRANCE

7

The Foremost Cultural Country

FRENCH CULTURE may have radiated at various times from Paris throughout the world, but of cultural *rayonnement* in the provinces there was precious little for centuries. In Attica there was Athens; in France, only Paris and that was all. The rest was a cultural desert with a few oases. After the capital had attracted and absorbed most of the intellectual and creative ability of the nation, little was left in the provinces which had to content themselves with living in a darkness only relieved by the brilliant gleam of the capital on the far horizon.

This depressing state of affairs was finally recognized by the Fourth Republic. The preamble to its constitution stated that all citizens were to be guaranteed equal access to the culture of the country but in 1946, to take the example of theatrical activity alone, there were fifty-two theatres in the capital and only fifty-one in the rest of France. To remedy the situation, a policy of theatrical decentralization was started. While Jean Vilar was made director of the Théâtre National Populaire in the Palais de Chaillot, resident dramatic centres were set up at Saint-Etienne, Toulouse, Rennes and Strasbourg. How little France outside Paris was a country of culture could also be seen from the way in which the governments of the Fourth Republic devised plans for a network of 'houses of culture' which would eventually cover the whole country. Towns which had previously been obliged to content themselves with the few crumbs tossed to them from the banquet table at Paris and such modest fare as the occasional visit of a lecturer, an itinerant theatre group, a musical comedy and a well-worn play, and a sleepily administered museum of antiquities or painting (exceptions being made of a few really first-rate museums at Lille, Nancy and other large towns), were to be given the means to become artistic centres in their own right.

After De Gaulle had come to power, a significant appointment was made. Culture was recognized as being essential to France's new policy of self-assertion in the world. To bring the culture of Paris to the under-privileged provinces was all very well but to combine such a policy with a prestige offensive abroad—what could be more opportune? The man to carry out such a task was at hand. He had a literary reputation in the world, he had been writing about art and culture for years and he was a fervent, prolix supporter of the new régime. On July 24, 1959, the government decided that the new Ministry for Cultural Affairs was to be headed by the glamorous figure of that ex-adventurer, ex-archaeologist-explorer, ex-revolutionary, ex-novelist and now fanatical Gaullist, André Malraux, whose ability to make stirring speeches about France's recovery and mission was an asset to the administration.

By his appointment, Malraux thus became France's official spokesman for a 'certain idea of culture' which was to be indissolubly linked with De Gaulle's own 'certain idea of France'. His mission was clear enough. It was to give France a cultural face-lift at home and abroad, to decentralize the arts in France and, as Malraux repeated for the umpteenth time ten years later, 'to end the privilege of Paris, to encourage artistic diffusion and creation, to conquer a public who until now did not go to the theatre, the cinema, the museum, thinking that these manifestations did not concern it' (56). It was also to make French culture, so long extolled to the world abroad, an element of foreign policy.

What the Minister's own ideas of culture were it is less easy to determine. His sybilline utterances on the subject were often as resistant to precise interpretation as De Gaulle's. For Malraux, culture was to be 'the resurrection of the nobility of the world' and art was defined by him as being 'that in life which should have belonged to death. That which should have been lost and which we rediscover in a fraternal communion. It is the domain of things immortal—the only things which can face up to the powers of night'. (57)

From the beginning of his term of office, there was no doubting Malraux's activity. The budget allocation for the arts which had been only about 0.1% under the Fourth Republic was raised to about 0.4% of the national budget. Paris's great buildings began to be scrubbed clean while pigeons were systematically stupefied with harmless chemicals and carted off *en masse* to the forest of Fontainebleau so that they might no longer sully Paris's buildings (unfortunately the pigeons returned). The moat in front of Perrault's façade of the Louvre was dug clear again. Innumerable projects were hatched: a hundred masterpieces of French painting were to be reproduced life-size and distributed free among the town halls of provincial France (58). Huge exhibitions were to be held. Malraux became a globe-trotting emissary for French culture, telling his bemused and fascinated hosts in Japan, Mexico and French Canada of France's mission, the significance of art, the meaning of culture and man's destiny in the face of the powers of darkness and death. But always behind his speeches was the idea that France was resuming her mission as the cultural leader of the world that so needed her.

In 1963, after Leonardo da Vinci's 'Mona Lisa' had been loaned to the National Gallery of Art in Washington, Malraux spoke with emotion of how he had seen Americans admiring the painting: 'And in Washington, a city with a black majority, I saw children, their eyes lowered, raise them towards the picture and then move off in the crowd: millions of beings came to thank France after a certain fashion.' (59)

France bore the 'responsibility for man's destiny', he later added in the same speech. But he denied that there could be such a thing as any 'intellectual nationalism'. Artistic nationalism must have been a different matter since, a few years later, the Italian 'Mona Lisa' was moved from its place of honour in the great long painting gallery in the Louvre which then became filled only with French masterpieces. But it is still the most popular painting in the whole museum.

As for the famous 'houses of culture' to which he was to pay particular attention, they too were to enhance France's glory in a world which, as De Gaulle had said, had its eyes firmly fixed on France. In a speech in parliament (60) Malraux said that there should be one house of culture for each department in France in ten years. After pleading that each such house would only cost as much as twenty-five kilometres of roadway, he declared that 'for the price of twenty-five kilometres ... we maintain that France, which has become the foremost cultural country in the world in its time, and which is now repeating experiments on which the entire world has its eyes fixed, France can, for this miserable sum, again become the foremost cultural country in the world'.

Speeches in honour of Le Corbusier, the repainting of the ceiling of the Odéon by André Masson (despite the protests of the descendants of its original decorator, J. P. Laurens) and that of the Opéra by Chagall (so unsuited to the surrounding style of decoration), the inauguration of French 'houses of culture' abroad and the signing of pacts were not enough to encourage 'the creation of works of art [in France] and the spirit which enriches them'. The idea of the 'houses of culture' which had been born under the Fourth Republic was taken up again. They were to be made into cradles of creativity, 'authentic birthplaces of French contemporary art'. They also became used as political slogans by Gaullist candidates in local elections. Electoral programmes included the building of these *maisons de culture* and the development of some aspect or another of artistic activity. Apparently France was to be legislated into a new Renaissance.

After ten years of De Gaulle and Malraux, seven 'houses of culture' had been built (Paris: Théâtre de l'Est Parisien; Amiens, Bourges, Caen, Le Havre, Thonon, Firminy), five more were in the process of being constructed and four more were being planned. Each house was equipped with a theatre, a cafeteria, rooms for a library, a record library, art galleries and lecture halls. Not only was each *maison de culture* supposed to bring the best in French art and Parisian culture to the public in the region, but in some not very clear way it was to act as a stimulus to local artistic creativity. Inaugurating the Amiens *maison de culture* in March 1966, Malraux had declared:

> There is not, there will not be any house of culture on the basis of the State, nor, moreover, of the municipality. The house of culture—it is you. It is a matter of knowing whether you wish to make it or if you do not wish it. And if you wish it, I say to you that you are attempting one of the finest things that have ever been attempted in France since then, in less than ten years, this hideous word 'province' will have ceased to exist in France.

The first great *maison de culture* to be opened was that at Bourges, in June 1964. In May 1965, it was the object of an official visit at the highest level. It was a great occasion, sanctified by the presence of De Gaulle who praised Malraux as being the man best qualified to create the *maisons de culture* since he was also the man 'most qualified to understand, to desire and know what the human spirit is' (61). After briskly striding through the entrance hall, engraved with an aphorism of Malraux's which stated that 'all thought that really justifies the universe becomes degraded once it is anything else than a hope', and a cursory inspection of the premises, De Gaulle let

Malraux continue to give his fellow countrymen an idea of the culture being brought them:

> The chief problem in the modern world is this: the immense dream factories which have been created have summoned all mankind to something which they did not know lay so deep within them and which, from those moments we call leisure, delivers them over to the oldest demoniacal powers in the world: blood, sexuality and night. Facing these powers we have understood that there is only one other power. In front of death, there is only that which resists death. In front of the powers of night, there is only immortality.
>
> For reasons that are mysterious enough, all the people who are here have understood—at times with anguish and at times with laughter—that that which has survived for centuries was the best weapon to be found against that which was menacing them. (62)

An even more splendid cultural centre was opened at Grenoble in February 1968. It had a library for books and records, the usual snack-bar-cafeteria, a theatre and art gallery which loaned paintings, sculptures, engravings and wall-hangings by modern artists to members of the centre who only had to pay a modest six francs' annual fee. More than 30,000 joined. Its cinema club and dramatic activity were some of the liveliest anywhere in the provinces. But by the end of the year, it seemed obvious to many people who had been watching the process of cultural decentralization with interest and sympathy that the policy had run into trouble.

Malraux had made it clear that the *maisons de culture* were to be used by the working classes. They were proletarian institutions. 'Like the Paris métro, they are used by proletarians, white-collar workers, and many other people' (63). He pointed out that 'we know that 3,000 workers go to the Maison de la Culture at Bourges' and a few moments later added that some 12,000 people had joined the centre. Who were the other 9,000? Disconcertingly, the facts became clear: the proportion of workers, their families, and peasants from the rural regions who attended various manifestations at the *maisons de culture* in France was disappointingly small. The proportion at Bourges was unusually high. Most of the people that Malraux had wished to see participating in the cultural activities of the nation stayed away. In a country which had boasted for so long of its culture, it seemed that the majority of the population were still convinced that they were not 'concerned' with it. 'Culture' was for the 'others', the France that had no need of *maisons de culture*. Investigations and surveys were made. Polls were taken and analysed. All too often, the worker or the farmer interviewed made the same distressing reply: 'Yes, theatre, exhibitions, etc., are all very well but they're not for *us*.'

But there was even worse. By November 1968, the newspaper *Le Monde* could publish an important article (64) saying that the *maisons de culture* had reached a 'dead end', and that 'almost everywhere in France, questions are being asked about their use, their cost, their vocation, their destiny . . . and the whole problem of decentralization'. Most of them had become merely 'a theatre plus a cafeteria'. Two months later, the weekly *l'Express* observed that 'outside Paris, the lights of mass culture are shining no more brightly. Most of the *maisons de culture* and the dramatic centres have either suspended their activities and closed their doors for an undefined period, or, in the better cases, considerably reduced their ambitions and discreetly replastered a modest programme achieved willy-nilly in the saddest financial indigence'.

What had happened to Malraux's great ideal? In the first place, it was to be noticed that the main basis of most of the *maisons de culture* had been that of theatrical activity and that participation in the centres' activities had consequently been overwhelmingly passive. With art teaching in its lamentable state, in a country where young art students were not even given a chance to design posters for the public transport authorities, and in which their activities at college were scarcely ever publicized outside the walls of their establishment, how were the cultural centres ever expected to stimulate, let alone increase, the rate of artistic creation? Were the peasants, workers and lower-paid white-collar employees who were supposed to come flocking to them expected to discover suddenly their own creative gifts and return home, inspired and ennobled by some exhibition of a few paintings on loan from the Louvre, to produce works of their own that might hope one day to end up in some grandiose exhibition of 'Fifth Republic Art'?

In the second place, these theatrical activities which were so often the main aspect of the centres' activities were attacked by the local authorities and the population. Schoolteachers in small towns and the country might do their best to instil some notions of French civilization and the culture of Corneille, Molière, Delacroix and Debussy into the heads of their charges, and adolescents facing the dreaded *baccalauréat* might be asked to compose essays on 'philosophical' themes ('culture is truth': discuss); but when it came to the local cultural centre—financed by both the state and the local authority—putting on plays by *avant-garde* or foreign authors, then it was a different matter altogether. There were many only too ready to agree with such an impassioned supporter of traditional and 'entertaining' French theatre as that eminent Academician Pierre Gaxotte.

He had made his views on the 'Malraux' idea of dramatic culture known in the *Figaro* in a sneering attack on the so-called 'cultural' theatre, at the time when the Odéon was presenting Genet's play *The Screens*. Playwrights were to be divided into two categories: into 'ex-gaolbirds and friends of the people, into entertainers and judges, into champions of gaiety and servants of nightmare, in brief, on the one hand, on the side of the boulevard, on the other, on the side of culture'. Feydeau, that prominent exponent of boulevard theatre, was to be performed at the Odéon, Gaxotte had learned. He was therefore being given cultural status although not, perhaps, at the same high level as 'M. Genet, that subsidized moralist of the Fifth Republic'. But even Feydeau's cultural promotion did not prevent him from being very good theatre: 'Feydeau fills the theatres and . . . his cultural vaudevilles (beds, nightdresses, cuckolds, *cocottes*, mistakes, undressings) often come to the rescue of a box-office compromised by integral culture (tortures, S.S., F.L.N., death camps) . . .' (65)

The difference between the Gaxotte idea of French culture and that of Malraux was reflected in the disputes that arose over the programmes of the *maisons de culture*. At Saint-Etienne, such a bitter quarrel broke out between the director of the *maison de culture* there, Jean Dasté, and the town mayor, M. Durafour, that as *Le Monde* remarked, for a long time 'only the central heating was active in the centre'. The modern premises had been built at great expense on the side of a hill on the outskirts of the town. They contained a crèche, an enormous restaurant, a main theatre and a smaller, experimental theatre. No sooner was the centre built than it was shut since the local cultural centre (ironically named 'Association of friends of the *maison de culture*') and its president clashed with Dasté on the issue of who was to choose the programme of theatrical events. It was a long quarrel that was only resolved by a patched-up compromise in August 1968.

A *maison de culture* had been inaugurated at Thonon in the French Alps on June 4, 1966, with an exhibition of paintings by Braque,

Utrillo, Picasso and other leading painters in France. In 1968 it was virtually closed, being demoted to a mere *'centre culturel'* like so many others in France where the main activity was centred around table tennis competitions and other such events. The mayor of Thonon had said that the cost of financing the centre had become 'unbearable' for his town. He had asked for more state aid only to be reminded that the municipality and the state had agreed to share expenses equally. After a unanimous vote in the town council, the decision was taken against continuing the centre.

In 1964, the *maison de culture* at Bourges had been treated as a 'pilot' and had received considerable attention and publicity both in France and abroad. During the events of May 1968 there had been a clash between the director, Gabriel Monnet, who had been directing a 'national centre of dramatic art' there since 1961, and the mayor. There had also been a strike of the personnel, with occupation of the premises. In November 1968, the town denounced the convention that linked it with the *maison de culture* and refused to renew it.

But the worst case of all was that of Caen, where a particularly well equipped and attractive *maison de culture* had been built in 1963, and where there had been a remarkably inspired theatrical programme. From the start there was a long-running battle between Jo Trehard, the director of the *'théâtre-maison de la culture'* as it was officially called, and the town council led by the mayor, M. Louvel, a senator and rich industrialist who was managing director of an important electrical firm. The mayor had opposed the idea of a cultural centre for Caen from the beginning but had had to accept it. He had constantly insisted that the dramatic policy of the centre should be one of 'entertainment' as well as 'culture', thereby showing the similarity of his views and those of M. Gaxotte. Not for him plays by that foreigner Shakespeare and all those *avant-garde* writers that Paris wished to foist upon his townsfolk! Backed by many fellow-citizens, he reproached Trehard for not giving enough place in his programmes to shows of a 'diverting' nature and echoed the widely spread feeling that it was intolerable that the council should have no control over the centre.

Jo Trehard refused to compromise. He was in full agreement with Malraux's original aims and refused to lower the high quality of his programmes which were bringing excellent audiences to his theatre of a thousand seats and which had encouraged twelve thousand people to become members of the centre. The town council hit back. It also had the advantage of being the proprietor of the centre's premises. In March 1968, it denounced the agreement linking Caen with the *maison de culture* and took back the theatre to organize its own cultural fare, condescendingly agreeing that Trehard might continue to put on the plays he pleased elsewhere in the town.

On August 8, 1968, Malraux's Ministry for Cultural Affairs had to recognize the state of affairs by publishing a communiqué saying that 'the state has recognized the impossibility of pursuing a cultural action in conformity to the principles which had justified its intervention, in the present framework of the *Théâtre-maison-de-culture* of Caen'. Furthermore, from January 1, 1969, the state was no longer to finance a cultural centre at Caen but only to subsidize Trehard's theatrical company, henceforth called a 'national dramatic centre'. The cultural centre was now virtually non-existent. In October, the town council closed the centre finally and dismissed some thirty employees.

While Trehard and his company tried to establish themselves in a disused skating rink, the mayor and his friends decided to give themselves the theatre they really wanted. Impresarios specializing in theatrical tours and operettas were invited to provide entertainments. Unfortunately for the new 'municipal theatre', one of the plays put on was Ionesco's *The King Dies*. It only lasted for one night, attracted a derisory audience and was marred by the vociferous protests of some students who had come to show their displeasure at the way Trehard had been treated.

On January 21, 1969, a 'safe' entertainment was to be offered to the people of Caen: Rostand's hardy old warhorse, *Cyrano de Bergerac*. The town council decided that this time they were not taking any chances. 'Chuckers-out' were enlisted; ticket buyers were carefully 'scrutinized' before being allowed admittance, and the police were called in. To make sure that enough of the 'right people' were present for the performance, some policemen were given seats and a large number of free tickets were given to employees of the council and their families. Nonetheless a few students managed to get past the mayor's watch-dogs at the theatre door and soon made their presence felt by noisy protests. They were picked out from the rest of the audience by locals, clubbed, bludgeoned, kicked and punched by the police and expelled. More violent scenes took place outside the building and the police behaved with habitual 'firmness' which was approved by many of the population although not by two local papers who protested energetically, on the following day, against the brutality of the 'repression'.

In February 1968, at the Grenoble *maison de culture*, Malraux had said: 'The first *raison d'être* of this *maison de culture* is that everything essential that happens at Paris should also take place at Grenoble.' It did. In May 1968 the staff of the centres at Grenoble and Bourges went on strike and occupied the premises. At Villeurbanne, on the outskirts of Lyons, some thirty directors of 'popular theatres' and cultural centres all over France demanded a new policy for culture and attacked the official conception of the *maisons de culture*. In short, they were refusing a cultural policy imposed from above. But how could it be otherwise? A policy of decentralization had been conceived in Paris by a ministry which belonged to an undeniably authoritarian government dominated by a single personality who wanted to impress his idea of France upon the nation around him. As for his subjects, there was not much sign that the great majority were begging for their share of the cultural riches so long denied to them. In 1968, *Le Monde* printed a revealing story in this connection. The proposal to convert part of the ground floor and basement of a modern low-cost housing estate at Ménilmontant in Paris into a socio-cultural centre for the tenants was put to a vote. The residents were asked whether they would agree to an increase of 0.60% of their basic rent, an increase which would have worked out at between 2 and 4 francs a month, to pay for the centre. The number of voters was 487: 133 voted 'yes', 177 voted 'no' and the remaining 177 abstained. The project was cancelled.

In November 1968, the state allocation for the arts and cultural affairs was increased in the annual budget but the grant for the *maisons de culture* was cut by thirty-nine million francs. It was a sad setback for Malraux. French culture and artistic creativity remained largely centralized around Paris. Furthermore that culture which was to be handed down and distributed from on-high was not always accompanied by the liberty necessary for flourishing artistic creativity. When questions had been asked in the National Assembly on October 15, 1965, about the proposed performance at the Théâtre National Populaire in Paris of a play by Armand Gatti, *A song for two electric chairs*, based on the Sacco-Vanzetti affair, and the responsibility of the state-appointed director of the theatre, Malraux had defended him, saying: 'When we are talking exclusively about aesthetics, we have only one way of assuring liberty and that is carefully to choose those we have entrusted with a task and, from the moment we have entrusted them with this task, to leave them alone.' (66)

Three years later, the director of the theatre, Georges Wilson, was refusing to work any more as director given the political pressures he had to face; Gatti's anti-Franco play had been forbidden at the theatre after direct government intervention, while the Foreign Minister Debré went to Spain, perhaps to exchange congratulations with Franco over order again being restored in their respective countries; and Jean-Louis Barrault had been peremptorily sacked from the Théâtre de France at the Odéon following his hasty remarks during the student 'occupation' of the premises. Earlier, three months before the student riots and the general strike in France, the government had behaved in a typically high-handed manner by dismissing the director, the creator even, of the Paris Cinémathèque, Henri Langlois. This brutal dismissal brought protests from all over the world, from leading film-makers and actors.

The government remained firm. The Cinémathèque was to be 'organized'. The director of the 'national centre of French cinematography', André Holleaux, a government man, wished to exercise total control over Langlois's 'museum of cinema' which had been run by a board containing several government members and, at a session of the board, held in Henri Langlois' absence, a new director had been found: M. Pierre Barbin.

There were demonstrations outside the Cinémathèque and the protesters were charged by the riot police, the *C.R.S.*, on February 14, 1968. There were clubbings and beatings. The director Jean-Luc Godard had his glasses smashed and there were several injuries. A week later, a second demonstration of protests was held outside Langlois' former offices in the Rue de Courcelles. Again the protesters found themselves faced by the police, truncheon in hand. 'Give us culture without clubs,' the young demonstrators cried. Malraux's ministry washed its hands of the affair: it was not their 'responsibility'. What was Malraux doing all the time?

Malraux had more than once stated his deep mistrust of the cinema. He had said that the cinema was a 'machine of dreams' and that 'never before has a civilization had at its disposal such powerful means for the dissemination of dreams, above all the film. Those with the biggest dream factories at their disposal are not saints but men, who want to make money' (67). And how did these men make their money? By concentrating on sex and violence. For Malraux, presumably, Antonioni, Ingmar Bergman, Kurosawa and Truffaut were to be considered on the same level as any hack director of war or crime films. It was a curious attitude for a Minister of Culture to take—especially one so preoccupied with the civilization of 'the image'. It is true that Malraux had reacted against the Minister of Information's banning of Rivette's film *La Réligieuse* by sponsoring its entry at the Cannes film festival of 1966. But in the main, ever since he first took office, he had reserved most of his attention for the less controversial treasures of the past. While the problem of reforming art-teaching in France remained unsolved, he concentrated on an established élite in the world of painting and sculpture and, when the basic liberties of the press and publishing were undermined, when books were banned and magazines seized for daring to protest against attacks on the values which Malraux had once fought for in Spain and in the French *maquis*, the voice of the author of the *Voices of Silence* was often that of Olympian silence.

Like the régime he supported and the government he had joined, Malraux gave the impression of being aloof and remote from ordinary mortals. When he was not having old buildings scrubbed clean or extolling French culture abroad, he was delivering chauvinistic speeches, liberally strewn with references to cathedrals and crusades, but he was silent when the manifesto of the '121' was signed in protest against France's treatment of Algerians and when many of his country's foremost writers and artists were banned from the state radio and television. He was the vociferous prop of Gaullism, living in some cloudy world of rhetoric and philosophical musings on death, immortality, art and culture, but unable to communicate with the mass of his fellow Frenchmen. The man who wrote so stirringly of human fraternity and comradeship in struggle against tyranny now seemed only able to talk to a mythical France of which his master saw himself as the inspired incarnation. The writer obsessed with ideas of death and eternity now seemed to soliloquize in a wilderness or perorate in a void. Well might it be said of him that 'what the mouth of darkness tells him is truly of greater interest to him than what the mouths of men might stammer. Malraux's real conversation is one pursued in the desert, facing the sphinx, his true interlocutor who, however, keeps silent' (68).

From his behaviour, and even his non-behaviour at times, Malraux would seem to have forgotten his earlier self, his revolutionary activities, his appeals for fraternity and human dignity, his defence of intellectual liberty, his fight for Republican Spain and his days in the *maquis*. Had they all become phantoms of a past that never really existed, ephemeral memories of another self that might flicker now and again through his consciousness before becoming lost again in his grandiose visions? At times, he would busy himself with more mundane matters. There was a ministry to be run, there were grants to be decided for this or that cultural project, the cleaning of a monument to be arranged, the selection of a well-established artist for a largely irrelevant commission. There was a living world around him and he had to play his part in it before lapsing again back into his dreams, erring like a lost soul in some vast mental landscape filled with towering ruins, Maya temples, Khmer friezes, great cities half buried by desert sands, world-famous paintings brushed by hands that had given their owners a form of immortality before being stilled by death, to emerge once more into the artificial radiance of a Gaullist France which was half myth and where culture served chauvinism. The *Canard enchaîné* was more right than it knew at the time when, in June 1958, it published Malraux's 'obituary' under the heading:
    'André Malraux, the great writer, is dead.'

*

What of the people in France who were being so spectacularly reminded by their official cultural spokesman that they were supposed to be one of the most cultured races on earth? The majority may have remained unmoved by Malraux's lofty notions of art but one passion they did share with him was a mania for the past—particularly that of France.

Most countries teach their children a deplorably one-sided view of their own history. France, being pre-eminent in chauvinism, laid even greater emphasis on the subject and her schoolchildren have learned that Joan of Arc saved France, that Louis XIV gave culture to the rest of the western world, that the Revolution gave liberty and democracy to France, that Napoleon gave her glory and a modern administration, and that France won World War I. They have also learned a mass of historical trivia including anecdotes about Saint Louis and Clovis, and their ancestors the Gauls, a spirited and warlike race, supposed to have embodied a spirit and virtues which are specifically French.

How widely the history of France is assumed to be known to every French man and woman may be seen from such quiz programmes on the radio as the daily *Jeu des Mille Francs* on France I with its abundance of such questions as 'Who gave the Tour de Nesle its reputation?', 'Which famous eighteenth-century encyclopaedist did this or that?', 'Which of Napoleon's marshals said something or other at the battle of ****?' and 'Which king's mistress became the Duchess of X?'. History magazines like *Historama* and *Historia* sell in large numbers from every newspaper kiosk, picture books of history sell in thousands, large-circulation Parisian newspapers such as *France-Soir* are full of comic strips of 'historical' subjects while popular magazines offer their readers '*grands récits historiques*' and serialized adaptations of popular historical romances while, as we have seen, the spokesmen of the régime have seemed incapable of making any speech about France today without dragging in some reference to the glorious France of yesterday.

Since France is apparently so much in love with its past, it is not surprising that this history-mania should have spread into everyday life and tastes. French 'popular' culture—be it represented in reading habits, furniture or architecture—is profoundly imprinted with it and with their taste for the antique, the old-fashioned 'traditional' and the historical, a vast number of French people seem fiercely determined to live in their country's past as far as it is humanly possible for them to do so.

On the other hand, the French might well be history-minded and have a preference for old architecture and furniture—when they can afford it—in view of the vulgarity and ugliness of much of 'modern' France with its shabby country *bistrots*, its garish modern cafés, its brutally designed housing estates, the appalling standard of poster design, the noticeable lack of any kind of a modern furniture tradition, and the astronomical prices charged in the few shops which do try to sell well-designed contemporary furnishings from abroad. Visit almost any French village or country town and try to find one attractive modern building or piece of design—one visually pleasing modern hospital or school. Generally, all you will find aesthetically pleasing will be the church, an old mansion or a few medieval or Renaissance houses. The rest will be a cross between a slum and a nineteenth-century workhouse. French railways may be among the fastest in the world but the seats in the second-class carriages are desperately uncomfortable and the stations are a disgrace, although airports are generally a welcome contrast. French books on new architecture are few, public taste or demand for modern shapes is virtually undetectable, and the planning of new urban centres is crushingly monotonous when not done for a prosperous clientèle in private-apartment estates. French architectural training is now under some reform, but until recently, it was a joke and the highest prize that a student at the Fine Arts school in Paris could win was a Prix de Rome entitling him to a three-year stay in that city where he could draw Roman palaces to his heart's and his academic tutors' content. Apart from a few ambitious projects, as at the Rond Point de la Défense on the outskirts of Paris or near a few industrial centres, the most distinguished modern structures in France in the last two decades have been churches.

While a 'certain' France has been prospering among a population of which one wage-earner in five in commerce and industry was still earning less than 580 francs (£50) a month after the wage agreements of June 1968 (69), a tidal wave of archaic middle-class taste has been sweeping across the country. A 'traditional' old-fashioned French fishing village has been built in the south of France (Port Grimaud), newspapers advertise such architectural attractions as 'Le Capitou' (an old Provençal word), a 'village which will recreate exactly the ambience of the old villages of the deep countryside, without having the inconvenience of a lack of comfort. Each house, known as a *bastidou*, is built in hard stone in the *provençal* style', and the rich businessman who could afford to hire a modern, adventurous architect (assuming one could be found) will have as his life's ambition the acquisition of some old mill or farmhouse, to be patched up for his days of retirement.

When this craze for an old farmhouse or derelict but 'typical' medieval cottage cannot be satisfied, bourgeois aspirations to culture can be satisfied by ransacking country junk-shops and the Paris flea market. Most young couples will no sooner marry and move into their recently built apartment than they will rush to the nearest antique stall to find some old bit of iron, some disused coffee-grinder or flatiron to adorn their walls and shelves. To look through the pages of almost any French magazine on home decoration is to become convinced that apart from holding a few books (André Castelot's life of Napoleon in handsomely bound collectors' editions, a Prix

Goncourt, a few paperbacks), a bookshelf's main function is to hold as many bits of quaint or historical junk as possible. A drawing-room may not be comfortable but above all it must produce a certain 'effect' with its little knick-knacks stuck here and there on the walls, its old painting (no matter what subject), an Epinal print, a pewter plate or two, its bare wooden floor, and a few 'antique' chairs and table, looking for all the world like a set for a school play.

In Paris the situation is no better. Flats already cost the earth but they cost the sun and the moon as well if you want an old studio with 'visible oak beams' or an apartment in a house built with '*pierres de taille*', and furniture in the antique shops is as much for decoration as investment. While the Louis Quinze style dominates the 'smart' quarters of the city, a 'folk-lore' or rustic 'old provincial French' style reigns in young middle-class flats elsewhere. After all, is this not the *real* France as far as interior decoration is concerned? What can be more reassuring for the man of property than to stand in his drawing-room, every detail of which is cunningly arranged to produce the most imposing effect on the visitor, and lovingly run his hands over the knobs and scrolls of his Louis XV/XVI armchairs? They give him a feeling of continuity and a pleasant reassurance that his taste is both safe and impeccable, since it is so unmistakably and traditionally 'French'. If he is a *nouveau riche* and without time or inclination to hunt around the shops, or without family heirlooms and grandfather's furniture, then he can call upon a decorator of prestigious reputation, like Jansen in the Rue Royale, who will give him all the Second or First Empire, Louis XIII or XIV grandeur he or any other client could wish for until each customer has become his own De Gaulle, proudly surveying his domestic version of the Grand Trianon and gloating over its high 'standing'.

Open a copy of the magazine *Paris-Match* and you will find advertisements saying 'My dream, which is going to be fulfilled, is to live at VERSAILLES GRAND SIÈCLE—the new prestigious quarter of Versailles'. Versailles, Elysée II, Marly, Parly II—all so many names reminiscent of regal sumptuousness and the glories of French history! Even motor-cars in France bear names recalling the splendours of the Sun King: 'Versailles', the 'Trianon' . . . The working classes, who can't afford anything better, will have their unlovely housing estates set down in wastelands, but the prosperous businessman or young executive can have both a comfortable modern flat *and* a sense of sharing in historical grandeur through being close to some royal residence of the *ancien régime*. Sometimes he can even have his own 'Paris' *plus* Marly-le-Roi.

In 1967 some fifteen million French were estimated to be badly housed. The government's economic policy had been to reduce public financing of building by asking private capital, represented by the banks, to take over much of the task of rehousing. The result was predictable: new buildings were erected which were totally unsuitable for the majority of those without a decent home, as they were well beyond their means. Anyone can find a flat even in the most historic and beautiful part of Paris if they have the money. Some 50,000 Paris flats (of which about 14,000 are new) have been unsold for several years. Meanwhile, clever businessmen like Robert de Balkany, backed by leading banks, have gone outside Paris to promote projects capable of satisfying a middle-class craving for residential status symbols. Balkany's new city was launched with great publicity. It was to be a new Paris outside the old city and was to house 20,000 people. It was to be called Paris II. After the Paris municipal council had protested, the name was changed to Parly II —a hybrid of Paris and Marly-le-Roi.

Parly II, the public was told, would offer 'an art of living unique in the world'. It might be expensive but it was going to be democratic. *Everybody* would be living there: who knows, but you might be living in a flat next-door to a famous film star or a millionaire? There would be drugstores, shops, nightclubs, swimming pools— everything. All you had to do was to put down some money quickly. As for such banal details as rates, schools, crèches, population density, facilities for driving to Paris quickly, parking and traffic density on the roads that would lead there—little was said. The project began in 1964. Land was bought near Versailles. There were to be 5,200 dwellings, a large church, tennis courts and clubs. At first the project was turned down by the authorities but eventually the then Prime Minister Pompidou (no stranger to the banking world that was backing Balkany) overruled the adverse decision and gave the go-ahead. Now Parly II offers flats ranging from a double-living-room plus bedroom for nearly 80,000 francs to a seven-room apartment for nearly 300,000 francs. There are already a drugstore (designed by Slavik), a *miniracer* for miniature racing car enthusiasts and a discothèque. There will be a huge shopping centre, two cinemas and four restaurants. As the advertisements breathlessly proclaim: 'No other residence in the world (including the U.S.A.)

can offer its inhabitants: the Printemps (a branch of the Paris store), the château of Versailles, the B.H.V. (branch of Paris's Bazar de l'Hôtel de Ville), eight swimming-pool clubs, a two-hundred-acre garden-city, a giant drugstore open at night, schools, two cinemas, a view over the museum of trees [*sic*] of 450 acres, 120 luxury shops, tennis courts, a discothèque, a riding club, etc. How could you think of buying a flat anywhere else than in Parly II?'

Balkany has come a long way since his first success in 1961 with his Elysée I estate. Other projects are in the pipeline and what grandiose names, suggesting, 'the most beautiful pages in France's history', they will have: the residence Matignon, the Montjouy, the Parc Saint-Cyr, the Vendôme, the Montaigne!

The vulgarity and appeal to snobbishness of the advertising of every such estate is breathtaking. Thus, the advertisements for the new commercial flat estate at Les Hauts de Saint-Cloud announce that it is built for 'an élite'. A historic site, a great name and the assurance that 'the entrance hall is *le standing*'—what more could anyone want?

The true culture of the France that is seduced by these offerings is certainly that of 'standing'—a detestable word which so well expresses the aspirations of a bourgeoisie which may not read much but which knows its school-book history and such essentials of civilized life as the absolute necessity, if you are 'anyone', to have your visiting card printed *in relief*.

Even gastronomy is burdened with history. The south of France is full of pseudo-*provençal*-style restaurants with red tablecloths, distorted lumps of wood tortured into candle-holders and ashtray holders, cartwheels and farming implements on the walls and a picturesque gloom made even gloomier by the smoke wafting from raw beef-steaks overdosed with aromatic herbs and from sizzling pans of fried potatoes. In Paris, the Left Bank and the Ile Saint-Louis are equally full of cavernous restaurants or restored cellars in the 'Louis Treize' style, which means an abundance of iron work, rusty implements, suits of armour, swords, Gothic lamps, chunky tables, great fireplaces and overall 'Three Musketeers' décor.

Those who wish for 'modernity' turn to America. In cinema, eating or living, to be up to date and progressive is to be American. The obsession with America is the reverse of history-mania, except where the Wild West is concerned. It has also been denounced in France by upholders of French culture and deplored abroad by people who seem to find increasing difficulty in detecting the France of their memories or myths.

In the early years after the war, Malraux had spoken enthusiastically and generously of an 'Atlantic' culture, only to fall back in defence of French and European culture after taking office. Etiémble, in his book *Parlez-vous Franglais?*, attacked the invasion of the French language by Anglo-Saxon words and expressions but seemed to ignore the fact that if there was an invasion, then it was one the French had brought upon themselves by being so ready to adopt a terminology that no Englishman or American had ever tried to foist upon them. Sartre was only one intellectual of supposedly cosmopolitan views who lamented American influence. Indeed, after an interview with the Greek composer Mikis Theodorakis (before the putsch in Greece), published in the Athens press, he had attacked 'the Americanization of daily life in the West' and added that 'to let a foreign culture be imposed on oneself is to accept to live the life of another'. Sartre went on to tell Theodorakis that 'we are suffering, like you, from Americanization of culture and its depersonalization . . . For reason our fight is the same: for you, as for us, these objectives are inseparably linked: democracy, national sovereignty, autocthonous culture.' (70) As De Gaulle might have said, in culture too Europe must be the '*Europe des patries*'.

The fascination felt for the United States is often accompanied by virulent anti-Americanism reinforced by the conviction that in France people know how to live better and are more 'mature'. Most Frenchmen may have learned practically nothing of America's history but when the Right bemoan the loss of the old French values through American influence, and the Left publicize the horrors of the American past, the agreeable feeling that France still has much to teach the New World in civilized values is strengthened. Thus, while a writer like Max-Pol Fouchet may attract much publicity with his book *The Americans—are they adult?*, there have been plays in Paris dealing with the Sacco and Vanzetti case, one performed at the Théâtre Récamier in 1964 by a touring company, the other at the Théâtre National Populaire (Armand Gatti's *Song for two electric chairs*), and in 1968 Alain Decaux's well-received play on the Rosenberg affair. In the world of books, a novel like *Mandingo*, a hefty American saga of slavery and sex in the Deep South largely destined for the same public that reads Harold Robbins in paperback, was a best-seller and in 1969 William Styron's novel on the life of a slave,

The Confessions of Nat Turner, was serialized in the magazine *l'Express* and also sold well in France. American violence may be condemned but American thrillers sell in quantities, followed by a flood of French thrillers and spy stories which borrow their inspiration, gadgetry and fashions from transatlantic models. As for Western films, so great has their popularity become that France has had to import vast quantities of 'Westerns' made in Italy.

American foreign policy has been attacked and deplored with a vigour and consistency lacking in French attacks on their own government's behaviour abroad. While newspapers and magazines have dwelt with relish on American setbacks in Vietnam, race riots and crime, little has been said of France's continued sale of arms to South Africa—a flagrant defiance of world opinion and the United Nations, and a strange contradiction of a France that boasted of upholding man's dignity in the world—and her outrageous attempts to dominate her Common Market partners, not to speak of exchanges of governmental courtesies and commercial deals with Franco's Spain and De Gaulle's visit to Latin America where he swopped compliments with the dictator of Paraguay, General Stroessner.

American influence on French culture has often been denounced. American materialism and preoccupation with money-making are attacked in a country which reads far less than the United States, where the gold *louis* is an object of profound veneration to millions of Frenchmen, and where you can rarely eat in a provincial restaurant or spend an evening in a country *bistrot* without hearing at least one of the customers talking about his own economic affairs, his property and his financial transactions. American influence on the French language is denounced but when English is taught to air hostesses and young business executives it is usually done so with the accents and inflexions of the United States. As for publishing, nearly half the shares in one of the most successful French publishing houses, Robert Laffont of Paris, have been bought by the *Time-Life* group and some of the best-selling books on recent history have been those written by such American historians as Cornelius Ryan.

While, according to *l'Express*, 1,300 million bars of chewing-gum were masticated in France in 1966, and nearly 10,000 self-service stores had opened in the country since 1948, it was being lamented that an essential vehicle of French culture, the book, was being sadly neglected. It is also to be noted that the advertisement which extolled the attractions of Parly II made no mention of either a bookshop or a library. Evidently, a book was not one of those 'cultural needs' of which so much has been spoken by Malraux and other politicians.

Most of France does not read and if it does buy a book now and again it is either because it has been selected as the winner of some literary prize, because it is handsomely bound and is therefore a decorative and prestige-conferring object, or because the television set has broken down. The number of new books published is well below that in Western Germany; books like Burckhardt's history of the Renaissance or Praz's *Romantic Agony*, which one would have thought essential reading for any cultured Frenchman interested in art, history or literary history, have had to wait for a scandalously long time before appearing in French translation or have still not been published or, if they have, only in insignificant numbers. On the other hand, no other country has such a number of literary prizes. Apart from the four 'greats', the Prix Goncourt, the Fémina, the Renaudot and the Interallié, France has several hundred other minor prizes, of which a substantial majority are awarded in Paris. It also has a book tax of 10% on turnover: the highest in Europe.

When M. Jules Milhau presented a report on books sales and reading habits in France to the *Conseil économique* on March 22, 1966, it was found that 58% of the adult population never read a book at all, and an earlier report by the national publishers' union in 1960 estimated that only about 14% were regular readers, and that this minority read 75% of the total production. Worse, only 6% of the population who had reached reading age were registered as members of a public library as against 20% in the United States, 28% in Great Britain and about one-third in Russia. There was a fearful lack of proper, central libraries for *lycées* and colleges throughout France: only about a hundred whereas there was a need for no less than seven thousand (71).

As a result of the dreadful figures disclosed by the 1966 report, an association called *Lire* was created with the co-operation of the publishers' union, booksellers and other bodies, and headed by several eminent literary men, all members of the French Academy and including such well-known writers as André Maurois and Henri Troyat. A national campaign to 'attract the attention of the French to the benefits of reading' was begun and a 'national reading week' organized from May 9 to 15, 1966. Huge vans loaded with book-displays toured the countryside; posters were put up bearing the image of a man and his double with a caption saying: 'a man who reads is worth two'; there was a publicity campaign on behalf of reading on the State radio network and Radio Luxembourg broadcast interviews with such famous authors as François Mauriac and Georges Simenon while listeners were invited to send them questions.

By June that year, the campaign was quietly acknowledged to have been a flop. Moreover, several French publishers had refused to participate. In their great majority, the French had shown that they were still unenthusiastic about 'literature' as opposed to stories of pure entertainment. The latest ferments in Paris's literary world did not concern them or change their tastes. Spy stories by San-Antonio, Jean Bruce and Paul Kenny continued to sell in hundreds of thousands. Lovers of history as fiction went on reading highly coloured romances. A demand for sentimental love stories set in a fairy-tale world of châteaux, fast cars, and glamorous aristocrats was satisfied by the sagas of Delly whose twenty-five or more novels had sold more than three million copies, mostly in the provinces. Other big sellers were war stories and established modern 'classics' —as in any other modern Western nation. Finally, with such other culturally under-developed countries as Greece, Spain, Italy and Portugal, France showed a voracious appetite for 'photo-romances' as could be seen by inspecting the contents of any country book and paper shop or railway stall.

The French might be reproached for being materialistic and apathetic about their country's cultural activity but materialism was also to be found at the top of the literary pyramid, in that peculiarly Parisian world in which there seems to be so little real life, in which the idea for its own sake so often predominated, became fashionable and was handed around as though it were some exotic object in the hands of courtiers unmindful of the world outside the palace gates.

Few of the recent novels that qualify as 'literature' in France give any picture of life today in that country. One is Georges Michel's *Timides aventures d'un laveur de carreaux*, another is Claire Etcherelli's *Elise, ou la vraie vie*, but they are rareties. The people in France, the divisions between classes and groups, political and moral issues, the changes in society no longer seem to interest 'serious' French writers. It was all very well for the newly-constituted 'writers' union' in 1968 to occupy the premises of the old-established *Société des gens de lettres* during the euphoria of the May 'Revolution' and for a group that included Sartre, Beauvoir, Leiris, Nadeau, Claude Roy, Mandiargues, Pingaud and Faye to issue a manifesto declaring that their union intended to 'contribute to the building of a new society of the socialist type', but few gave any sign that they were contributing to a culture capable of radiating throughout the country. Like Malraux, they too were spellbound by their visions and myths, and while they made their grand gestures, the mass of their fellow Frenchmen continued to imbibe a culture of the image by watching what their government allowed them to watch—on television.

8

The Image and the Word

THE FRENCH may neglect the printed word but they still remain attached to the culture of the image, brought to them by cinema and television.

It is not part of the scope of this book to deal at any length with the achievements and successes of the French cinema since the war. Much has already been said abroad about French films. In this domain of the nation's culture, there has certainly been more to applaud than in that of literature. A great deal of vitality and genius has gone into the making of films. Both old and young directors have produced works which have delighted audiences throughout the world, which have won prizes, become classics and moved critics to rapture. Films like *Jules et Jim*, *Monsieur Hulot's Holiday* and *Hiroshima mon amour* have been praised as masterpieces, and those of Jean-Luc Godard are a highbrow's delight or hate in London, Rome and New York. But few other directors have shown signs of being greatly interested in the France around them, and in the dramas and lives of a nation of fifty million people. Godard has been buzzing around the many facets of contemporary France, picking up scraps here and there, making his own intermittent comments, interjecting his own satirical, savage or political-extremist views, and generally filming the trivia and ephemera of life in a breathless, jerky style which has fascinated and irritated audiences all over the world. But as for his films being a part of a wider French culture—accessible to all in France and widespread in appeal—has he not said 'Culture doesn't mean anything ... Art should be the voice of reality and the people. Today, movies are like parliaments—they are not really representative'? (72)

What could be less representative of reality in France than a film about 'ordinary people' by another, fervently politically-minded film-maker, Agnes Varda? She may take part in jointly-produced films about Vietnam and be very good at shooting heroic peasants silhouetted against grey skies made menacing by the drone of bombers, but when it comes to a film about the working classes in her own country, a film like *Le Bonheur*, she perpetuates a caricature. Is it supposed to be real life, a fairy-tale with a bitter ending or an allegory—this odd saga of a handsome young workman with his pretty young wife whom he drives to suicide by succumbing to the charms of a ravishing blonde in a local post office, who dresses so well, lives in a marvellously modern and comfortable flat with Dostoevsky in paperbacks on the wall, and who prances hand in hand with her lover through sunlit woods to the music of Vivaldi? Certainly none of the characters in it seems to be living in a real France.

However, even if they did want to make serious films inspired by some of the more disturbing or unattractive realities of their country, film-makers have not had much liberty left to them. The list of films prohibited for mainly political reasons in France is an impressive one: *Battleship Potemkin* was banned for years; *Paths of Glory* was banned; *Jeux interdits* was banned; Godard's *Le Petit Soldat* was banned; and Vadim's *Les Liaisons dangereuses* was a prohibited export for years. Ninety prefects and nearly forty thousand mayors throughout France have the power to ban films on their 'territory' and no film can be shown from the beginning unless it has been given a visa by the *Commission de contrôle*. When the commission was created in 1916, half its members were government representatives; in 1961, the government proportion rose to two-thirds. A film-maker may also have to contend with the army authorities. When Jacques Laurent, who writes the *Caroline chérie* romances under the name of Cecil Saint-Laurent, was making a film on the 1914–1918 war in 1968, the War Ministry asked him to cut some twelve seconds of scenes showing corpses because 'the military are horrified by the thought that one can be given the idea that wars kill. Show them five hundred cannon being fired and they won't say a thing. Show the effects of their bombardment or even a single corpse and there you are—being accused of ill will' (73).

The decisions of this commission can be either imposed or contradicted by the Minister of Information. In an officially secular Republic the thought that Rivette's *La Réligieuse* might offend practising Catholics and nuns' congregations was enough to send the Minister into a panic and for him to ban the film at the same time as the Minister for Cultural Affairs backed it for the Cannes film festival. When the censorship commission saw Laurent's film

Quarante-huit heures d'amour in 1968, they immediately demanded that it be banned. The Minister for Information, Joel Le Theule, saw the film and decided otherwise after asking that two scenes be shortened. He might have been acting in a liberal spirit. Anyway, another erotic film, *Benjamin*, had been shown and it was said that this story of a young boy's initiation into sex by a bevy of eighteenth-century beauties had highly delighted De Gaulle himself. The magazine *Paris Match* reported (74) that there were well-informed people in France who thought that there was another reason for this apparent loosening of censorship of erotic films. Sociologists and statisticians had discovered that television-watching was, with the birth pill, a factor in reducing the birth-rate. The government, alarmed by this threat to France's demographic expansion, were inclined to be tolerant while a new wave of eroticism swept into their nation's cinemas. Meanwhile, Jacques Tati's *Playtime*, a film of real genius which so well mocked a style of modern life, failed so badly in France that its brilliant director declared his intention to go abroad in search of a more congenial artistic climate.

But the foremost instrument for diffusing France's image-culture is undoubtedly television. Any examination of the visual culture offered to the majority in France must give it priority over the cinema (whatever its effect on the birth-rate), especially since Paris's wealth of good cinemas and 'art houses' is not shared by the rest of the country, as a visit to any provincial town will show.

At first sight, it would seem a curious anomaly that such an influential and far-reaching medium, with a great cultural potential, should have been largely ignored by the ex-Minister for Cultural Affairs. But then, it should be remembered that his interest in cinema and television was never absorbing and had often been tinged with distrust and hostility. His words, from a speech made to his Gaullist companions at the Salle Pleyel in Paris on March 5, 1948, are worth repeating: 'The values of Europe are menaced from within by techniques born out of the means of appealing to collective passions: newspapers, cinema, radio, advertising—in a word, the "means of propaganda".'

Such techniques, according to Malraux, led to a disdain for the customer or voter and he added 'in the first place we proclaim that we shall stress not the unconscious but consciousness; not abandonment but determination; not head-stuffing [*bourrage de crâne*] but truth'. Twenty years later he still seemed to ignore the fact that

France had a television service with a viewing population of more than eight millions—small in comparison with other countries but still an enormous increase since he took office in 1958 when there were only about half a million. In the same ten-year period, there had been a good deal less truth and a lot more head-stuffing.

The fact that Malraux was not interested in television did not prevent the state from putting all its weight and authority behind it, or other politicians from expressing their views on the medium. Many intellectuals and teachers might still despise or disparage television but its importance to the government was never underestimated.

In 1966, the review *La Nef* asked a dozen eminent French politicians what role they thought radio and television should play in the diffusion of news and the country's political life and culture. M. Michel Debré (75) admitted that radio and television played an important part in French public life, but 'priority must be given to the examination of problems rather than to ideological discussions. We must learn to observe realities and to judge facts'. The rest of his statement must be given in full: 'Moreover, we must maintain the *national character of political and cultural inspiration* [author's italics]. No doubt, it is indispensable to give the French a taste for world affairs and a knowledge of foreign realities, but a radio and a television which do not give the men and women of a democracy the sense of their responsibilities to the collective destiny of France would be failing in their mission. Finally, we must seek for quality. The main aim, no doubt, is to please, but we must also have the determination to educate the spirit and raise the character. The present status of the radio and television is an excellent basis. It makes it possible for well-chosen personalities to prove their qualities of command and administration.'

As for Edgar Faure, then Minister for Agriculture, he voiced the pious protestation that mass media such as television should not be used as an instrument susceptible of political exploitation, but as far as head-stuffing was concerned, he did not think that there was any great danger given the 'critical spirit of the French and the level of their general culture'.

The first well-chosen personality given the chance to prove his qualities of command and administration over the radio and television was the Minister of Information. Governmental control of television did not date from the Gaullist régime alone since, five months before it, the writer and journalist Max-Pol Fouchet had to declare: 'In its present condition, the *R.T.F.* (the *Radio-Télévision Française*—now the *O.R.T.F.*) is the voice of the government. It usually reflects a thinking which I would not call official (for that would imply that there was an "official thinking"!) but officious' (76). Max-Pol Fouchet was only one of many who had had trouble with the authorities controlling the radio and television services. He had been asked to submit programme scripts to officials before they were accepted and had refused. As for the lamentable state of France's information services—state and private—during the Algerian war: they do not need emphasizing. Eleven years later, the story was exactly the same. The ex-Gaullist writer and journalist Maurice Clavel was not allowed to appear on a Sunday interview programme on television by the administrative authority and said that he had also been dismissed from his post by the peripheral and so-called 'independent' Radio Luxembourg organization because of his remarks and, in particular, those concerning France's Prime Minister.

While De Gaulle was in power, heads were rolling in the television organization. Of three recent chiefs of the *O.R.T.F.*, one was an adviser to the government on foreign affairs, another an official dealing with finance, and a third, an inspector of the 'administration of the interior'. In the same period there were seven successive directors of the television news service—a service whose policy was decided every day in direct consultation with the Ministry of Information and government officials. The head of the news service was not even master of his own budget: if he wished to send a team to report on some important event which had suddenly occurred in the outside world, he had first to obtain a visa from the director of the *O.R.T.F.*, which meant, in effect, from the government.

In handing over television to the Ministry of Information, the government had shown that their main preoccupation was with the news that the medium would present to the nation. And what a news service it was! To watch an average television news programme under De Gaulle was enough to suggest that you were living in an occupied country. Practically every item was pressed into the service of official chauvinism. There was a concentration upon French successes in the most varied fields, on the comings and goings of foreign personalities coming to do homage to the President of the Republic, and on military ceremonies. The watcher was deluged with platitudes and regaled with endless scenes of obscure emissaries from mini-republics declaring how happy they had been to have had frank and cordial discussions with France's masters about the eternal links between their countries. Whenever there was a financial or political crisis in which France was involved, nothing was more depressing than the antics of the smooth-speaking commentators and so-called 'journalists' and experts of the *O.R.T.F.* During the 1968 financial crisis, for instance, a complacent announcer, sitting behind his desk and repeating the usual official French thesis on monetary reform, would introduce two financial 'experts' who popped before the camera like vacuum cleaner salesmen, to explain the mess the other countries had got themselves into by not heeding the wise advice of France, with all the gravity and conviction of a pair of smirking pederasts extolling heterosexual love. As for foreign affairs and the war in Vietnam in particular, what a wealth of detail was shown of each battle, what shots of carnage, horror and destruction, what an emphasis on each successful Vietcong attack on the Americans or South Vietnamese, and what reiterated statements to the effect that it was a 'filthy war' when, eight or nine years earlier, that other 'filthy' war in Algeria was presented as a French crusade, in defence of civilization!

The news is depressing on French television for what it *is*, in the form of its presentation. The cultural aspect is mostly remarkable for what it is *not*. The magazine *L'Express* might complain that 'the young French know the code of honour of the American Far West better than that of the knights of the Middle Ages; they acquire their vision of the world from cinema and television'; but the vision of the world they do acquire from this medium is singularly limited. There has been an astonishing absence of any *real* France from television programmes. There has been nothing to remind viewers that theirs is still a country with anguishing social problems, a country with a large poor minority, some of the worst-paid hospital staff in Europe, the highest hospital expenses, and a tuberculosis mortality rate of 18.4 per thousand compared with 14.4 in Italy and 6.5 in England (77), a hideous housing problem, deep social divisions and dangerous prejudices which may erupt into violence. There have been none of the spontaneous debates and forums with persons involved in important social problems speaking their minds as in England with its admirable documentaries and special-feature programmes on mental care, living conditions in modern housing estates, drugs and the young, sexual problems and local political issues.

There have been plays, many historical, and serials on French television but few real people. In England, the producers seem at least to realize that a good majority of their audiences are working class or lower-middle class with their own special sympathies and interests. In France, the idea of a 'Coronation Street' programme seems inconceivable. You may see everything except 'people like us'. It is simply no good objecting that a comparison with English television is unfair: in a country which has prated for so long, from the highest levels of authority, about its intelligence, culture and sophistication, its education and intellectual maturity, what should we expect but the best television in the world instead of a sorry apology for a cultural policy and a grotesque travesty of that information without which no country can ever call itself truly 'cultured'? No wonder that so many Frenchmen locked themselves up in their literary Byzantium or intellectual cloister if the television news was 'a window opening on to nothingness' (78), when the occasional fifteen-minute programme allowing an opposition leader to state his views was presented as proof that France was a free democracy, and when, with the paltry fare that was offered for entertainment, the mass of the viewers should have been so enthusiastic over a 'popular' programme as deliriously chauvinistic as *'Impossible n'est pas Français'*! French television may not have had much to offer in the way of culture (the word being used in its widest sense) but it does have colour—French colour. When it was a question of the European countries choosing a common colour system for international transmissions, De Gaulle made the French S.E.C.A.M. colour process and its adoption a personal affair of prestige. While most European countries (in the West) chose the German P.A.L. system, derived from an American procedure, the government poured millions into its own S.E.C.A.M. project. The countries which adopted the French system were mostly such staunch upholders of freedom of culture and information as Russia and the Eastern European countries, Algeria or French ex-Africa and Greece, and they did so for largely political reasons. The result is that if you live in Alsace-Lorraine, French-speaking Switzerland, Belgium, Luxembourg or Monaco you need two colour systems, the S.E.C.A.M. and the P.A.L., to receive all international transmissions.

And yet, the awful, depressing truth is that many Frenchmen will still tell you that their television is 'not bad'. They will point at a musical programme, an adaptation of a well or little known play, a literary programme or a profile and hail it as evidence that France can still do 'these things well'. They will agree that the news service provided by their television has been less than satisfactory and still be able to talk of culture. But what culture *could* there be when it was taken for granted that the transmission of information should be so tyrannically controlled and slanted and when the basic right to be informed impartially was so disgracefully neglected? There can only be the *kultur* of chauvinism, a pseudo-culture that became vastly popular, judging by the many letters received concerning a controversy in 1969 over the discontinuation of a popular and harmless series using models and cartoon techniques, *The Shadoks*. When viewers were asked to write in about the programme, many of the 5,000 who responded could think of nothing better to replace it than interludes on the touristic beauties of *la belle France* which they begged for with a fervour that would have been better employed in protesting against the scandalous state of their information services: 'Show us our beautiful churches, our beautiful rivers and our beautiful bridges. And don't forget that France is the country of Napoleon and Louis XIV.' (79)

They could rest assured: early in 1969 there was no question of letting them forget that France was the country of Napoleon. As for it being the country of De Gaulle, had it not been announced by the authorities that a fervently Bonapartist writer, Roger Stéphane, had been given the task of producing a television celebration of the thirtieth anniversary of De Gaulle's appeal to France on June 18, 1940? And had not Stéphane proudly declared (80) that 'the general has already seen some nine hours of projection. It pleased him—we may say that it amused him'?

*

Although the image may be controlled on television and the word on radio, the French language remains at the free disposal of fifty million men and women. Most have been taught to believe that their language is one of the glories of their civilization. They have been taught to believe that French is the greatest, most civilized, classical, clear, concise tongue in the world. It is the direct product of France's grandiose culture during the century of the Sun King, when it became finally purified, and it is the first instrument of French cultural and political *rayonnement*.

The Frenchman's language is one of the glories of his race, together with his abilities as a cook, a lover, an arbiter and creator of taste. It is believed to express such national virtues as a passion for order and measure, and an abhorrence of any kind of extreme or excess. It is esteemed as the perfect vehicle for the communication of diplomatic messages, expressions of love and any thought inspired by that most sublime form of intelligence which is, was and can only be French.

For France to radiate abroad, French must be taught and spoken. The necessity for its continuance as one of the world's great languages has been emphasized in advertisements in the French press urging Frenchmen to defend their language and promote its diffusion by giving financial assistance to the Alliance Française schools abroad—an advertisement, it might be added, produced by the British firm of Young and Rubicam. The continuity of a tradition of 'pure' French, obeying certain rules and rejecting foreign imported words, has been the aim of the members of the French Academy ever since the first half of the seventeenth century.

The French that is regarded as the only *real* French worthy of the nation's culture is essentially a formal and traditional language and it bears an authoritarian stamp inasmuch as it echoes an autocratic determination to impose order and discipline over something unruly and undisciplined. It was formalized and forced into a certain mould after being freed from impurities and foreign elements in a process which started with the reaction of French grammarians to the untidy and pedantry-ridden state of their tongue in the seventeenth century. It was confirmed by the French Academy which started its long life during the reign of Louis XIII, and which has led a fight against neologisms and what the French still call 'barbarisms', in other words anything that is not *good French* and is unsuitable to express a French thought.

These purists and partisans of a French which should be *really French* did a good job. It was admirable of them to tidy up and refine their language, but a certain narrow nationalism sometimes lay behind their endeavours and many of their achievements were accomplished under the shadow of that chauvinism which is rarely absent when French culture is being talked about. The French

Academy and the linguists were at work in a century when many Frenchmen had a feeling of artistic, linguistic, literary and general cultural superiority over other nations and when this conviction of France's pre-eminence was agreeably reinforced by the growing grandeur and power of the royal court and military triumphs abroad. There was no doubt that in politics as in the arts this was the great age of France. One consequence was that while French became the universally accepted language of diplomacy, French critics were scornful and disparaging of the languages and culture of their foreign neighbours. A common sentiment which has persisted until the present day was voiced in 1672 by the grammarian Gilles Ménage when, in his dedicatory preface to his *Observations on the French Language*, he said: 'Indeed, Monsieur, since the establishment of the Académie Française, our language is not only the most beautiful and most rich of all living languages, it is also the most restrained and most modest', and added that, since the conquests of King Louis XIV, the French language had become the 'principal study of all foreigners'. (81)

This new French language which had been made purer and more profoundly national was thus both the creation and symbol of a monarchy which was convinced of its country's supremacy in international politics and culture. It was a language of the Court which became the final arbiter of taste in this as in so many other respects. It was moulded at a time when royalty, the centre of all authority in the country, was expressing its power and aims not only in administrative matters but aesthetically. It encouraged a passion for carefully calculated great vistas, geometrical lay-outs, symmetry and rigid planning, severely designed gardens to mark the triumph of autocratic human will over the untidiness of nature, and a strictly codified social etiquette and protocol to discipline the untidiness of human conduct. The language of politics and diplomacy also became that of a drama praised for its loftiness, dignity and restraint, and ability to present noble ideas clothed in a no less aristocratic language. To some extent, we may say that French was a political product in an autocracy which knew precisely what it wanted and which was making its aims perfectly clear. The French language became part of French grandeur and when you venerated the one you automatically venerated the other. The same idea has been heard often enough today.

At the same time, while becoming more national, French also

remained dominated by an idea of a culture of classical Graeco-Roman Antiquity which was held to mirror and exemplify the virtues which were those of France. Ever since, French has continued to groan under the weight of the classical heritage which was foisted upon it when not already there from the beginning. This may be seen by reading almost any front-page article in the newspaper *Le Figaro* when it is written by an Academician, with its wealth of allusions to classical history, mythology and poetry, and even in some of the short front-page leaders and commentaries in *Le Monde*. A similar fondness for classicisms is to be found in countless other articles throughout the press and magazines, in humorous or satirical commentaries on literary or political events, in guide books and encyclopaedias.

A music historian may write of such and such a composer's musical ideas being made to fit a 'procrustean bed of dodecaphonic form', and a gastronomic journalist may begin his article by saying 'before embarking with your fair companion for Cytherea first make a pilgrimage to that classical temple of gastronomy which is the . . .' An example of a less facile use of such a classical-culture-laden speech is the way in which the newly elected Academician Paul Morand concluded his address of acceptance after invoking the memories of his predecessors in the seat he was about to occupy:

> Messieurs, our promenade in the Elysian fields is ending. I believe I have not left any of my heroes' ashes unhonoured. After having journeyed through this illustrious charnel-house, I feel these dead growing as familiar as characters in a novel, as saints in the calendar. I am become almost their companion and I do not regret it; let us recall these words of Joubert: 'the evening of life brings with it a lamp.' I hope I may raise again, for one more instant, that Olympic flame which already burns the fingers of the runner at the entrance to the stadium. (82)

French is still a deeply history-conscious language, impregnated with a veneration for the past. It is an élite language, a creation of a Court, and when written, the use it may make of classical or post-classical historical references is meant to be immediately understood by a cultivated public whose knowledge of history is as thorough as their knowledge of French. Thus, the reader of the article on gastronomy is expected to understand a reference to Cytherea; and when Robert Escarpit in *Le Monde* (March 21, 1969) concluded his brief comment on the Sino-Soviet quarrel, and on the problem of making an alliance against two nationalisms with a third one, he would write, 'There remains the tactic of Jean le Bon, who shielded himself from the right and then shielded himself from the left according to the indications of his son the prince Philippe', assuming that this trivial but striking incident of the battle of Poitiers is known to every reader who has been to school in France.

But French does not only venerate the past: it has a passion for clarity which was stated to be the first requisite as early as in the seventeenth century. Anything that could not be understood at first hearing or reading was 'not French'. The first demand upon the user of the language was that he be immediately intelligible. Other demands were that he never make use of a foreign word or foreign constructions, that he keep his sentences short, and that he always observe a sense of measure and restraint.

A delightful example of this clarity in which absolute lucidity is allied with perfect economy and grace is to be found in the beginning of Voltaire's *Candide*. It is the description of Candide's first sentimental encounter with the heroine of the tale, Cunégonde, at the castle of the baron of Thunder-ten-Tronckh:

> Elle [Cunégonde] rencontra Candide en revenant au château, et rougit; Candide rougit aussi; elle lui dit bonjour d'une voix entrecoupée, et Candide lui parla sans savoir ce qu'il disait. Le lendemain, après le diner, comme on sortait de table, Cunégonde et Candide se retrouvèrent derrière un paravent; Cunégonde laissa tomber son mouchoir. Candide le ramassa; elle lui prit innocemment la main, le jeune homme baisa innocemment la main de la jeune femme avec une vivacité, une sensibilité, une grâce toute particulière; leurs bouches se rencontrèrent, leurs genoux tremblèrent, leurs mains s'égarèrent. Monsieur le baron de Thunder-ten-tronckh passa auprès du paravent, et, voyant cette cause et cet effet, chassa Candide du château à grands coups de pied dans le derrière.*

A perfect paragraph. Voltaire is not writing about ideas, or formulating a thought, but all the qualities demanded of perfect French are there in his short and humorous description. The same qualities are also present in his philosophical writings, as indeed in those of so

---

* She met Candide on returning to the château, and blushed; Candide also blushed; she said good-day to him in a stammering voice, and Candide spoke to her without knowing what he was saying. The next day, after dinner, as they were leaving the table, Cunégonde and Candide met behind a screen; Cunégonde dropped her handkerchief. Candide picked it up; she innocently took his hand, the young man innocently kissed the hand of the young woman with a very particular vivacity, sensibility and grace; their mouths met, their knees trembled, their hands strayed. Monsieur the baron of Thunder-ten-tronckh passed by the screen, and, seeing this cause and this effect, chased Candide from the château with great kicks in the behind.

many other writers of his age and later. Together they all upheld the idea that French was first and foremost a language of clear ideas and expression. As Paul Morand said in his speech during his reception as a member by the Académie Française, the past writers who occupied his seat 'all have a point in common: they have written in that French which, despite attempts at a dislocation of language, aims at saying briefly and clearly everything that man has thought. To write in French is to watch the flowing of a mountain stream compared to which all other languages are muddy rivers, it is to live in a crystal palace'. (83)

In view of the respect with which their language has been treated and the thoroughness with which it is taught, it is not surprising that the general level of spoken French is high throughout France. A workman in the provinces or a schoolgirl from the most hidebound middle-class family will express themselves with a confidence and a vocabulary which will put to shame the usual stumbling, semi-articulate speech of an English workman or the word-poverty of a member of the so-called 'upper classes' for whom English has apparently been reduced to a few hundred basic words and clichés for use at all times. But although the great ideal of clarity is being upheld in spoken French, the notion that the language cannot but be clear is a myth and, as countless books and articles testify, many Frenchmen find it all too easy to be obscure as soon as they put pen to paper.

The way in which French can be obscure, ambiguous or simply unintelligible, although, perhaps, grammatically correct, is not only to be seen in so many of De Gaulle's and Malraux's speeches but in much contemporary writing, whether it be about art, politics or ideas. Any translator who has laboured to turn swamps of French prose into the firm plains of English will readily cite examples of the vague, the high-flown and the obscure in French writing. To read some of the theorizing articles in a magazine like *Tel Quel*, or articles of literary criticism in an intellectual weekly, is often almost unendurable for anyone in search of a clearly stated idea. So many words, so many abstract nouns, such heavy, clumsy constructions and a disconcerting lapse at times into the vaguest poetry—can this be the flowing mountain stream of which Morand spoke?

Consider the following piece of modern French. It is an extract from a newspaper article. The writer is dealing with an author, Henri Raynal, who has achieved some success with three novels of which one is an erotic tale. Raynal's vision, the article tells us, embraces all marvels and expresses the 'rigorous necessity to speak faithfully of them'. After referring to a statement in which Raynal declares himself 'proud of that which is', the critic continues:

> L'être immense et subtil qui le presse d'écrire, en fait inspire aussi toute parole. Qu'il y ait de l'être au monde, et que toutes nos pensées n'en soient que les reflets changeants, les chatoiements, les aspects divers et renouvelés, c'est ce que nos contemporains ne veulent pas croire.
>   Il leur plaît d'inventer un espace idéal, un vide où l'esprit par ses œuvres pourrait de toutes pièces secréter le nouveau.
>   Mais le nouveau, en dépit de nos efforts, le monde en est prodigue avant nous. Dans un ravissement, une adoration émerveillée, le poète qui est aussi voyant espère, plus que tout, répondre à l'instance de l'être.
>   L'inspiration est un état d'urgence. L'être veut être dit, par celui-là, tout de suite—et mieux et mieux encore. Et l'ingrat labeur—mais plein d'heureuse espérance, est d'aller au point où par grâce et travail le langage enfin, rejoint et enlace justement cet instant qui ne voulait pas seulement être entrevu ni savouré mais glorieusement enchâssé dans l'or précieux des mots.*

Such writing is by no means uncommon in France today. It is notorious to foreign publishers and journalists, students and translators. It is French 'waffle' and an example of that love of words for their own sake of which the French have so often been accused.

Another characteristic of much French writing and speechmaking is its orotundity. French is often said to be rhetorical and indeed, much fun has been made of the way in which French leaders and spokesmen indulge in grand words and compose phrases that are often more sonorous than meaningful. This verbal grandiloquence, the passion for the majestic and imposing rather than the

---

* 'J.D.', 'Henri Raynal, témoin de la beauté du monde', *Combat*, June 24, 1965.
A literal translation attempt:
  The immense and subtle being which urges him to write, also inspires every word in fact. That there may be being in the world, and that all our thoughts are nothing but its changing reflections, its gleamings, its diverse and renewed aspects, this is what our contemporaries do not wish to believe.
  It pleases them to invent an ideal space, an emptiness in which the spirit by its works could at once secrete the new.
  But despite our efforts, of the new the world is prodigal before us. In a rapture, a marvelling adoration, the poet who is also a seer hopes, more than anything else, to respond to the instances of being.
  Inspiration is a state of emergency. Being wishes to be said, by him, at once—and better and even better. And the thankless toil—but one full of happy expectation, is to go to the point where by grace and work the language finally rejoins and exactly enfolds this instant which did not merely demand to be glimpsed or savoured, but to be gloriously inset in the precious gold of words.

plain and simple, is often apparent in the French use of language whether dealing with art, politics or love. It gives French an old-fashioned air; the grand manner in language is now out of date but it still survives tenaciously.

Other Latin languages share this tendency towards the rhetorical but they never underwent quite the same degree of pruning and disciplining as French. In many ways, French rhetoric is a complete anachronism. But it is also a product of that chauvinism connected with the purification of French in the seventeenth and eighteenth centuries, and its exaltation above all other languages.

If you venerate your language and believe it to be one of the splendours of your homeland and a proof of national genius, you may wish to illustrate its supremacy and capabilities. You will resort to virtuosity and this, in its turn, will culminate in rhetoric. Thus, the French Academician, whose use of his language has brought him membership, will celebrate the fact in a ritual piece of rhetoric which is at the same time a proof of his own virtuosity and evidence of the virtuoso-like capacities of French. And in this rhetoric, a distinguishing characteristic is the respect for the *word* which has been carefully selected as the only one that will perform the task assigned it and whose meaning in the total context is assumed to be shiningly clear. Thus admiration of the overall virtuosity of a passage will bring as its corollary admiration of the *mot juste* whose selection has been determined by that same virtuosity.

We may see this in Racine. He wrote his plays at a time when nobility was regarded as an essential quality for style and when a royalty-inspired chauvinism led to a taste for displaying the virtues of the national language in the two most dramatic and interlinked forms possible: drama and rhetoric.

In Racine's plays with their steady flow of carefully worked out alexandrines, there may be detected the elevation of the word within a majestic and rigorously measured context. The form is antirealistic and bound by an extremely strict set of conventions but emotion is communicated not only by this stylized language but by the regular use of certain words. Those, for example, like *honneur, ardeur, flamme* (for love) and *devoir* all relate to noble sentiments and moments of high drama. With their long final syllables which fade away so resonantly like the last note of a trumpet call, they are like chords in music which are designed to strike the right corresponding notes in the scale of the listener's sensibilities and, as the bells in

Pavlov's experiments with dogs, are expected to elicit the appropriate emotional responses.

The language of Racine, like that of so much French speech-making, is a narrow one. The consequence is that all the more power and significance are accorded to the few words used. The same is evident in the language of chauvinism, with its words that are so often repeated and relished like *gloire, grandeur, honneur, fraternité, liberté* and *souveraineté*—all polysyllabic words suitable for solemn or impassioned declamation.

As for the language which 'finally rejoins and exactly enfolds' an instant or a theme in the 'precious gold of words', this gold is none other than that of rhetoric whose task is to heighten the splendour of the language that *expresses*.

That this French tendency to rhetoric has been fostered where French is taught there is no doubt. Anyone who has been to a French *lycée* or *collège* will know how pupils are encouraged to write essays and compositions on themes which call for the use of certain key words and metaphors, to write elegantly about cloudy subjects which are themselves metaphors, to incorporate polysyllabic words and classically constructed sentences which enable a formal compression of meaning to be made. This writer remembers how, in the penultimate class before the *baccalauréat*, he found himself having to compose essays on such subjects as one school of French poetry representing a 'marriage of convenience' between two others or some aphorism by an eighteenth-century writer. The object was not to express original thought but to make the language perform in accordance with strictly traditional rules. All too often, this encouragement to write pseudo-intellectual essays in a classic style will end with the immature pupil turning readily to all those ready-made phrases which abound in spoken and written French today, and fitting them together in a kind of linguistic jig-saw.

The result of this enthusiasm for a literary and classical French may be seen in the number of clichés so often heard and read in French. Even the simplest and most sincere statement will sound pompous; even the most banal opinion will seem intelligent and profound. The language of art and literary critics is full of words like *puissance intérieure, épanouissement, délire, liberté intérieure* and *recherche de l'absolu*. A writer's works will be 'bathed' or 'impregnated with poetry'; an artist will have 'followed the movements of his soul' or 'obeyed the inner impulses of the spirit' and a historian or novelist will have 'painted a vast fresco of history'. In one standard history of French literature, you will be told that in some works by a famous writer 'the heart of France beat in unison with the heart of the most gifted and—maybe—the most typical of her children' (84), and in another history, you learn that the same writer's style 'makes the stars sing. It strikes sparks from the smallest pebble on the path'. (85)

You have only to turn on the radio and listen to a cultural programme in French to hear such language currently used. Books on art are cluttered with such verbiage; a journalist asked to turn out five hundred words of copy on a new restaurant cannot resist the temptation to indulge in this second-hand literary style. An author writing a book for a large public, dealing with the most straightforward subject, will endeavour to show his writing ability by resorting to the hackneyed metaphor and the irrelevant detail in order to give 'colour' to his style and by opening a chapter with a rhetorical flourish or a dramatic inversion. Thus, in a book on Greek civilization, intended for a student or schoolboy, the author will begin a section on a Greek temple in the following 'lyrical' vein: 'Une colline ensoleillée, quelques colonnes d'une blancheur éclatante qui se détachent sur le bleu perpetuel du ciel parmi des herbes parfumées de thym, tel se présente aujourd'hui le site du temple de Zeus, témoin d'un passé prestigieux et d'une civilisation éblouissante, etc., etc.' On the radio, an announcer will breathlessly begin his account of the latest battle in Biafra or Vietnam by saying: 'Des quartiers en ruines, des rues jonchées de cadavres, l'odeur âcre des bombes, des routes encombreés de refugiés, un nuage noir de fumée qui monte au ciel, tel est le triste bilan de . . .'

To parody such a style is easy. It often reads like a parody of itself. The line of demarcation between the pompous-rhetorical and the ridiculous is never very clear in French. But this type of language which can be so cold and formal or so grandiloquent, which admits the use of so many ready-made phrases and in which it is easier to write or speak 'good French' than express yourself spontaneously, intimately and originally, is burdened by the traditions created at a time of royalty-inspired chauvinism. It is still a court language. You cannot play tricks with French; you cannot play with it as you can with English. The language is an idol, a living monument, and to be told that something is 'not French' is to be accused of a crime approaching sacrilege. If language is an expression of national genius and virtues, as has been often suggested in France, then *notre langue* may no more be trifled with than the national flag or anthem.

As for those great words which are set upon pedestals, like statues which need no label to explain their precise significance, words like *honneur*, *gloire*, *l'esprit* and *grandeur*, what need is there to ask what they mean to the Frenchman who has heard them so often? To repeat Von Moltke's famous remark, the French people often tend to take the word for the fact. They have been doing so for a long time. It is enough for many Frenchmen to hear a word repeated for him to be convinced that it expresses a reality. The motto for this allegedly Cartesian-minded individual might well be, 'It is talked about; therefore it *is*'. As for *what* it is, does it not suffice that it be French?

9

Anti-France

GENERATIONS OF Frenchmen have been taught to believe that their country's culture is both unique and universal, that it embodies a spirit which is called 'French' and which combines creativity, tolerance, readiness to welcome innovation and to experiment, intellectual integrity and audacity, a sense of measure, lucidity, and a tendency to give primacy to reason rather than to emotion and prejudice.

They have been told that since the Revolution, which set France free, Frenchmen have at all times been determined to fight in defence of the ideals without which there can be no civilization worthy of the name. All these qualities are inherent in this French spirit, which is reflected in a culture shared by all Frenchmen and from which the idea of intelligence is inseparable.

Such convictions have led to the idea of the supremacy of French culture. Many foreigners have been won over to the concept that French culture is, of all others, the one which most clearly displays human intelligence at its most refined. They have been told and believe that the French are too individualistic, too non-conformist as a race, too sceptical, too clear-minded, too rational for them ever to be ruled by blind prejudice or swayed by unreason. The French way of thinking is 'cartesian' it has often been said; the French attitude to all that is meant by the word 'culture' is said to be open-minded, discerning and knowledgeable. France is the true home of the spirit, and a country in which art and literature and every other manifestation of the creative human mind is held in the deepest respect by the people as a whole.

And yet, in this country which has prided itself on its respect for intellectual accomplishment and artistic creation, the forces of reaction and philistinism have always been strong. The Gaullist government might declare it a part of official policy to stimulate intellectual and artistic life and to diffuse French civilization abroad, but there was no lack of Frenchmen who shared their leaders' chauvinistic ideas while remaining violently hostile to part of that culture which was said to be their pride. Just as they had acquiesced or remained silent when humanitarian ideals were being outraged at home or abroad, so they ridiculed or attacked those fellow-countrymen of theirs who had innovated and created in art and thought.

By one of those curious paradoxes which abounded during the Gaullist period of rule, the government-controlled radio provided a daily forum for years on end for all that was the antithesis of what has been believed to be the 'French spirit'. The voice of reaction, ignorance and prejudice was allowed relentlessly to revile and mock every sign of intellectual courage, non-conformism, and genuine creativity which had honoured France and maintained the traditions of her true civilization. Millions listened and many agreed with what they heard, just as many in Nazi Germany must have applauded Goering or Goebbels when they sneered at 'decadent' art, literature, and music. The voice they heard, and which expressed so vigorously what many thought, was that of Jean Nocher, one of the best-known and most popular speakers to have broadcast while De Gaulle was in power.

Like Malraux, Nocher had his idea of French civilization and the national genius and it was one immediately comprehensible to millions of Frenchmen who found it inspired by that common sense and refusal to be misled or mystified which are held to be national attributes. Whereas Malraux used his verbal gifts to proclaim his own grandiose cultural ideas, Nocher spoke for the so-called average Frenchman. Whereas Malraux's ideas might tend to become lost in a swirl of cloudy rhetoric, Nocher's style was earthy and trenchant. If Malraux's conceptions of art and culture were often unintelligible to the man in the street, Nocher's were plain and categoric. We may say that he stood at one extremity of the cultural spectrum in France with Malraux at the other. When he spoke of art, literature or philosophy, he seemed to speak for millions of plain, blunt Frenchmen exasperated by the extreme esotericism, over-intellectualism and preciosity of a minority culture represented by Paris's cultural cliques. Like Malraux's, Nocher's views were often politically inspired but they reflected those of a far greater proportion of the population.

Such was the freedom he enjoyed to speak his views, on the rigidly controlled state radio, that he must be considered as much a voice of the régime as the Minister for Cultural Affairs, although he held no official position. Unlike Malraux, he received a vast mail, most of it flattering and approving. Had he stood as a candidate in a referendum organized to decide France's next cultural spokesman, the number of votes cast in his favour would doubtless have been impressive.

His real name was Gaston Charon. He had been a pupil at the prestigious Ecole Normale Supérieure in Paris in the company of the young Pompidou and Julien Gracq, and then became a teacher before moving to journalism. He wrote for the left-wing newspaper *L'Oeuvre* and supported the Popular Front government in 1936. When the war came, he served first in the air force and then, like Malraux, joined the Resistance. He was imprisoned for fifteen months at the fortress of Montluc, near Lyons, and he wrote a number of poems during his captivity. With the Liberation he became editor of a daily paper, *L'Espoir* of Saint-Etienne. He also began to write for radio and in February 1946 had produced a remarkable script on an imaginary atomic war, *Platform 70*, which, like Orson Welles' *War of the Worlds* programme in the United States before the war, caused a public sensation.

Charon was politically active and joined De Gaulle's *Rassemblement du Peuple Français* which had been created in 1946 and in which so many people detected authoritarian if not Fascist tendencies. In 1951 he was elected as a Gaullist-sympathizing member of parliament for the Loire district, but two years later he was expelled from the *R.P.F.* for contesting a seat against the party's official nominee and in 1955 he lost his seat.

With the Fifth Republic he came into prominence as a broadcaster, with programmes about youth and, above all, his daily talks '*en direct*' (i.e. 'live') which were regularly heard by an estimated five million people. They were a fantastic success. Letters came pouring in to Nocher (as he was always known) at the rate of 300 a day. Of these listeners' letters, 95% were approving, only 4% were hostile and 1% threatening.

In 1960 Nocher was in trouble because of the sneering, slanderous way he had referred to the prominent Opposition member, M. François Mitterand, on whose life an attack had been made in Paris. In the midsummer of that year the administration of the *Radio Télévision Française* stopped his broadcasts, by order of the Director-General, on the grounds that his statements had been 'incompatible with the neutrality which must be shown by a national information service'. But soon afterwards, listeners who had sent in thousands of letters protesting at Nocher's removal were reassured by a communiqué from the Ministry of Information which explained that this 'interruption' was only temporary, 'being part of a reorganization of the services of the televised news'. Two months after his programme had been suppressed, Nocher was back on the air in September 1960, apparently as a result of the direct intervention of the Minister of Information over the head of the Director-General who had sacked Nocher in the first place.

The reasons for this curious reinstatement seem to be clear. The Ministry had thought Nocher's words important enough to be heard every night by millions of Frenchmen. It was the period when the Algerian war was at its most intense. Intellectuals, writers and journalists were attacking the government's policies with increasing vehemence and being silenced by censorship with increasing regularity. Demoralization and disillusionment were widespread. Nocher's speeches were both moralizing and optimistic and castigated an opposition which had no right of reply nor any chance to defend itself on the radio or television. It was also to be noted that many of Nocher's talks went beyond everyday subjects of topical interest and were constantly embracing the domains of culture and morality.

For the next seven years Nocher was given 'peak listening time'. Five minutes every day, before the main evening news broadcast, listeners to the France-Inter (now France I) network, could hear an announcer saying '*Et maintenant, en direct avec vous—Jean Nocher!*' ('And now, direct to you—Jean Nocher!'). For close on five minutes they would hear a plain, blunt voice declaiming at top speed, hardly ever stopping to take breath, speaking of some aspect or another of life, art, culture, morality and politics in a tone which might be sneering, jovial, coarse, ironic or deploring and which, to many listeners, was the tone of voice of the 'good, honest Frenchman'—a little too blunt, perhaps, at times but always the voice of a common sense inspired by traditional *esprit Gaulois* and that Gallic scepticism which knew that Picasso and existentialism were nonsense and a fraud and that what really mattered were the family, patriotism, a pretty girl and a good glass of wine.

They would hear a speech like the one in which Nocher began by reading a letter from a distraught mother whose son, a pupil at a *lycée*, had shot himself, leaving a letter in front of book-shelves 'garnished with the whole of existentialist literature and philosophy, on the uselessness of effort, on the negation of will, on the denial of moral values'. Why had the boy killed himself? He had been happy at home, surrounded by love and care; he had no complexes, no love troubles. But, said the mother, he had been 'killed, destroyed, demoralized, by the masters of death who have only one aim: material and moral destruction'. He had been the victim of false philosophers and their evil books who 'instead of teaching him wisdom had systematically pushed him towards despair'. He had been writing an essay on the theme of 'Oh death, how great is your deliverance!' and his notes had been filled with 'quotations from the so-called masters of thought who had perpetrated this murder'.

Summing up this sad case and drawing the conclusions which seemed to be in order, Nocher then declared that 'this "auto-destruction" is in fact what we might dare to call a perfect intellectual crime . . . Should an intelligence which is good only for destroying, degrading, reviling, bringing despair, corrupting and disintegrating . . . continue to wreak its havoc not only in literature, in art, in politics or in philosophy but in the very heart of French culture?' He would not go so far as to ban certain 'ideologies and certain writings which are, moreover, legally subversive and morally degrading', but should youth not be taught to live rather than to die? (86)

But as for dying, what about the murderer who had stabbed a woman taxi-driver who had seven children and who had escaped the death penalty? In another speech, Nocher took up the time-honoured theme of the law 'showing more pity for the murderers than for their victims and the orphans that were made', and reminded his public that 74% of the French people were in favour of the death penalty. Anti-militarism? Nocher could assure his listeners that when 'one professes the faith of anti-militarism and unbelief, it is in order to join the enemy army and embrace the new political religions. When you call yourself an intellectual, an aesthete or a philosopher, it is to send your fellow-men a message of despair, of ugliness, of evil and death leading to suicide and to nothingness'.

As for the '121' who had signed the famous manifesto protesting against France's Algerian war, what were these so-called philosophers and self-styled intellectuals but '121 carriers of suitcases with the *fellaghas*' bombs in them'?

But despite Nocher's constant inveighing against the 'enemies of France' who had become wedded to 'the ideologies of subversion and tyranny', and all those whose only aim was to destroy their country and its youth, despite his refusal to allow France to 'be attacked by self-styled humanists who betray humanity at the same time as their homeland', his defence of the French colonialists in Algeria who were being attacked and accused by 'a part of French opinion which is, in reality, radio-controlled by a certain partisan spirit' and his countless sneers at the 'intellectuals of the anti-France', it was the state of French culture and, more specifically, its effect upon French youth that seemed to preoccupy him the most.

He more than shared Malraux's distrust of the 'dream factories', those 'so-called *avant-garde* machines which take us from rottenness to poisoning with films in which we see a procession with neither head nor tail of images already seen in Buñuel or Bergman, interspersed with pseudo-philosophical vapidities and distorted truths'. He also took up his verbal arms against 'so-called nonconformist novelists' who had 'sullied the homeland, the family, honour, faith, plain common sense and even ordinary civility' and who, of course, were supported by those intellectuals and pseudo-aesthetes who saw themselves as an élite and attacked 'all that the people loves: the good, goodness, the true'.

Once he had been to observe the debates held at a 'Week of Marxist thought' and had been delighted to hear a Soviet filmmaker reproach French directors for the amount of sex and violence in their films. This moved him to exclaim against 'our artistic intelligentsia which devotes so many themes to the destruction of the family, the negation of morality, the denial of the homeland, the preaching of revolt, violence, terrorism, defeatism, desertion or, more simply, boredom, despair, disgust for the most sacred institutions and the subversion of all French and human values ... These cineasts of horror, these desperadoes of literature, these painters of nothingness, these musicians of madness that are being sent to destroy our minds, to make us lose our souls, Stalin would have none of them and he was quite right: he would have exterminated them for decadent deviationism and anarchistic nihilism. Then why should they be imposed on us if not to corrupt our minds and turn our stomachs?'

Even fashions were not spared Nocher's verbal lashings. No more trousers and boyish clothes for women! Give us back real women again, for to guess the sex of these dressed-up girl-boys had become 'horribly difficult even for an intellectual used to all the gymnastics of the *avant-garde*'. And what did the attraction of this type of ambiguous 'semi-femininity' in women's clothes reveal if not 'the impotence of an epoch in which true, solid, honest virility is becoming increasingly rare, if not in life at least in the arts, in literature and in society, i.e. in what we now agree in calling the élite of intelligence'?

No wonder there was so much delinquent, demoralized and disorientated youth in France! No wonder a gang of 'leather boys' had broken into a café in which ex-colonialists were trying to meet the youth of Paris and the repatriates from Algeria in 'a perfectly honourable dancing club'! Look what the self-styled élite of French culture were feeding young minds with: 'Ionesco, Audiberti, Adamov and Picasso'! And what did he find in a list of suggested books in a school for training women teachers, for students aged between fifteen and seventeen, but Gide's *Faux-monnayeurs*, *L'Immoraliste*, and *Caves du Vatican*, Laclos' *Liaisons dangereuses* and Sartre's *Diable et le Bon Dieu* and *Huis Clos*, and even *Oedipus Rex*! But what else could you expect when the young were brought up to despise or ignore the 'acts of heroism or of grandeur of their grandfathers or even of their fathers'? What did they learn at school and what did they find out of school? Nocher was deeply disturbed to see 'bands of young people wandering on the pavements, idle ... or scouring the suburbs every evening, looking for some mischief to be done with an intensity both ridiculous and touching, learned as much from literature as from the cinema and art—that art which so often takes its nourishment from ugliness, anomalies and vice'.

Such daily warnings to the nation were not enough. In a world of a 'sordid materialism' in which eternal values were being forgotten and the country's youth were being systematically pushed to the edge of nothingness or even to suicide by so many philosophers, self-styled intellectuals and effete aesthetes, the young had to be taught again to admire greatness and the virtues of their country. This Nocher did in various programmes for youth. One, in particular, was broadcast every week on the France II programme under the title 'Youth broadcast'. A series called 'Rendez-vous with heroes' represented the quintessence and apotheosis of Nocher's thought.

A group of young people, including Nocher's own son, François, would meet before the microphone to talk about the youth that the newspapers seemed to ignore—the youth that 'has something else to do than to suffer its own boredom and filthy complexes, which aspires to raise rather than lower itself'. After asking why they had gathered together, five youths all under twenty and Jean Nocher, the answer was given: it was because youth wished to say what it had in its head and its heart and what was weighing down its mind. But let a part of the broadcast speak for itself:

> JEAN (*Nocher*): I agree with you. You have accused a whole culture which lowers you instead of uplifting you . . .
> (*Decadent, whining and sad, muffled, jazz music*)
> FRANCOIS: That's right! Above all, we have stigmatized a sick century which has given us nothing but bad advice, bad examples: first, the years of horrors revealed by the war and its aftermath, and then the publicity given to crimes, the corruption of the arts, literary decadence, thugs and gangsters made into film heroes, the cowardice and laziness of a deficient régime, the feebleness and demagogy of which it has given proof, the abandonment of universal or eternal values, dignity trampled underfoot . . .
> (*The jazz gives way to a very muffled rending melody*)
> JEAN: Almost nothing, in short! (*laughter*) And where does it lead us?
> DOMINIQUE: Well, to that drama of youth which may perhaps be explaining its sickness: it is not given something to love . . .
> LISE: Rather, something to which it can devote itself . . .
> GEORGES: Something to fight and give oneself for . . .
> DOMINIQUE: To work for something!
> FRANCOIS: Or even, for lack of a great task, a hope . . .
> JEAN: Yes, our children who should be our hopes are themselves without hope . . . A pile of letters here bears witness to it . . . The last messages of adolescents overwhelmed by life and who gave themselves death, leaving on the river-bank from which they dived, or under their shattered heads, the latest murder story by some prefabricated novelist, the essay by a philosopher of demoralization or even, alas, the work of a Nobel prize-winner on the meaninglessness of existence . . . (*Music ends*) And it is to end with all these surrenders, all these abasements, all these degradations, all these degeneracies and, how shall I put it, with . . .
> FRANCOIS: With all this cowardice . . .
> JEAN: Yes! There's the true word: to finish with the cowardice which delivers this world up to fear, egoism, laziness and facileness, we have tried to rediscover the path in life *par excellence* by making a rendezvous with those who gave their all to live better if not to die better.
> DOMINIQUE: And it is thus that we have tried humbly to resuscitate great lives . . . At present we must tear ourselves away from them. How shall we have the courage?
> GEORGES: By once again holding out our hand to the best, to those who are dearest to us . . .

JEAN: That's a very good idea. Before we part, let us ask ourselves to whom we would like to make a last farewell . . .
FRANCOIS: First, to the greatest of them all: to Saint-Exupéry!
DOMINIQUE: Yes, he's our master.
GEORGES: He's our brother.
LISE: He's our friend.
JEAN: He is Man. It is he who saves morality from a *fin de siècle*. Remember his key-message.
(*Softly, Tchaikovsky's concerto, tortured and then triumphant*)
SAINT-EXUPÉRY (*François' voice, reverberating*): We have lost man because we have ceased to give. Now, if I aim at giving only to myself I receive nothing for I build nothing of what I am and therefore I am nothing, etc., etc., etc.
(*End of concerto*)

The programme continues in the same vein with due honours being paid to Jean Mermoz the pilot hero, the Resistance heroes, Alain Bombard the sailor, interspersed with the 'Song of the Partisans' and Bach organ cantatas. It was broadcast in September 1963.

Not unnaturally, the 'self-styled intellectuals' and 'pseudo-humanists' protested against Nocher's broadcasts. They could not reply to his attacks on the same medium but they could still counter-attack in print. This they did in a number of articles mostly in weekly magazines, with clamorous titles such as 'Malraux, rid us of Nocher!' Malraux never uttered a word about the matter but Nocher, as might have been expected, revelled in the attacks made on him by his detractors. Everything they said confirmed his thesis that they were the enemies of France and only represented the anti-France of a subversive, so-called 'élite'.

Had Nocher not said that there was more common sense to be found in a metalworker than in all the 'self-styled philosophy of Sartre' and that for all the world's evils the supreme panacea was France? He admitted it joyfully. After all, did not five million people listen to him daily and express their approval of his speeches in a flood of letters that never dried up? Who listened to the 'intellectuals'? The answer was clear: 'If people don't listen to them, who are so intelligent, and if people do listen to me, who am so stupid, isn't it because there is a point of contact between us which they do not have: pure and simple common sense, always, and sometimes a little of that spirit which people abroad rightly call "French"?' (May 21, 1962).

To investigate this 'editorialist' of the State radio whose popularity was so phenomenal and whose words were echoed by so many listeners, the weekly *L'Express* sent a young woman reporter to interview Nocher (87). It must have been an alarming experience.

Nocher expressed himself freely to the reporter with a colourful imagery and a wealth of coarseness which would have been too much on the air, even for the Minister of Information. He began by defining himself as a 'scientist. I don't know why, now, I was with the fools at the Normale [the Ecole Normale]. I did literature for two years. Ridiculous. All those who don't know how to do anything, who are good for nothing, they do literature'.

Why did he change his political sympathies? Simple: 'now Fascism is communism.' Why did he attack intellectuals? Because 'intellectuals are fools . . . I'm an intuitionist. I would never reflect before acting. I don't believe in an intelligence which reasons'. What were his views on the world and on society? The answer was simple: 'All capitalisms are condemned. Communism like the others . . . As a matter of fact, all the problems of production are solved but not the problems of distribution. Ah! Mathematicians should be castrated . . .'

What about the arts? 'The cinema is disgusting. Nothing but people fornicating everywhere.' Creativity and modern forms of creation? Again, to Nocher 'intellectuals are fools . . . they never invented a thing . . . all the people who invent new forms are mad. They are hollow forms. The other day I saw a lad who had made a hole with his finger in a canvas. This was, it seems, a picture . . .'

Asked about the future, Nocher who had declared that 'I am a humanist' swore that he had foreseen everything himself, especially in his scientific programmes, even the Russian Sputnik twenty-two months in advance 'with scarcely 5% of error in its weight, speed and everything'. And as a final message to his interlocutor, he declared 'if they don't listen to me, in 1966 there'll only be one chance in ten thousand of survival'.

Nocher had spoken. He went on broadcasting to the nation until his death, the perfect eloquent representative of a France that was and is an 'anti-France', as he would say. As his publisher said in a preface to one of his collected speeches, the book was the 'living reflection of that spirit which we call French and which was his own'. In his words, 'the millions of men and women listeners to Jean Nocher will find the echo of their own thoughts'.

His popularity was enormous. Did Nocher ever reflect that in his ideas on culture, youth and the spiritual regeneration of the French people, he was faithfully reflecting the views of another Frenchman who had dwelt at length on similar themes of morality, work, the family and the homeland. When Nocher spoke of the 'anti-France', there were millions ready to agree with him. When a real anti-France had been in power, during the Occupation, millions had accepted and agreed with Marshal Pétain.

*

Jean Nocher may have been a Fascist-minded megalomaniac but he was quite right when he said that he spoke for millions of his fellow-countrymen. He was certainly a representative figure. By allowing him to broadcast, the Gaullist government at least performed the service of showing how great was the opposition and antipathy to much of that modern French 'culture' which was an essential part of France's continuing *rayonnement*. The letters which came pouring in showed how widespread was this 'Nocherism' in the country and how great was the gap between many 'ordinary' Frenchmen and the culture they were all supposed to share. Even though Nocher's views may have been too extreme for many people, they reflected commonly-held prejudices and a popular distrust of the nation's 'intellectuals'. Ionesco, Gide, Sartre, Boulez and Picasso might be ambassadors for the French genius abroad, but for Nocher and his vast audiences they were un-French or even anti-French. The culture against which Nocher raised his spiteful voice was widely believed to have been created by a minority who formed a body apart from the rest of the nation. By his vicious attacks, Nocher had shown how a large part of the country supposed to worship intelligence and thought has remained deeply suspicious of a culture that does not immediately flatter its chauvinistic vanity, and has tended to place the creators of this culture in a special category, denying it the quality of 'Frenchness'.

But what is this 'Frenchness'? How is it that so many people in a country divided politically, socially, religiously, physically and economically will generally agree that certain qualities of the spirit are especially French and then proceed to deny 'Frenchness' to those who display them to the highest degree?

The concept of 'Frenchness' has often been determined by chauvinism. The whole myth of France's cultural and spiritual radiance and her mission in the world has been based upon the conviction of the specialness of the French race, upon the belief that it possesses qualities and virtues to a greater degree than other peoples. But when it is a matter of deciding which of their compatriots share this Frenchness, Frenchmen have tended to disagree violently.

The Frenchman from the north of France and his fellow-countryman from the Pyrenees may both have listened approvingly to Nocher's speeches and have shared the same notion of national genius and characteristics. Both will believe that by virtue of being citizens of France they are in possession of a secret of a way of life that no other country can ever share or rival. Both will believe that their race has produced a culture unrivalled in the world and which reflects qualities to be found from one end of France to the other. Each will take pride in his *esprit gaulois*, his sophistication in the arts of living, his way with women, his ability to get along in life, his capacity for enjoyment, his innate intelligence, reasonableness, healthy scepticism and individuality. But at certain times, and according to his social type, each will regard the other as lacking true 'Frenchness' and as being an alien to the country he inhabits and to its traditions.

There may be one myth of France shared by most Frenchmen and by millions of foreigners, but there is certainly more than one France. There is the France of Paris and that of the provinces with the inhabitants of the capital revelling in their sense of superiority over the rest of the nation, and in the assurance that they are united by a complicity which can only be Parisian and which only they can appreciate. Outside Paris, the feeling that to be French is a concept which can only be understood, enjoyed and shared by Frenchmen is common to the provincial from Metz and the provincial from Narbonne, yet each will feel anything but oneness with his fellow-countrymen, taken as individuals rather than as an agglomerate, since he is still deeply divided from them by regional ties, politics, geography and his own view of France and her culture.

Many Frenchmen, including De Gaulle, have seen their country's history as something organic, as something profoundly *one*, which has formed their fellow-countrymen in a special mould. Similarly, French culture has been believed to represent an achievement in which all Frenchmen, in the past as in the present, have concurred. But even a brief glimpse at the history books will show that France's history has been characterized by a never-ending succession of struggles between various parts of the nation, each with their own local and political allegiances and ideologies. Even so, the belief is strong that all these divisions and differences inside France have somehow combined in a constructive manner to produce something unique of which all Frenchmen can be proud.

The myth has it that the French are a nation of individuals bound together by the unity of their culture and their 'Frenchness'. The truth is that they have tended throughout their country's history to form into factions and to fight each other. In this France in which patriotism has so often become chauvinism, in which myths of cultural and warlike grandeur have been assiduously propagated by rival groups, in which past history is never digested and seen to be the past, in which political divisions have never been counterbalanced by overall moral unity and a sense of national oneness, in which class resentments and enmities are so marked, no characteristic would seem more applicable to the French as a mass than a tendency to divide into certain well-defined types rather than individuals. Each type has seen itself as representative of France, its rivals as embodiments of the 'anti-France'. Each type has seen one part of the nation's creative activities as 'culture', the other as an 'anti-culture', before masking all these divisions and prejudices with the myth of a nation-wide 'Frenchness'.

This long-established tendency to gather according to type into factions within the nation and to take up extreme positions in politics and culture has been accompanied by a remarkable amount of violence. Such violence has been a product of the intensity of hatred that has so often been engendered by the rivalry and clashes between types. The degree of hatred in Nocher's attitude needs no emphasizing. Such hatred is common in French history—particularly since the Revolution. It has been an important factor in French politics, parliamentary life and class conflicts. At times it has exploded into a violence that has shocked foreigners.

The pleasant belief that the French are a somewhat frivolous people, more devoted to pleasure than to strife, to verbal argument rather than serious and violent enmity, is not confirmed by France's recent history. It is strange how often it is forgotten that the culture and way of life which have attracted so many admirers have been produced by a country with an extremely warlike, blood-stained past. Memories of various *belles époques,* the lure of Paris and the prestige of French art and literature have made people forget that this country which they find so civilized has a dark record of extremist behaviour, internal hatreds, and civil conflicts in which one part of the population reacted against the other with appalling ferocity and a passionate refusal to recognize that their enemies were also Frenchmen.

Such tendencies towards extremism and hatred have been seen in those occasional outbursts of xenophobia which are inherent in chauvinism and to which France has been prone at various times. Naturally, this hatred between social categories and political factions has often been directed against the most obvious 'anti-France' of all—the alien racial or religious minority within the country.

For a nation which has prided itself on its tolerance and which has, a long tradition of giving refuge to foreign exiles, the expression of racial hatred in the last hundred years has been remarkable in its intensity if not in its scale. Xenophobia is generally latent in France but apt to be expressed when the country is in economic or political confusion, and yet France now has a population of more than three million foreigners most of whom live quite amicably among Frenchmen and who, with the outstanding exception of the Algerians, are generally integrated into the country. Anti-semitic incidents have been extremely rare in France in the last few years and yet there is always a widespread underlying prejudice. A survey conducted by the French public opinion poll organization, SOFRES, in 1967 showed that, with regard to other races, the French were generally more anti-Negro than anti-Jewish and more anti-Arab than anti-Negro—a degree of bias well reflected in extremist papers like *Minute*. In 1964, hundreds of thousands of readers of right-wing papers could read alarming stories under sensational headlines (THE ALGERIAN INVASION OF FRANCE—THE ALGERIAN GANGRENE, etc.), about how the honest Parisian worker could no longer go with his family to enjoy himself at Pigalle or Montmartre without having his wife jostled by Arabs, how 'they invade our hospitals, burgle the Social Security, and discredit those who do work', how one pimp in three is an Algerian, one murderer in three, etc., how they bring T.B. and syphilis into France and generally demoralize the nation. In 1969, French government policy in the Middle East encouraged extreme anti-semitic organizations like *L'Oeuvre Française* ('against Zionization') and *Europe-Action*, and in the Gaullist demonstration in the Champs-Elysées a year before, cries had been heard of 'Cohn-Bendit à Dachau!'.

Happily, such manifestations of racial hatred are now very limited in France—but we have only to look back into not so distant history to see how vigorous and widespread they have been. Just as France's colonial history has been one filled with violence, torture and oppression, her history at home has, at times, been disfigured by a racism and an anti-semitism which, particularly at the turn of the last century and during the 1930's, were only surpassed in Russia, Germany, and parts of eastern Europe. Racialism and anti-semitism continued to rage in sections of the French press and political life until the Occupation when the French Vichy authorities collaborated in rounding up Jews with a zeal unknown in occupied Holland, Denmark, Norway or even in Fascist Italy. Furthermore, extreme anti-semitic sentiments were echoed not only by a few extremist fanatics but by writers and personalities of prominence, many of whom had contributed to France's cultural *rayonnement*.

France has had a long tradition of racist and anti-Jewish hatred expressed by well-known writers who were all thoroughly 'respectable'. In the 1870's Jews in France only amounted to 0.13% of the total population—one-fifth of the proportion in Germany (88). Yet a few years later, in 1886, when the French journalist Edouard Drumont published his five-hundred-page, hysterically anti-Jewish *La France Juive*, France was the scene of one of the greatest spontaneous explosions of anti-semitism in modern times. A vast number of Catholics disgraced themselves by the welcome they gave to the book; such great artists as Degas, Rodin, Renoir and Cézanne all showed their strong anti-semitic sentiments during the Dreyfus affair and some of France's most popular writers howled with anti-Jewish hatred.

Prominent among this sorry number was the Countess Sibylle Martel de Janville, who under the pseudonym of 'Gyp' wrote many best-selling novels of life in 'society'. The novelist Paul Bourget who was praised to the skies for his 'psychological' novels and who continues to occupy a prominent place in histories of French literature was another ardent anti-semite and super-patriot. The old-established firm of Flammarion, which had brought out *La France Juive* to its eternal shame, was one of France's leading anti-semitic publishers. So was the firm of Dentu. The Catholic newspaper *La Croix* joined in the anti-Jewish 'crusade' and naturally various rabid nationalists such as Paul Deroulède were as fanatically anti-Jewish as they were xenophobic, anti-German and militaristic in general.

Since the 1890's, the list of French writers of talent who continued to pour the poison of anti-semitism into the French system and the body politic is an impressive one. Edouard Drumont had as one of his greatest admirers the novelist Georges Bernanos. The historian Jacques Bainville was as anti-semitic as he was Fascist in his sympathies. Even the leading anti-militarists and anti-chauvinists were anti-semitic. Urbain Gohier, that eloquent bundle of contradictions and polemicist of genius, was as fiercely anti-Jewish as he was anti-militaristic, anti-clerical, anti-trade-union and royalist, although he defended Dreyfus against his accusers. Gustave Hervé, another brilliant journalist, began by attacking the army and colonialism and founded a militant Socialist paper, *La Guerre Sociale*, only to become an ardent patriot in 1914 and the founder of the anti-semitic and Fascist-inspired *Parti socialiste national* in 1927.

Maurice Barrès who wrote so many super-patriotic French sagas and whose reputation was immense throughout France had many ideas on blood, racial 'purity', the state and the individual which were put into practice by the Fascists and Nazis. Charles Maurras, whose reputation as a French writer is still strong, was able to write such passages as: 'It is necessary to be particularly on our guard against the Jews, a wandering nation . . . their harmful influence on the general morality of the country . . . national education, religious policies . . . the solidarity of the French family even . . . are strongly influenced by the intervention of the Jews . . . in the aim of obtaining the degradation and enslavement of the French' (*Action Française*, 1936).

The election of the Popular Front Government with Blum as Prime Minister provoked new outbursts of anti-semitism, with the *Action Française* newspaper (which had a vast circulation at the time) appearing with the front-page headline FRANCE UNDER THE JEW. Other novelists like Céline and Drieu la Rochelle disgraced themselves with their racist views. As for Jean Giraudoux, that most delicate, 'refined' French stylist, the author of *The Women of Troy* and *Siegfried et le Limousin*, he not only wrote anthology pieces but *Pleins pouvoirs*. This lesser-known work, published in 1939, contained every xenophobic and racist theme that the most rabid Fascist could wish for: Giraudoux recommended the creation of a more 'orderly, coherent French culture' which should have spectacular monuments, many children and 'rather fewer half-breeds'. He denounced immigration into France and attacked the 'greedy cohorts' from central and eastern Europe who 'denature France by their presence and action', adding that 'they rarely embellish it by their personal appearance. We find them swarming over each of our arts or over our industries, old and new, in a spontaneous generation which recalls that of fleas over a newborn dog'. Giraudoux wished to see the creation of a 'Ministry of Race' and fully agreed with Hitler when the latter had declared that a policy 'only attains its superior form if it is racial'.

The anti-semitic press which had flourished at the time of the Dreyfus case continued to spread its message of hatred until the end of Vichy France. Drumont's *Libre Parole*, founded after the success of his book, continued to scream at the Jews and to campaign for 'France for the French'. When Jewish refugees from Nazism came into France in 1938 and 1939, it sank to depths rivalling those reached by Julius Streicher's *Der Stürmer*, with articles under such titles as '*L'Invasion Juive*', '*Sous la botte juive*' and '*Les Français sont-ils chez eux?*'

The journalist Henry Coston, now managing editor of *Lectures Françaises*, issued a statement printed in the right-wing press in 1969 denying that he had created a 'united anti-Zionist front to fight against Jewish influences' as had been reported by the Agence France-Presse and a number of daily papers in France, but thirty-nine years before he had been one of the star journalists of the *Libre Parole*. His style was pure Drumont: 'The claws of the Jew gradually tear away what little remains to the Frenchman of his goods and liberties ... The Jew is the parasite who kills to fatten himself ... But the Jews are, by their nature, far from courageous, and they fear—with reason moreover—an awakening of the race—that old French race whose blood has so often flowed abundantly in the cause of liberty.'

Such an 'awakening' certainly occurred in Vichy France. The *Libre Parole* was able to celebrate its fiftieth anniversary in 1942. The French *Croix de Feu* member of parliament, Xavier Vallat, who had openly insulted Blum in the National Assembly ('For the first time in her history this Gallo-Roman country of ours is ruled by a Jew'—June 6, 1936) was responsible in 1941 for the congenial task of enforcing anti-Jewish legislation on behalf of the Vichy government. The great round-up of Paris's Jews on July 16 and 17, 1942, was entirely accomplished by French police. Most of the 9,000 engaged in this exploit collaborated without protest in the hunting of their fellow-citizens, although there were a few honourable exceptions, and were applauded by Maurras and the rightists. The journalist Lucien Rébatet, a self-confessed admirer of Hitler, a glorifier of Nazism and the S.S., wrote an enormous book, more than six hundred pages in length, *Les Décombres*, which attacked the Third Republic France which had 'gone rotten'. Condemned to death after the Liberation and then reprieved, this unsavoury character spent some seven years in prison before emerging again as leader-writer of *Rivarol*—a weekly paper whose sympathies may be deduced from the number of its articles whitewashing Pétain and Laval, its 'minimizing' of the Nazi death-camps, and its 'rehabilitations' of various prominent collaborators and Vichy writers. Another speciality of the same paper is its ferocious attacks on 'corrupt' and 'decadent' art, literature, plays and films, in the best Nocher vein. It has a circulation of 40,000 to 50,000 copies. But the sad truth is that such poisonous publications cannot be dismissed as merely being the mouthpieces of a cranky minority whose influence and numbers are on a par with Flat-Earthists and other such esoteric groups.

One only has to look at a copy of the *Libre Parole* or some other pro-Nazi and collaborationist periodical like *Je suis partout*, published during the Occupation, to see how great was the quantity of Fascist and anti-Jewish books and pamphlets published and written in those years by Frenchmen. Evidence is not lacking to show how strong and how widespread was the conviction among certain writers that Nazi Germany had come to the aid of the 'real' France, to fight against the 'anti-France' which had been corrupting French life and its 'glorious traditions' with its intellectuals of 'despair and decadence', its 'artists of decay' and its 'desperadoes of literature', aided and abetted by a proletariat who had become so much less 'French' than the peasants of that 'old France' so lovingly and often referred to by the senile Pétain and the Vichy gang. As with Nocher, as with the young extremists who stormed the stage and behaved like hooligans when plays like Genet's *The Screens* or Panizza's *The Council of Love* were performed in the last few years, modern forms of art and literature have become politically controversial and considered as products of the 'anti-France' by the racist, anti-semitic, chauvinistic Right.

Exaggerated as such attitudes are, and extreme as the behaviour in public life and politics of those professing them have been, there is no doubt that they have enjoyed the tolerance if not the active support of that 'other' France represented by the middle classes. Middle-class, *bourgeois* taste in art, architecture and living generally has already been referred to. On the whole, it is appalling and retrograde as it is in other countries which have yet to come to terms with modernity. In France, the expression of this antipathy and distrust for modern cultural achievements has always been liable to assume an extreme form, in which the danger of violence is permanently present. The ultra-Conservative housewife or retired army colonel of old-fashioned views in England may regard certain forms of modern culture as eccentric, disgusting, outlandish and incomprehensible but even so their prejudices will not be as politically charged as in France where even choices in art and literature are made under the influence of political inclinations.

For the right-wing French bourgeois, the culture that is attacked in a paper like *Rivarol* or reviled by a Nocher is not only aesthetically and morally repugnant in itself but seen as evidence of an 'anti-France' conspiracy against the 'real' France. The perpetrators of such a culture are regarded as enemies, if not as traitors, to their country. The culture which this reactionary bourgeois has in mind when he talks of France's civilization is one that directly appeals to his chauvinism. For the viewers who wrote to the French television authorities, begging for pictures of their 'beautiful France', for views of cathedrals, bridges and castles, culture was represented by relics of the past which were held to show the supremacy of the French genius. Like the conservative provincial Frenchman who will drive you to some village with its sign announcing 'its XIIth-century chapel; its Renaissance cloister; its Carolingian bridge', the vast majority of middle-class Frenchmen are not interested in architecture or painting, music or literature in themselves. In this old village, with its desolate main square, its decaying school, its lack of a public library, its dingy café, its restaurant advertising several kinds of gastronomic menus, you will be taken briefly to admire a historical monument and be told '*c'est beau!*' A moment later you are also likely to hear: '*c'est français!*' It is not the intrinsic beauty of the chapel or bridge that you are invited to see, but evidence of French supremacy and of a culture that may be extolled to a foreigner but readily ignored in favour of a seven-course meal by any self-respecting bourgeois who knows what 'counts' in life.

Because of this widespread bourgeois tendency in France to

equate 'culture' and a monument, it is hardly surprising that the intellectuals, artists and writers who flee to Paris tend to scorn the general public and to become willingly divorced from the rest of their fellow-Frenchmen, living like aliens, surrounded by a sea of philistines all lumped together in the category of bourgeois—a class to be scorned if not hated.

The hatred that the bourgeois have expressed for so many of their fellow-countrymen, aliens, Jews, workmen, communists, modern artists or intellectuals, has been returned with equal virulence by the objects of their antipathy. The ferocity with which the French middle classes have been savaged and pilloried in French art and literature is without parallel in any other western European nation. We have only to look at Daumier's caricatures, the drawings in a satirical periodical like *L'Assiette au beurre*, or to read novels by Zola and Balzac and a number of lesser-known writers to see that there is nothing kindly or gentle in such mockery. On the contrary, it is characterized by a hatred as intense as that animating the racist, chauvinist, and ultra-conservative right wing. Far from confining their hatred to such specific targets as the Fascists, the ultra-reactionary parties, royalists and clericals, this 'anti-France' has been constantly in arms against the whole middle-class population of France in general: in other words against a good half of the nation which they, in their turn, regard as being an 'anti-France'.

To read a late nineteenth-century novelist and journalist like Octave Mirbeau is to realize the authenticity and violence of this hatred for the owning classes, the snobbish country aristocracy, the shopkeeping classes and the little *rentier* whose spiritual life is null and whose morality is atrocious. Balzac in the nineteenth century and Mauriac in the twentieth have given unforgettable portraits of this France which has enclosed itself behind its own boundaries and which despises the rest of the nation to which it belongs.

Every now and again, because of political turmoil or threats to the Republican régime, this hatred flares up spectacularly. Thus, at the end of the nineteenth century, there was a flowering of great 'anti-France' polemicists. On the one hand there was the reactionary theatre critic Sarcey, whose complete inability to understand the best modern and foreign theatre, and his *a priori* detestation of it, was a perfect example of the bourgeois attitudes that Nocher repeated sixty years later; on the other hand there was an 'anti-France' enemy of society like Georges Darien, who expressed his views on middle-class France in *La Belle France* in 1901. For this fluent pamphleteer and novelist, the French bourgeoisie was 'the most ferocious, the most hypocritical, the most ignorant in the entire world, and also the saddest'. He could hardly find enough words to stigmatize the bourgeois taste and way of life: 'The bourgeoisie, in fact, imposes its tastes and its preferences upon the entire country which accepts them . . . the distinguishing characteristics of the products preferred by the bourgeoisie are a coarseness, a heaviness of form and a nullity of ideas which nauseate a man of intelligence and envelop him in an unspeakable boredom.' Education is seen as part of the bourgeois plan to impose its idea of France upon the other France: 'The system of instruction and education in France is the worst in the entire world. It is the worst because it is the most tyrannical. It has no other aim than to inculcate respect for authority; to maintain class differences, the spirit of hierarchy, discipline and abject obedience; to create, with platitudes, a uniformity of character; to hunt down originality and crush the individual. It tends not to form men but to wind up automata.' Such words could equally well apply to the traditional British public school system, but in England, such a reaction does not often become part of an anguished hatred for an entire threatening middle-class society which has, on occasion, approved the massacre of its fellow citizens. After Darien's great cry came other protests: Vigo's film *Zéro de conduite* in the early 1930's and the *lycée* revolts in the 1960's. Meanwhile, the more general hatred for bourgeois France continued to be expressed.

Aragon's cry against France, 'my country which I detest, in which all that is French revolts me in proportion as it is French', has often been repeated. The young Paul Nizan expressed his intense abhorrence of bourgeois France in his book *Aden-Arabie*, written in 1931–32 after a voyage to the Middle East to escape an image of a hated France that was pursuing him, and the recognition that there was no escape for him. For Nizan, the bourgeois society of France was his own, personal enemy. It had disfigured the France that *might have been*, beyond all recognition. For what was this France about which so much had been boasted and pontificated, and who were those fellow-Frenchmen of his? France was 'still filthy from the excrement and filth of its war, its moans about its poverty, its dignity, its spiritual mission, the smallness of its profits and the greatness of its good will. For it is led by hypocritical shopkeepers who hide the profits on their balance-sheets and who weep over the hardness of the times. Their voices repeat in her name that she is the capital of the spirit, the eldest daughter of the Church and the muse of democracy: thus they feed illusions to men to whom the hazards of marriage, of love and of journeys have given the quality of being French'.

The lives led by these bourgeois who have become profit-mongers and *rentiers* are sterile: they are non-lives lived in a non-France, and for France to be a France worth living in, the future offered by bourgeois society must be rejected: 'What lies in wait for us is not an attractive prospect. It is to become their like, with the shameful memory of having wished in one's youth to live like men: it is to become one of their servants, charged with tasks laid down by them and prescribed from beginning to end.' The only solution is to live in a state of constant revolution and unending war: 'it is a question of a destruction and not of a mere victory which leaves the enemy standing' and 'we must no longer be afraid to hate'.

For the last forty years, the anti-France to which Nizan belonged has certainly not been afraid to hate, in a nation in which the individual has so often been eclipsed by the type and in which, as Nizan wrote, the French 'flee from each other, detest each other, for they are living among each other like strangers. They are never anything else but accomplices'. The implication is obvious: at times of crisis, a nation where individuals are types rather than individuals finds itself on both sides of an armed barricade, each side intent on the destruction of the other, each with its own idea of nation.

During the Algerian war, this polarization between the two Frances again became manifest. In the middle, there was apathy and resignation, at each extremity of the social spectrum, enemies who might have come from different planets for all that they were nominally French. In Simone de Beauvoir's journals (89) there is that same feeling of living among an alien race. After seeing and hearing of the atrocities committed in the name of France in Algeria, and the behaviour of the police towards North Africans in her own country, and after witnessing the murderous hatred expressed by her fellow-citizens against herself, Sartre and all others protesting against what France had become, she could no longer bear her nation: 'I loathed it all—this country, myself, the whole world', and once again, from her pen, there came that anguished cry of hatred against the 'horrors of the French bourgeoisie'. It is a cry that can still be heard—scarcely any less loudly although the Algerian war is over.

Talk to a number of French intellectuals: after a while you may be certain of hearing at least one of them reiterating a hatred for France—'*La France, ça me dégoute!*'—as if the whole country had been ruined and distorted for them beyond all recognition and all hope of salvation.

That there should be such a tradition of violent hatred for the French bourgeoisie is not very surprising in view of their past behaviour. Quite apart from the way they have often treated their best artists and intellectuals, there remains the fact that on every occasion when there have been explosions of xenophobia and racial hatred in the country, when there has appeared the danger of a dictatorship, when the régime has been annexed by one man, when human rights have been attacked, when attempts have been made to curtail or violate elementary freedoms, when there has been a flagrant misuse of power by the nation's leaders, whether in a resort to torture or brutal police methods, the great mass of the French middle classes have either remained silent, from apathy or tacit approval, or applauded what has been done because they felt that their material interests were protected.

It happened during the Paris Commune repression, during the Occupation and, to a lesser degree, in 1968. After the riots and general strike, and after a conspicuous failure to protest publicly against police savagery directed against their own youth, they voted *en bloc* for the continuation of their régime and rushed abroad with their nation's money to change it into less fragile species.

This French bourgeois type who has aroused so much detestation in his country can be described without difficulty. He prefers to hoard money rather than invest it in his country's economic future. He is the first to succumb to the fever of chauvinism. His culture revolves around the 'gastronomic' menu rather than literature or living art. His intelligence lies in never being 'taken in' and his ability to make money breed money. He will vote blindly for any régime which he considers strong enough to safeguard the system that ensures his continuing prosperity, while affecting disgust for its leaders. He concentrates on growing more prosperous while hospitals, schools, low-priced lodgings and libraries remain scarce and neglected in a country where advertisements shamelessly appeal to the basest snobbery and a mania for historical grandeur, where appeals for public charitable donations at home and abroad are conspicuously absent from the newspapers, and where all the noble ideals spouted by his chosen political representatives have been regularly flouted and betrayed. This archetypal member of the conservative middle class with its obsession with property and hoarding, this direct descendant of Molière's middle-class characters who sneer at a learning and culture they cannot understand, can be a deadly dangerous animal. He has a capacity for hatred, distrust, prejudice, and approval of murderous violence used on his behalf that make the typical English 'Blimp' look like a sentimental spaniel by comparison. He is vicious, greedy, philistine and profoundly unpatriotic since he will see, and has seen, his country degraded and his fellow-people massacred either in his own interests or because of his failure and unwillingness to intervene on the side of all that is best in France. And as French history has shown, he has always been legion and his influence immense.

As a type he is reasy to recognize. You meet him everywhere. He has appeared on the television screen before millions of people, he has spoken on the radio with the voice of Jean Nocher and others, he has written newspaper editorials and magazine articles and has made speeches in parliament. He has been a Vichy supporter, a Gaullist, a Fourth Republic conservative, he has marched in the May 30, 1968 procession down the Champs-Elysées and may well be a supporter of some later régime if, by any catastrophe, a junta of army officers should take control. Unlike his pale shadow, the English conservative man of property or the working-class reactionary, who want negroes 'sent home', who mutter their disgust at long-haired youth and modern art forms, who support capital punishment and the British military presence in remote regions of the world, this French bourgeois has a penchant for hatred, for violence by proxy, and a loathing for his fellow-citizens that is peculiarly and historically *French*. Whereas the English archbourgeois may be seen as a figure of fun, as someone to be mocked without real hatred, to be partly excused because of his lamentable education, his upbringing, his inability to adjust completely to modern changes, his general ignorance and stupidity, the French bourgeois will be dangerous and vicious through greater rationalization and conscious choice. Where the Englishman will lapse into semi-articulate confusion when asked to justify his prejudices, the Frenchman will be fluent. The one will dislike because of his inability to comprehend, the other will hate as a matter of deliberate principle.

No matter how chauvinistic he may be—and chauvinism is a characteristic of his type—the French bourgeois can have little patriotic feeling since such a sentiment cannot be genuine unless accompanied by a feeling that, in the last resort, all Frenchmen are one, no matter what their differences, and that all share a common conception of a way of life and a culture without which France could not be French. He has no moral unity with the rest of his nation. France can only be his own class, a conglomeration of like types who will occasionally band together to defend their common interests which are the survival of the sum total of their individual material interests, but who otherwise live among each other and in the nation as strangers. Unlike the English or American conservative, he is never attached to his country in its totality, only seeing it as a vague, mythical entity which he idolizes in his chauvinism inasmuch as he believes it to be a magnification of his own virtues. As a consequence, the violence that has been perpetrated against a part of his country's population will never assume for him the tragic aspect of an extension of his own self being injured.

Thus, the thought of Frenchmen shooting other Frenchmen in a national crisis is never as unthinkable, as abnormal and as repellent to him as it is in many other countries. Nor is it unimaginable to many other fellow-countrymen. Behind this façade of one France, with one culture and one people, there has long been a state of civil war, in culture as in politics, with one France and one anti-France confronting each other over the barricades when they are not simply ignoring each other.

10

The Republic, One and Indivisible

THE FINAL sign that a people has been unable to reconcile its differences and has failed to agree on the form of the nation in which it must coexist is civil war. The danger of such a calamity has been recognized by some Frenchmen but it has not deterred others from advocating policies and maintaining enmities which, if pursued far enough, could not fail to bring it nearer. The possibility of civil war has been evoked more than once in recent years; at times it has seemed very close and at other times it has even broken out on a minor scale. France's rulers have raised the spectre to frighten their fellow-countrymen into voting for the continuance of their régime, and it was raised again* after De Gaulle's defeat in the referendum of 1969. Fortunately no civil strife of any nature followed De Gaulle's withdrawal from office but the fact that it could still be mentioned as a possibility was in itself significant. It was also a sad comment on Frenchmen's attitudes towards each other after a long history in which France was supposed to mature towards unity. It is sadder still that civil war has not become something to be regarded unanimously in France as an impossibility, as something profoundly abnormal, unthinkable and un-French. After all, are not civil wars for nations that have not yet grown up?

In September 1968, René Andrieu, a leading member of the French Communist Party and editor-in-chief of *L'Humanité*, spoke in an interview of the danger of another massacre of the country's working classes and the *avant-garde* of its middle classes by the conservative bourgeoisie should it feel its régime to be threatened. Andrieu was convinced that the middle class would not hesitate to strike if it thought it necessary and he was obviously thinking in terms of a civil war or a *coup d'état* such as that which had taken place in Greece.

Despite Andrieu's obvious bias and his allegiance to a party no less conservative in its way than its foe, and whose attitude towards the

---

* By Georges Pompidou in his Presidential election manifesto.

suppression of freedom in other countries has been ambiguous to put it mildly, he was voicing a widely-shared fear. He knew how deep was the enmity still separating many Frenchmen, and when he spoke of the possibility of them killing each other, he knew like his followers that such a catastrophe had already happened several times in France's history since the Revolution. We have only to look at the history books to see how often her people have been ready to resort to violence in order to impose certain ideas of France upon the rest of the nation.

Frenchmen have killed each other in the name of France in 1830, 1848, 1851 and 1871, and they came very close to doing so in the late nineteenth century and the period between the two World Wars. On each occasion, the mass of the middle classes had applauded when workers, revolutionaries and radicals were killed or seemed likely to be killed. In 1848, 1851 and 1871, the shooting of civilians and the suppression of less privileged classes were directed by violently reactionary generals who had never concealed their hatred for the Republic of 'liberty, fraternity, equality': Bugeaud, Lamoricière, Cavaignac, Saint-Arnaud and Gallifet. In 1968, after De Gaulle had conferred with his generals during the crisis, there had even seemed the possibility that General Massu might have added his name to the list.

Past civil strife has left a deep impression on the minds of successive generations of Frenchmen of the Left and the working classes. Of these memories, transmitted from generation to generation, the most potent has been that of the Commune of 1871, in commemoration of which some Frenchmen still make a yearly pilgrimage to the Père Lachaise cemetery where the movement was finally crushed. No better illustration of the way in which a preponderantly middle-class France acquiesced in the destruction of thousands of other Frenchmen can be found than the repression of the insurrectional Commune in May and June 1871. It is a horrifying story and has helped to perpetuate a tradition of social hatred ever since. Many books have been written on the subject, and although some may err on the side of political poetry and give an over-rosy picture of the aims, methods and ideas of the Commune's leaders, there is no exaggeration in their accounts of how the Commune's citizens were treated by the bourgeois, their government and their army.

Reading the history of these two months, it is difficult to decide which was the more sickening: the glee and hypocrisy of the middle-class French who backed the repression, and of their leader, the Prime Minister, Thiers, or the horrors of the killings in Paris after the insurrection had been militarily subdued. The same politician who had talked of France's great work in North Africa thirty years earlier publicly rejoiced in the fact that 'the cause of justice, order, humanity and civilization has triumphed!' after the Versailles army had begun to enter Paris. The generals leading the attack were 'great men of war'. Expiation would be 'complete' and it would take place 'in the name of the law, by the law, for the law' (90). When Paris was being bombarded as a prelude to the assault, there were extraordinary scenes on the heights near the city, as members of parliament, officers, civil servants and prosperous representatives of the middle classes, including elegantly dressed women, watched the shelling as though it were a circus spectacle. After the Prussians had allowed Thiers' army to reconquer the city and after some 20,000 men, women and adolescents had been shot *after the fighting had stopped*, Thiers declared that 'our valiant soldiers conduct themselves in a manner to inspire the highest esteem, the greatest admiration abroad'. (91)

How prisoners were humiliated, starved and shot out of hand was witnessed and described by observers from abroad. The correspondents of the London *Times* and the *Daily News* have left accounts of how army officers, accompanied by pretty women, would walk among mounds of corpses, boasting of their exploits, how wounded prisoners were shot, how massacres took place in prisons and barracks for days and nights on end, how convoys of prisoners were taken to Versailles in dreadful conditions and were mocked on the way by crowds of well-dressed spectators, and how the abominable prison camp at Satory was visited by the local society people who came to stare at their fellow-Frenchmen and Frenchwomen as though they were beings from some alien planet. We now know that the mass shootings of Parisians lasted until June 1 of that black year and that the Municipal Council of Paris paid for the burial of 17,000 corpses. We only have to look at some of the newspapers of the time to see how unrelenting was the hatred and vilification of the victims of the repression.

The massacres of prisoners were applauded by leading middle-class newspapers like the *Figaro* which begged for more shootings and greater harshness and which lavished praise on the army and its officers. The *Moniteur universel* called the Communards who had fought to the bitter end 'the most frightful monsters ever to have appeared in the history of humanity'. The Commune had shot less than a hundred hostages; after protesting in the name of the 'law', the Thiers government had shot 20,000 and deported thousands more, was applauded by a vast number of bourgeois and church dignitaries, and talked of saving 'civilization'. The *Figaro* finally deplored the shooting of so many female prisoners but then reflected that as the Commune had supposedly flung open the doors of all the city's brothels, they must mostly have been prostitutes and therefore victims of no account. Nearly 400,000 denunciations of Frenchmen by Frenchmen were received and of these denunciations barely the twentieth part was officially stated to have been signed. And yet, despite these horrors, there were many Frenchmen who remained convinced that the victims had been barely human, that they had been 'monsters' unworthy of the name of Frenchmen, whose existence had been like a gangrene in the body of the nation. Those who reviled and denigrated the Communards included many brilliant representatives of French middle-class culture such as Alexander Dumas the Younger, the playwright Sardou, the novelist Edmond About, the academician Jules Clarétie and the critic Sarcey. Their behaviour and the attitudes of the many who shared their views have never been forgotten by successive generations of the French Left. That the Commune occurred a hundred years ago is of no account: the Revolution happened eighty years earlier and is still an influential memory.

Although nothing comparable to the Commune has happened since in France, violence and expressions of intense social hatreds have persisted in French political life. Even the references to the *bourgeois*, the *concierges*, the people of the *seizième arrondissement* in Paris, the sneers at *ces gens là* that can be heard so frequently in France, are more than expressions of snobbery or resentment: they betray deep-rooted and long-held class hatreds and the feelings of one class that the other is an enemy and almost an alien. For the Frenchman who found his thoughts echoed by Nocher, the 'intellectuals' are among the enemy and the non-French; for the despairing left-wing intellectual, the bourgeoisie are a deadly enemy who stifle all hope of progress.

Each side is quick to detect some threat from the other and even, at times, to mobilize and prepare for the worst. One of the most significant passages in De Gaulle's speech of May 30, 1968, when he announced that he had no intention of retiring from the Presidency, was that in which he urged Frenchmen to form 'civic guards' to fight against subversion and Communist dictatorship. By such an exhortation he was dangerously intensifying divisions in the country and encouraging the resort to violence. One consequence of his speech was the rapid growth of the *C.D.R.* groups or 'committees for the defence of the Republic'.

The *C.D.R.* were officially baptized as such after De Gaulle's demand for the formation of similar civic groups in every French departmental region. They rapidly recruited supporters ready to make war on what they considered the anti-France. Even the Minister of Education at the time, Edgar Faure, called some of their attitudes 'Fascist'. They specialized in verbal attacks on university teachers and students, schoolmasters and trade unionists. They applauded police repression, saw signs of foreign-inspired subversion everywhere and enlisted ultra-Gaullists and right-wing extremists. Above all, they tended to speak with the accents of Nocher who so well mirrored this hatred of one France for the other. Thus, a M. Jouandin, President of the *C.D.R.* of the Haute-Vienne department, attacked 'the intellectuals of the left who only praise foreign writers like Brecht and Miller rather than Giraudoux or Anouilh' and branded them as people for whom 'only foreign imports are worthy to deliver "messages" even though they bear only darkness and turpitude' (92). Thus, the members of the Caen *C.D.R.* praised the police for their action after students protesting at the suppression of the *maison de culture* had been beaten up. They were symptomatic of a tendency noticeable in French history since its first republican constitution: a readiness to resort to unconstitutional forms of opposition and to think in terms of battle rather than debate.

The history of the long Third Republic, when France often came closer to being a democracy than at any other time, was filled with instances of political extremism, plots against the government, attempted *coups d'état* and unconstitutional opposition movements with a penchant for violent action. During much of the 1920's and '30's, France was in a state of latent civil war, a civil war that often simmered and threatened to break out, and her political life was poisoned by fierce hatreds and fears of revolution or reaction. The France that so many extremist parties fought for was always *their* France, not that of the nation as a whole. Not only the internal structures but the whole overall context of national life was under attack. The *Croix de Feu* organization, which at one time claimed a membership of more than half a million, was encouraged by its founder, Colonel de La Rocque, to fight for a 'purified' France. For Charles Maurras and his monarchist *Action Française* group, France since the Revolution was no longer France. To the Left, *their* France had been stolen by the anti-France of the Right and the bourgeois. Nothing is more revealing in this respect than the way the Communist propaganda on the eve of the 1936 elections made use of such themes as the *Marseillaise*, the Glorious Revolution of 1789, the 'sovereign people' and even Joan of Arc, rather than themes of international communism after the Russian example.

The violence, both verbal and physical, expressed against the Prime Minister of the Popular Front government, Léon Blum, was the violence of civil war. Organizations like *Action Française* and *Solidarité Française* were virtually inciting Frenchmen to murder Blum and, in February 1936, he was savagely beaten up by Royalists. A weekly Fascist paper like *Gringoire* reviled the 'Reds' and, while hypocritically denying that it was anti-semitic, purported to show how the Jews were in charge of the government. By the mid-Thirties its circulation was more than half a million and, as Alexander Werth, historian of this period, pointed out (93), together with other papers of similar tone, it did 'more than anything else to keep France divided, as far as possible, into two camps'. But nauseating as *Gringoire* was, it was widely read, had a large circulation, and even such distinguished contributors as the novelist François Mauriac used its columns to review the extreme right-wing Georges Bernanos's *Diary of a country priest* (May 24, 1936) while the front page preached hatred and violence.

What kind of country was this in which so many hostile groups were ready to fight to the death and in which France, for each faction, could only be France after part of its body had been destroyed, and after it had been purged as Giraudoux suggested in his *Pleins pouvoirs?* It was a France in which the Popular Front government evoked fears of a 'Red Terror' among the middle classes, in which the idea of workers' paid holidays seemed outrageous to Frenchmen comfortably living on their incomes, a France in which many people still longed for a restoration of royalty and the *ancien régime*, or a 'strong man', a country which sent a team to the Berlin Olympic Games where they were seen to give the Nazi salute as they filed past Hitler's grand-stand, in which refugees from tyranny could be treated as contemptible scum and in which many Frenchmen longed for a German-inspired and -led New Order which would revivify their nation and remould it nearer to their hearts' desire. It was a France sick with political poisons and nostalgias and it was not so very different from the France of the nineteenth century when the same hatreds, rivalries and violence were so often conspicuous. It was a France of deadly divisions and it has not changed so greatly today.

The danger of another eruption of civil strife is constant in France. That political violence is always latent in French society has been recognized by Frenchmen like Jacques Fauvet who, when writing of anti-constitutional movements in France, and of 'authoritarian, Bonapartist or Boulangist' movements, said 'there exists an underlying state of mind in France which from time to time breaks out like a rash. The attacks are sudden and violent, and it is not always possible to tell how they start or why they end' (94).

Such rashes have broken out several times since the war. There have been bloody riots and *O.A.S.* terrorism. The police have more than once shown themselves to be possessed of what can only be called hatred. Election campaigns have been marked by occasional shootings, explosions and beatings-up, bookshops and offices of political parties have been attacked and damaged. Extremist groups like *Occident* or *Jeunesse Révolutionaire française* continue to find recruits and correspond to this long tradition of political hatred and fanaticism. Right-wing students talk of 'smashing the Bolshies' and go armed with clubs to break up left-wing meetings. Universities and *lycées* are contaminated with violence. No less an authority than Pierre Bertaux, a former Director General of the *Sûreté Nationale*, has confirmed the survival of this disease in France: 'There has always been in France a ferment of the extreme right which plots permanently. We know it and, if we wish to, we keep watch on it. It is an illusion—particularly nourished on the left but not there alone—to believe that it is a matter of some temporary illness, some abscess which we can eliminate by surgery. For me it is rather a constant secretion of the French body. What convinces me is precisely the constancy of the phenomenon. In the past forty years, I have seen the *Camelots du Roy*, the *Croix de Feu*, the *Cagoulards* recruit from every generation numbers as constant as the number of plums harvested every year from the same tree, of boys of the same age, the same state of mind and character, and belonging to the same milieux' (95).

The numbers and strength of such groups may vary: what remains unchanged is the hatred which so often inspires them and the readiness to use violence. They provoke the same reactions, they inspire the same violent counter-movements, they keep alive the idea that one day there will have to come a bitter, deadly reckoning when physical strength will prevail. Every time a shock group or a 'commando' raids a *lycée* or a university, every time another plastic bomb is set off, a civil war is being fought in miniature and in deadly earnest. We have seen how such conflicts can escalate in a crisis.

Part of the reason for this violence and intensity of political passion, which can make the French political and social climate so tense and electric, is a long refusal to admit or coexist with an opposition within a commonly accepted system. For many Frenchmen, an Opposition is not something with which you conduct a dialogue or engage in a debate: it is something wrong, alien and threatening and therefore something to be destroyed, by violence if necessary. Violent hostility to dissent has always been marked in Republican France and although Frenchmen have on the whole subscribed to the idea of democracy, those attempting to apply one of its first principles, the right to oppose, have often been treated with scorn, hatred and ferocity. To the chauvinist, dissent is treason and it is worth remembering that during the French Revolution, which was supposed to be conducted in the cause of liberty, the Revolutionaries decreed that there was to be 'no liberty for the enemies of liberty'.

*

Ever since 1789 there has been in France the myth of a Revolution made by 'the people' representing France as a whole. The myth has helped to keep France divided. The majority of Frenchmen have been taught that the 1789 Revolution was something in which most of France shared, that it was a sudden, nation-wide struggle for those ideals resumed by the words 'Liberty, Equality, Fraternity' to be seen everywhere in France's public buildings, that it created a united France symbolized by the tricoloured flag of the people rather than the Bourbon lilies of the monarchy.

A succession of French liberal historians has been embarrassed by the excesses, brutalities and massacres of the Revolution which so often assumed the appearance of civil war; but they have praised its achievements. The great historian Michelet helped to create the myth of a truly national revolution which created a new France and in which 'the principle actor was the people'. The Declaration of the Rights of Man has been seen as a product of this people as a whole. The Revolutionary wars have been interpreted as a sign of a united nation fighting for its new life. The Revolution has often been presented as a great popular movement expressing that passion for freedom, social equality and justice which is ascribed to most Frenchmen. It was a great movement of 'fraternity and reason', born out of oppression and reactionary authoritarianism.

For a hundred and fifty years at least, a considerable portion of the French population has seen the Revolution as a marvellous event which bettered the conditions of the people and united them. It was violent and it succeeded even if many of its aims were later frustrated by reactionary and conservative forces. But it still overthrew an old order.

The Revolution has even become acceptable to many people who would have resisted it violently at the time by its being presented as a subject for patriotic pride—as a national expression of the French genius, as proof of French love of freedom and progress, and evidence that France is always in the vanguard of all great movements in the world. The whole period, which saw so many great hopes disappointed, a political turmoil followed by an authoritarian terror, civil war, massacres and mass denunciations, followed later by a dictatorship, a militaristic empire, twenty years of costly wars and a long period of reaction, ended by creating a mystique of the 'people', the 'sovereign people' who alone are France.

The inevitability of the Revolution is another influential historical myth and has helped to keep the idea of further revolution respectable to many Frenchmen even if they will not admit it openly. The myth has served historians and theoreticians who have idolized this 'people' as the only body entitled to express its will and shape the nation's destinies. The Revolution has long been a cult; it has been romanticized and it has produced floods of political poetry and its own folklore—a poetry and a folklore that again appeared during the so-called 'May Revolution' of 1968 which, like other such movements, distinguished itself by its verbosity.

There has long been observed a tendency to fight over words and ideas rather than concrete facts in France. Thirty years ago, D. W. Brogan wrote that French politics had acquired the character of 'art for art's sake' and noted the extreme verbal violence of people whose views themselves might be quite moderate (96). His remark still applies today. The great ideals voiced by so many Frenchmen have become, to some extent, concepts to be visualized aesthetically. The word 'fraternity' which is so often used in politicians' speeches and which is so conspicuously absent from French life is itself a poetic notion. We may say that it is a translation into the language of art of an idea which simply means democratic political and legal equality. 'Liberty' is often an abstraction, a pure idea to be intellectualized, or a poetic notion to give colour to a manifesto. 'The people' all too often means 'those who think about France as we do and who share our political beliefs'.

This verbal extremism and political poetry has led foreigners to mock this aspect of France's political life and to see in it a Latin tendency to exaggerate and be carried away by rhetoric. But the violence of the word and the poetry of the slogan often reflect passionately-held views and a readiness to express them in acts of violence if the need should arise. The majority of Frenchmen are reputed to be conservative and completely un-revolutionary. Indeed, conservatism is generally regarded as a major French characteristic. But such recent opinion polls as those taken in 1969, which showed that 67% of the population were satisfied with the present state of their departments (97) and that only a tiny minority regarded change in their provincial regions as a matter of urgency, or that which showed that the majority of French youth between the ages of sixteen and twenty-nine were more or less content with their lot (98), do not change the fact that the minorities determined to change the life and structure of their country are still vigorous and powerful.

The students who fought the police, who painted and shouted slogans by Marcuse, Marx or Mao Tse Tung, who formed 'revolutionary' committees and talked of tearing down the whole structure of French society, are descended from Frenchmen who also shouted slogans, declared their radical aims and fought for them. Although the verbal exaggerations of professed revolutionaries may lend themselves to caricature and derision, their seriousness of purpose should not be underestimated. Moreover, French history is full of examples of people dying and killing in their country for their revolutionary ideas and poetical words. Both the young Frenchman who talks of destroying the university and the class system and the middle-aged conservative who expresses the hope that the 'reds' and 'anti-French' will be crushed, are perfectly serious. At each end of the political spectrum there are vigorous and powerful minorities who share a common determination to change the whole rather than a part of their country.

Instead of concentrating upon immediate, specific objectives, the latest generation of young revolutionaries in France has, like other extremists, demanded *another* kind of France which cannot be created without a violent civil war, and has consequently widened a dangerous split in the country. By echoing Nizan's resolution to live in a state of 'constant revolution' and his conviction that 'it is a matter of destruction and not of a simple victory which leaves the opponent standing', it has hardened the will of its opponents to fight relentlessly for *their* France. Its ideas of France are more potent than facts and admit of no compromise and, as Fauvet remarked of his fellow-countrymen whose conduct he had observed for a long time, 'in every situation the Frenchman tends to give precedence to pure ideas'. Its aims and attitudes inevitably suggest the possibility of another convulsion, be it minor or major, in which one France and one anti-France will continue a struggle which has continued since the Revolution and which still makes it difficult to know exactly what we mean when we speak of 'France'.

*

The background to all those achievements in democracy and culture which are credited to France and form part of her national myth has been one of constant dissension and periodic turmoil. Between the Revolution and the First World War, France had two great dictatorships, several periods of reaction, three serious outbreaks of revolution, several epidemics of bellicose nationalism, several attempted *coups d'état* and a long series of bloody colonial wars. In the past fifty years, dissension has continued. France has been the scene of bitter conflicts between Fascists, Monarchists, Communists, Radicals and neo-Bonapartists, and outrageous epidemics of anti-semitism and xenophobia during the 1920's and '30's. A Nazi-occupied, Fascist state was accepted and even supported by many Frenchmen during the war. The later 1940's and '50's were marked by bitter strife between Left and Right with the genuine danger of a Communist attempt to seize power. The later '50's and first three years of the '60's were poisoned with colonial wars which threatened to destroy all freedoms, and France returned to a period of personal rule which revived every great chauvinistic myth of the nineteenth century.

In this divided land, every democratic achievement has been due to the passionate, articulate and courageous way in which determined individuals and militant minorities have campaigned from one generation to the next for ideals which many governments failed to respect when they were not simply violating them. When Dreyfus was acquitted and rehabilitated after years of struggle, the myth that France was the homeland of justice seemed confirmed abroad, but justice was only done in the face of violent opposition from people who were some of the most racialist, chauvinistic and reactionary in western Europe. Similarly, much of modern art was born in a country distinguished by gross philistinism and complacency in cultural matters, and social progress in the 1930's nearly precipitated a civil war.

That the Third Republic survived for so long with all its faults and yet with all its virtues, and that France managed to avoid surrendering to extremism from Left or Right, was not so much because of any great national unity or because of any widespread enthusiastic support for it, but because the strength of opposing extremist forces never allowed supporters of the Republic to take it for granted. Instead they had to fight hard for it, while the prospering middle classes whose conservatism and materialism have so often been attacked provided a stabilizing force. But still a vast body of Frenchmen remained hypnotized by myths of national grandeur. Too often they failed to protest at the degradation of civil liberties and democratic ideals and too often they failed to adapt by maintaining social attitudes which no longer corresponded to realities. They fostered myths of France's mission in the world and her culture, while often scorning, attacking or ignoring those who did defend democracy or contribute to the nation's culture; and when their chauvinism led them to glorify France's achievements they credited them to the people as a whole while perpetuating social divisions and prejudices.

In 1958, after years of political chaos and at a time when the behaviour of France's armies and police were mocking any claim to be a 'civilized' country, France agreed to be ruled by a single man and again showed that many Frenchmen tend to care more for nationalism than democracy. As has happened in other countries, the man who made his providential appearance and promised to renovate the country encouraged his people to turn back again towards a mythical past. Once again, a people believed to be violent in defence of its liberties surrendered to the call of chauvinism.

De Gaulle's Fifth Republic claimed to restore unity in the country and to be making a break with the previous disorders of the previous régime. But precisely the same disorders and signs of disunity survived. There was still censorship, there were still police brutalities, there were still unconstitutional forces working in the nation, culture became harnessed to vainglorious foreign policy, cliques still exploited the régime for their own ends, and there were still irreconciled social divisions. There was material progress and De Gaulle could boast of the Concorde aeroplane and France's atomic reactors, but they would have been there without Gaullism just as France would have prospered industrially without her Revolution. The state of the Republic oscillated uneasily between semi-democracy and semi-dictatorship. Admirers of France could indicate the number of left- and right-wing publications freely on sale on bookstalls and at the lack of political prisoners in the country as a sign that France was still democratic. Critics could point out that France's protesting intellectuals and opposition parties had been conspicuously ineffective and that the two most powerful means of communication, radio and television, had been captured by the régime. France seemed to have acquiesced in her semi-democracy, lulled by her comforting myths, until the events of May 1968 showed how fragile the apparent unity of her society had remained and how the most visible opposition tended towards an extremism that could cause all the old hatreds to explode again and revive the menace of civil war. The near-revolution had diminished the glamour of their leader and it was because De Gaulle had lost stature as a mythical figure, not because of any sudden longing for real democracy, that France voted against him in his referendum. When the interim president, Alain Poher, spoke of restoring Republican freedoms, destroying the 'mafias' of the régime, dismantling the clandestine police networks and investigating the huge sums that had been squandered on illusory shows of grandeur, only a minority voted for him. By abstaining from the second round of the presidential election, by seeing both Poher and Pompidou as enemies on the other side of the barricades, the Communist Party maintained the tradition of unconstitutional opposition and the dangers of a serious future clash.

The more reactionary features of Gaullism may be removed in France but the divisions remain and the myths have been given a new lease of life. The conflict between one France and another will continue and may lead to more bitterness and violence should each France regard the other as the 'anti-France' and think in terms of winning a victory rather than of conciliation. The revolutionary tradition is still alive and the forces of a reaction that cannot accept the present are still powerful. The dreamer has gone but the dreams persist. The tendency for France to conduct a monologue rather than a dialogue with the rest of the world is still present. A time of silence is needed—not the silence of a country bemused by grandiose visions of her own importance and mission but that of a country healing its wounds, reassessing its place in the world, and collaborating in creating the only real civilization today which is international. Should the myths prove too strong for France, then she will remain divided and apart from the rest of the world, isolated by a spirit which she may call 'French' but which, as one of her writers said of Gaullism, 'proceeds from the intransigence of a wounded soul which stiffens in its pride and immures itself in legend in order not to accept the lessons of history' (99). To free herself from her myths she still has a long way to go, but as De Gaulle said, in a different context:

> La route est dure, mais elle est belle.
> Le but est difficile, mais qu'il est grand!

Notes

(1) The quotation is from Marcel Thiébaut, 'En lisant M. Blum', *Revue de Paris*, Vol. 3, 1937, pp. 355-356.
(2) He used the expression during a speech at Mostaganem, Algeria, June 7, 1958.
(3) Speech in Paris, June 18, 1959.
(4) Speech in Nevers, April 17, 1959.
(5) Press conference, Paris, October 23, 1958.
(6) Press conference, Paris, June 25, 1958.
(7) Speech in Rio de Janeiro, reported by *Le Monde*, September 1, 1959.
(8) Speech in the Assemblée Nationale, Paris, November 11, 1963.
(9) Pierre Alix, *My France*, Jarrolds, London, 1939.
(10) Reported by Raymond Tournoux and quoted in *Paris Match*, March 30, 1968.
(11) Maxime Du Camp, *Souvenir d'un Demi-Siècle*, Paris, 1949.
(12) Urbain Gohier, *l'Armée contre la nation*, Paris, 1898.
(13) André Masson, *Histoire de l'Indochine* (*Que sais-je?* series), Presses Universitaires de France, Paris, 1950, pp. 83-84.
(14) Augustin Bernard, *l'Algérie* (*Histoire des Colonies Françaises et de l'expansion de la France dans le monde*, Vol. II, edited by Gabriel Hanotaux of the Académie Française and A. Martineau, Professor at the Collège de France), Plon, Société de l'Histoire Nationale, Paris, 1930.
(15) Press conference, June 22, 1951.
(16) Speech in Oran, Algeria, June 6, 1958.
(17) Speech to the nation, Paris, January 25, 1960.
(18) Speech in Mexico City, April 8, 1960.
(19) Quoted by A. Bernard, *op. cit.*, pp. 210-211.
(20) All extracts from Bugeaud's letters to Thiers are from *Lettres inédites du maréchal Bugeaud, duc d'Isly, annotées par le capitaine Tattet*, in the Bibliothèque Nationale, Paris.
(21) Quoted by Urbain Gohier, *op. cit.*
(22) Raousset Boulbon, *De la colonisation et des institutions civiles en Algérie*, Paris, 1847.
(23) Quoted by A. Bernard, *op. cit.*
(24) *Le Matin*, August 10, 1907.
(25) Andrée Viollis, *Indochine S.O.S.*, Paris, 1935.
(26) 'The president of the Republic is the foremost personage in the State. Whether we like it or not, M. de Gaulle has succeeded in becoming such. But then, are we not diminishing him by designating him by the appellation "General de Gaulle", even more so as history books are in no danger of being weighed down by the recital of his "warlike exploits"?'—letter from a French ex-serviceman (veteran of Verdun and other places), *L'Aurore*, January 25-26, 1969.
(27) *La Gangrène* was one of the most famous denunciations of torture in France and Algeria in the late 1950's and was published by Editions de Minuit, Paris, in 1959.
(28) Speech to the French Senate, June 25, 1959.
(29) Fully reported in P. Vidal-Nacquet, *La Raison d'Etat*, Editions de Minuit, Paris, 1962.

(30) P. Vidal-Nacquet, *op. cit.*
(31) *Figaro Littéraire*, November 15, 1961.
(32) Assembled and published by the 'Commission Témoignages et Assistance Juridique' of the student union UNEF and the teachers' union SNESUP in *Ils accusent*, Editions du Seuil, Paris, 1968.
(33) *Sunday Times*, London, May 26, 1968.
(34) Published in *Ils accusent*, Paris, 1968.
(35) Budget speech on the maintenance of public order made in the Assemblée Nationale, Paris, November 14, 1968.
(36) His relations with the 'Prospective' group were stressed by the highly informed satirical newspaper *Le Canard enchaîné* in an article, 'Un Papon de Paris' by Jean Manan, January 3, 1962.
(37) The expression is that of Jacques Fauvet in his book *The Cockpit of France* (English translation of *La France déchirée*), London, 1959.
(38) André Passeron, *De Gaulle Parle 1962–1966*, Fayard, Paris, 1966, p. 92.
(39) *Fodor's France*, MacGibbon & Kee Ltd., London, 1968.
(40) *op. cit.*
(41) *op. cit.*
(42) Vincent Cronin, *The Companion Guide to Paris*, Collins, London, 1963.
(43) From Julien Gracq, *La littérature à l'estomac*, Paris, 1950, translated by A. M. Sheridan-Smith in Maurice Nadeau, *The French novel since the war*, Methuen, London, 1967.
(44) David Noakes, *Boris Vian*, Classiques de XXe Siècle, Editions Universitaires, Paris, 1964.
(45) Alain Jouffroy, 'Le testament du Marquis de Sade', in *Une Révolution du Regard*, Gallimard, Paris, 1964.
(46) Quoted in 'Le Style Slavik', *Vogue*, Paris, June 1965.
(47) *Nouvel Observateur*, December 31, 1964.
(48) 'J'ai rêvé que tu pleurais à chaudes larmes tandis que je te sodomisais, et quand je m'écartais un fleuve s'échappait de toi par derrière et d'innombrables petits éléphants y nageaient . . .', Arrabal, *Une chèvre sur un nuage, Théâtre panique*, Christian Bourgeois Editeur, Paris, 1967.
(49) Interview published in the *Nouvel Observateur*, April 26, 1967.
(50) *Idem.*
(51) Jean-François Revel, 'Les stylistes au pouvoir', *France-Observateur*, 1958, reprinted in *Contrecensures*, Jean-Jacques Pauvert, Paris, 1966.
(52) Claude Elsen in *Dimanche-Matin*, August 29, 1954.
(53) 'A note on the Story of O' by André Pieyre de Mandiargues, translated by Sabine d'Estrée for the American translation of *Histoire d'O* published by Grove Press, New York, 1965.
(54) *Nouvel Observateur*, February 23, 1966.
(55) *Nouvel Observateur*, July 5, 1967.
(56) Speech to the Assemblée Nationale, Paris, in November 1968.
(57) Speech in Mexico City, April 8, 1960.
(58) Reported by André Brincourt, *André Malraux ou le Temps de Silence*, Editions de la Table Ronde de Combat, Paris, 1966.
(59) Speech to the Assemblée Nationale, Paris, November 1963.
(60) Speech to the Assemblée Nationale, Paris, October 1966.
(61) Reported in *Le Monde*, May 19, 1965.
(62) *Idem.*
(63) Interview published in the *Nouvel Observateur*, October 14, 1968.
(64) Claude Sarraute, 'La crise des maisons de la culture', *Le Monde*, November 1, 1968.

NOTES

(65) Pierre Gaxotte, 'Le côté "culture" ', *Figaro*, May 11, 1966.
(66) Speech to the Assemblée Nationale, Paris, October 15, 1965.
(67) Interview in the *Nouvel Observateur*, October 14, 1968.
(68) Claude Roy, reviewing Malraux's *Antimémoires* in *Le Nouvel Observateur*, September 27, 1967.
(69) *Le Monde*, economic supplement, September 17, 1968.
(70) Reported in *Le Monde*, November 10, 1965.
(71) Reported in *Le Monde*, May 7, 1966.
(72) Quoted in the *Listener*, London, December 12, 1968.
(73) Quoted in *Paris Match*, November 23, 1968.
(74) *Idem.*
(75) 'L'information politique', *La Nef*, Paris, May–July 1966, no. 27.
(76) Quoted in *L'Express*, January 16, 1958.
(77) Figures provided by the World Health Organisation and reported by *Le Nouvel Observateur*, January 4, 1967.
(78) Henri Jeanson, 'Basile au secours de Machiavel', *L'Aurore*, January 21, 1969.
(79) Reported in 'Les Shadoks divisent la France', *L'Express*, February 17, 1969.
(80) Reported in *Le Monde*, January 31, 1969.
(81) Quoted by William L. Wiley, *The Formal French*, Harvard University Press, Cambridge, Mass., 1967.
(82) Paul Morand's speech was reproduced in its entirety by *Le Monde*, March 21, 1969.
(83) *Idem.*
(84) J. Bédier and P. Hazard, *Littérature Française*, Vol. II, Larousse 1946. The reference is to Giraudoux.
(85) Another reference to Giraudoux in Louis Chaigne, *Les Lettres contemporaines* (*Histoire de la Littérature Française*), Del Duca, Paris, 1964.
(86) Broadcast on June 7, 1962.
(87) Interview with Michèle Manceaux, *L'Express*, March 22, 1962.
(88) Robert F. Byrnes, *Anti-semitism in modern France*, Vol. I, Rutgers University Press, New Brunswick, New Jersey, 1950.
(89) Simone de Beauvoir, *Force of Circumstance* (*La Force des choses*), translated by Richard Howard, André Deutsch and Weidenfeld and Nicolson, London, 1965.
(90) Speech by Thiers to the Assemblée Nationale at Versailles, March 22, 1871.
(91) Speech by Thiers to the Assemblée Nationale, May 24, 1871.
(92) Quoted in 'C.D.R.: La milice du régime', *Dire* (*La nouvelle revue de la gauche socialiste*), no. 4, February 1969.
(93) Alexander Werth, *The Twilight of France*, Hamish Hamilton, London, 1942.
(94) Jacques Fauvet, *op. cit.*
(95) Pierre Bertaux, 'On a la police qu'on mérite', in *La Nef*, 'La police en France', no. 14, June–September 1963.
(96) Introduction to Alexander Werth, *op. cit.*
(97) Result of an opinion poll taken by the firm of *Sema-Sofres*, reported in the *Nouvel Observateur*, January 20, 1969.
(98) Result of an opinion poll undertaken conjointly by the Institut Français d'Opinion Publique (IFOP) and the weekly magazine *L'Express* which reported the findings in its issue of February 17, 1969.
(99) Louis Rougier, *La France Jacobine*, Brussels, 1959.

Index

A

Abadie, Claude (band-leader), 104
Abd-el-Kader (Algerian leader), 24
About, Edmond (novelist), 222
Academy, the French, 184–185
"Action Française" (monarchist group); its newspaper, 209; incites to violence against Blum, 224
Adamov, 200
Algeria, 16; suffering in, caused by French colonisation, 21; conquest of and atrocities in, 23–28; torture used in, 30, 36–38; amnesty for French brutalities in, 38; war casts shadow over Paris, 106
Algerians; concentration camps for, in France, 40; massacre of, in Paris (1961), 42, 55; treatment of, by police, 50; manifesto against treatment of, in France, 164, 198; hostility to, in France, 207
Algiers, Bey of; insults French ambassador (1827), 23
Algren, Nelson (novelist), 106
Alix, Pierre, 10–12
"Alliance Française" (French schools abroad), 184
Alsace-Lorraine; clamour for recovery of, after 1870, 17; nourishes war mania, 20
Alsop, Joseph, 16 fn
Aly Khan, the, 70
America, United States of; French modernism linked with, 170–171; French hostility towards, 171–172
Amiens; House of Culture at, 156
Andrieu, René (Communist Party member), 219
Annam, North, 31
Anouilh, Jean, 223
Antonini (film director), 164
Apollinaire, Guillaume (poet), 58; gives impetus to the Sade cult, 116
Aragon, Louis, 135, 137; his "detestation" of France, 214
Arc de Triomphe, 3–5, 67, 72, 73
Army, the French; as quintessence of national spirit, 15–16; its use of torture in Algeria, 37; record white-washed, 37–38
Arrabal; plays of, 125–126
Atget; photographs prostitutes, 90
Audiberti, 200

B

Bainville, Jacques (historian); anti-semitism of, 209
Baj (artist), 130
Baldwin, James (writer), catches tragic atmosphere of Paris, 77
Balkany, Robert de, 169–170
Balthus (artist), 120, 144
Balzac, Honoré de, 70, 76, 213
Barbin, Pierre; appointed director of Paris Cinémathèque, 163
Bardot, Brigitte, 86
Baron (Director of the Sûreté in Madagascar), 34, 35–36
Barrault, Jean-Louis, 163
Barrès, Maurice; his ideas and the Nazis, 209
Bastille, the, 4, 9
Bataille, Georges; writes on de Sade, 116; his life and work, 142–144
Baudelaire, Charles, 117
Baylot, Jean; becomes Prefect of Paris police, 50; and the "Communist Plot", 51–52
"Bazar de l'Hotel de Ville" (Paris store), 170
Beatles, the, 99
Beaufré, General; on the army's dwindling prestige, 15–16
Beauvoir, Simone de, 104, 129, 175; on the "horrors" of the bourgeoisie, 215

Belleville (Paris), 74: Rue de, 75
Bellmer, Hans (German artist), 120, 126
Belmondo, Jean-Paul, 86
Ben Barka affair, the, 56, 60
Benoît, Jean (French Canadian painter), stage ceremony in memory of de Sade, 113-115
Bergman, Ingmar (film director), 164, 199
Bernanos, Georges (novelist); anti-semitism of, 209
Bertaux, Pierre (ex-Director General of Sûreté); on right-wing plots, 225-226
Billetdoux, François (playwright), 105
Blake, Peter (artist), 124
Blum, Léon (Socialist Prime Minister); expresses French chauvinism, 7; butt of anti-Semites, 209; insulted in National Assembly, 210; beaten up by royalists, 224
Boer War, the, 29
Bogart, Humphrey, 99
Bombard, Alain (sailor), 202
Bon, Jean Le, 187
Borges, José, 92, 130
Boulanger, General, 17, 19, 20
Boulbon, Raousset (writer); on appropriation of land in Algeria, 27
Boulez, Pierre (musician), 204
Bourgeade, Pierre, 145; his "smart" erotic stories, 146; 147
bourgeois, the French; cultural chauvinism of, 212; pilloried in literature and art, 213; reaction against, 213-214; diatribe against, by Paul Nizan, 214-215; description of, 216-217; lack patriotic feeling, 218; exultation of, in suppression of Commune (1871), 221-222
Bourges, Yvon (Minister of Information), 56
Bourges; House of Culture at, 156-157, 160
Brauner, Victor (artist), 113, 119, 124
Brecht, Berthold, 223
Breton, André; ruler of original Surrealist group, 113; takes up the Sade cult, 116; quoted on despair, 117, 118; creates a new bourgeois taste, 119, 120, 129, 141, 143
Brogan, D. W., 227-228
Bruce, Jean (thriller writer), 174
Bruckberger, Father; on Greeks' disappointment in France (1969), 40
Brunius, Jacques, 125
Buffet, Bernard (artist), 125
Bugeaud, Thomas Robert, General (19th century conqueror of Algeria), 22, 24-26, 37, 220
Buñuel, Luis; popularity of his films in Paris, 120; influence on Arrabal, 126, 199
Burnand, Robert, 12-14
Bussoti, Silvano; his opera *Passion of the Marquis de Sade*, 117 *fn*

C

Caen; House of Culture at, 156, 160-161, 223
Caillois, Roger (anthropologist), 69, 119, 145
Cain, James, 105
Caldwell, Erskine, 105
Cambodia; penal code of, 30
Camus, Albert, 70, 129
Canada, French, 155
Canard enchainé (periodical), 165
Candide (by Voltaire), 187
Carbuccia, the brothers; of, 48
Carré, John le; popularity of his thrillers in Paris, 99
Carroll, Lewis, 98, 117, 125
Casablanca; French landing at, 29
Castelot, André, 167
Cavaignac, General, 220
Céline, Louis-Ferdinand (novelist); racist views of, 209
Cézanne, Paul; anti-semitism of, 208
Chagall, Marc, repaints ceiling of the Opera, 156
Champs-Elysées (Paris), 73, 82
Chardin, Teilhard de, 57
Charles X (of France), 17
Charon, Gaston—*see* Nocher, Jean
Charonne, métro station; rioters killed by police at, 42, 55, 60

INDEX 239

Chase, James Hadley, 105
Chauvin; originator of "chauvinism", 6
chauvinism, French, 7, 8, 9, 10, 18, 28, 165, 180–181, 182, 183, 184, 190, 191, 195, 207, 212, 216, 218, 230
Chavannes, Puvis de, 72
Chiappe, Jean (Paris Prefect of police), 48
Chirico, Gidrgio de (painter), 79
Cinema, the French, 176–178; repressive censorship, 177; erotic films excepted, 178
Cinémathèque, the (Paris), 163
Cité, Ile de la (Paris), 88
Clair, René, 74
Clarétie, Jules (Academician), 19, 222
Cocteau, Jean, 85
Colonial mission, France's; the myth of, 21–23
Combat (newspaper), 105
comic strip, the; vogue for, 123; and eroticism, 146–147; and history, 166
Commune, the Paris (of 1871), damage to buildings during, 71, 75, 78; atrocities in its suppression still remembered, 220
Compagnies républicaines de Sécurité C.R.S.—riot police); brutality of, 41–42, 44; founded as right-wing force, 49, 163
Conciergerie, the (Paris), 78
Concorde (aircraft), 12, 56, 231
Concorde, Place de la (Paris), 69, 72, 79, 82
Coppée, François; praises books glorifying war, 19
Coppet, General de (Governor of Madagascar), 34
Corbusier, Le, 155
Cordier, the Galerie Daniel, 124
Corneille, Pierre (dramatist), 73, 158
Coste-Floret, Paul (Minister for France Overseas), 36
Coty, René (President), 38
Cournot, Michael (film critic), 117
Croix, La (Catholic newspaper); joins anti-Jewish crusade, 208

Croix de Feu, la (right-wing nationalist organisation), 17 *fn*, 210, 224
Cruelty, Theatre of; dominated by de Sade, 117
Culture, Houses of, 90; set up by Gaullist régime, 155–157; their failure, 158; controversy and closure, 159–162

D

Daladier, Edouard (Prime Minister), 4
Darien, Georges (novelist and pamphleteer), 29; quoted against the bourgeoisie, 214
Dasté, Jean (cultural director at St. Etienne), 159
Daumier, Honoré, 213
Davie, Alan (artist), 124
Déat, Marcel; converted to Nazism, 12
Debré, Michel (Prime Minister); attacks book exposing use of torture, 41, 163; on role of radio and television, 179
Debussy, Claude, 158
Decaux, Alain; his play on the Rosenburg Affair, 171
Defence of the Republic, Committee for the (C.D.R.); development and activities of, 223
Degas, Edgar, anti-semitism of, 208
Delacroix, Eugène, paints Liberty as a woman, 8, 9, 158
Delly (writer), 174
Deroulède, Paul; war-mongering of, 20; anti-semitism of, 208
Dides, Jean (Commissioner of police), fosters right-wing tendencies of police, 50–52
Dien Bien Phu, 32
Dior, Christian, 70
Doré, Gustave, 70
Doucin, Joseph; gives evidence on prisons in Indo-China, 31
Dreyfus Affair, the, 20, 208, 209, 230
Driant, Captain; his best-selling war books, 19
Drumont, Edouard (journalist); anti-semitism of, 208, 209, 210

Dubois, Maitre, Camille; describes police brutalities (May, 1968), 44
Dumas, Alexander (the Younger); reviles the Communards, 222
Durafour (Mayor of St. Etienne), 159

E
Eiffel Tower, the, 76, 88
England; Fashoda incident with, 29; propoganda against in Boer War, 29
Ernst, Max (artist), 119
Eroticism (see also de Sade); in Surrealism, 119; cult of erotico-sadism, 120–121; in France and modern French literature, 137, 138–147
Escarpit, Robert (journalist), 186
Estienne, Charles; his novel *O et M*, 141–142
Etcherelli, Claire, 174
Etiemble; his book *Parlez-vous Franglais?*, 171
"Europe-Action" (anti-semitic organisation), 207
European Convention on Human Rights, 60
Express, *L'* (newspaper), on Houses of Culture, 158; on Americanisation of youth, 181; interviews Jean Nocher, 203

F
Faithfull, Marianne, 132
Fanny Hill, 138
Fashoda, 29
Faure, Edgar (politician), 54, 179, 223
Fauvet, Jacques, 225, 229
Ferrier, André (literary critic), 124
Ferry, Jules (Prime Minister), 29
Feuillère, Edwige (actress), 70
Feydeau, Georges (playwright), 159
Figaro (newspaper), 14, 15, 186, 221, 222
Fini, Léonor (artist), 119, 129
Firminy; House of Culture at, 156
Flammarion (publishers), 208
Foreign Legion, the, 28; in Indo-China, 31–32; in Morocco, 31; in Madagascar, 33
Forrest, Jean-Claude; his comic strip adventure "Barbarella", 146 *fn*
Fouchet, Max-Pol; his book *The Americans—are they adult?*, 171; on government influence in radio and T.V., 180
Franco-Prussian war, the; subject for painters, 19
Fry, Roger (Minister of Interior), 55

G
Gabriello, Suzanne (singer), 127
Gaillard, Félix (Prime Minister), 55
Galliéni, General, 29
Gallifet, General, 27, 220
Gandrène, La (book exposing police and army atrocities), 41
Gassiot-Talbot, Gérard (art critic), 122
Gatti, Armand, 162, 163, 171
Gaulle, ex-President de: his idea of France, 3; incorporation of the French myth, 7–8; pronouncements on the destiny of France, 9; philosophy not new, 10; pre-war anticipations of his style and thought, 10–14; quotation from his war memoirs, 13; raising France to the "summit of the world", 14; and relations with the army, 16–17; as champion of France Overseas, 22–23; his near-dictatorship, 39; decorates Prefect of Paris police, 46; represents anti-democratic tendency in French history, 58–59; on his total powers as President, 59–60; increase of repressive measures under, 60–63, 82; great "stylist", 137, 156; enjoys erotic film, 178, 183; obscurity in his speeches, 188; view of French history, 205, 219, 220, 222; loses stature as mythical figure, 231
Gaulle, Madame de, 88, 138
Gaullist régime, the, 14; role of police under, 40–53; its authoritarian machinery, 63; the arts under, 63–64, 91; dullness and

respectability of, 99; sets up Ministry for Cultural Affairs, 154; government control of culture under, 162-163; and television, 179-181; encourages anti-cultural broadcaster, 195

Gaxotte, Pierre (Academician); his views on French theatre, 159, 160

Genet, Jean; his play *Les Paravents* (*The Screens*), 127, 159, 211

Geneviève, Saint (patron saint of Paris), 88

Gestapo, 40

Gèze, General, 37

Giap, General, 32

Gide, André, 200, 204

Giraudoux, Jean; racism in his *Pleins Pouvoirs*, 209-210, 224, 223

Godard, Jean-Luc, 176, 177

Gohier, Urbain (writer); on the horrors of French colonisation, 29; anti-semitism of, 209

Gourmont, Rémy de; protests against sabre-rattling patriotism, 20; on the ugly aspects of Paris, 71, 75

Gracq, Julien; on atmosphere of literary Paris, 96; attends de Sade ceremony, 113, 115, 196

Grandière, Admiral de la, 22

Graziani (Corsican painter), 121

Greco, Juliette, 70, 85

Greece; police terror in, 40

Grenoble; House of Culture at, 157, 162

Grimaud, Maurice (Paris Prefect of Police), whitewashes police actions (summer, 1968), 45; on "electric atmosphere" in Paris streets, 82

Grimauld, Port, 167

Gringoire (Fascist newspaper), 224

Gueydon, Admiral de; urges French dominance in Algeria, 28

Gyp (novelist)—see Janville, Countess Sibylle Martel de

H

Halles, the (Paris), 76, 85, 90

Hanoi Legionaries; trial of, 31-32

Haussmann (architect); commissioned to beautify Paris, 70; his heavy-handed method, 71; districts spared by, 76-77, 85

Havre, Le; House of Culture, 156

Heine, Maurice, 116

Hemingway, Ernest; on Paris, 68

Herriot, Edouard (radical minister), 10

Hervé, Gustave (journalist); his book *C'est Pétain qu'il nous faut*, 58-59; anti-semitism of, 209

Hiquily (sculptor); his sexual symbolism, 121

"Hiroshima mon amour" (film), 176

Ho Chi Minh, 32

Hockney, David (artist), 124

Holleaux, André; and the Paris Cinémathèque, 163

Hôtel Dieu, the (Paris), 71-72

Hugo, Victor, 70, 75, 76

Huysmans, J-K., 132

I

Indo-China; French colonisation in, 21-22, 28; atrocities in, 30-32, 51

Invalides, the (Paris), 72, 81

Ionesco, 161, 200, 204

J

James Bond; popularity of books in Paris, 99

Jansen (interior decorator), 168

Janville, Countess Sibylle Martel de (the novelist "Gyp"); anti-semitism of, 208

Jaurès, Jean (Socialist leader), 29

Jazz Hot (French jazz review), 105

Jemappes; French victory at, 15

Joan of Arc; her statue at Rouen, 12, 165

Jouandin (provincial C.D.R. president); quoted against "intellectuals of the Left", 223

Jouffroy, Alain (art and literary critic); describes ceremony in memory of Marquis de Sade, 113-115, 118, 128, 131

Jules et Jim (film), 176

K
Kabyle (tribesmen); massacre French colonists (1871), 27
Kabyila (mountains in Algeria), 26
Kaplan, Nelly (writer); her Surrealism, 121, 128
Kenny, Paul (thriller writer), 174
King Kong (film), 117
Klossowski, Pierre, 116, 121, 144, 145
Koestler, Arthur, 69
Kubrick, Stanley (film director), 37
Kurosawa (film director), 164

L
Labisse, Felix (artist), 120
Lacassin, François, 123–124
Lachaise, Père (Paris cemetery), 220
Laclos, Choderlos de, 200
Lafayette, Marquis de, 39
Laffont, Robert (publishers), 172
Lamartine, Alphonse de (poet); condems conquest of Algeria, 26
Lamoricière, General (conqueror of Algeria); 22, 220
Langlois, Henri; dismissal of, as director of Paris Cinémathèque, 163
Language, the French, 183–193; virtues it is believed to express, 184; teaching of, abroad, 184; "purified" by French Academy, 184–185; a symbol of French pre-eminence, 185; dominated by Graeco-Roman culture, 186; deeply history-conscious, 186; passion for clarity in, 187–188; can be obscure, 188–189; lends itself to rhetoric, 189–192; literary artifice in spoken French, 192; as a living monument, 192–193; words taken for facts, 193
Laniel, Joseph (Prime Minister), 51
Latin Quarter (Paris), 68, 69, 77, 82, 87; riots break out in (May, 1968), 101
Laurens J. P. (artist), 155
Laurent, Jacques; his films cut by censor, 177, 178

Lautréamont; his "chants de Maldoror", 117, 129
Laval, Pierre, 211
Layon (legionary); his testimony in trial of Hanoi legionaries, 31
Lebel, Robert, 113
Left Bank (Paris), 82, 91, 170
Leiris, Michel (anthropologist), 143, 175
Lely, Gilbert (biographer of de Sade), 116
Le Pen (right-wing extremist), 52
Liaisons Dangereuses, les (film); temporarily banned in France, 63, 200
Libre Parole (anti-Jewish newspaper), 210–211
Lichtenstein, Roy (artist), 124
Lille; museum at, 153
L'Isle Adam, Villiers de, 132
Littlewood, Joan, 100
Loi Marthe Richard, the; closes French brothels, 138
Louis, Saint, 165
Louis XIV, 165, 184, 185
Louis Philippe, King, 5, 17, 23, 24
Louvel (mayor of Caen), 160
Louvre, the (Paris); poor architectures of, 71, 72; parterres of, 80
Luxembourg, the (Paris), 80, 81
Lyautey, General, 30

M
Madagascar, 28; massacre of French settlers in (1947), 32–33; violence of French counter-measures, 33–36
Madeleine, the (Paris), 72
Magritte, René (artist), 119, 120
Maillol, Aristide (sculptor), 72
Malesherbes, Boulevard (Paris), 73
Malraux, André (Gaullist Minister of Culture); propagates France's cultural mission, 7, 9, 12; on the benefits of French colonisation, 22, 137, 138, 139; activities as Minister, 154–165; and Houses of Culture, 155–163; condemns sex and violence in films, 164; vociferous prop of Gaullism, 164; visionary dreams,

INDEX

165, 173, 175; distrust of cinema and T.V., 178-179; obscurity in speeches of, 188, 195, 196, 202
Mandiargues, André Pieyre de, 113, 118; partisan of Surrealist tradition, 121; represents culture of Gaullist France, 128; literary career of, 128-137; his poems and stories, 129-132; his novel *La Marge*, 132-135, 139, 141, 147, 175
Mandingo (American novel), 171
Mansour, Joyce; holds de Sade ceremony, 113, 121
Mao Tse Tung, 228
Marais, the (Paris), 69, 75, 77, 78; its historical atmosphere, 79
Marchand Mission (of 1898), 29
Marcuse, Herbert, 228
"Marianne"; female figure representing French Republic, 3-64; depicted as warrior on Arc de Triomphe, 4-5; as mother of civilisation and liberty on coins and stamps, 5-6, 9; in Burnand's book *Je suis français!*, 12-13; as conqueror bestowing culture, 17-23; the Mother of Arts, 64
Marseillaise, La (anthem), 5, 224
Marx, Karl, 228
Masson, André (artist), 143; repaints ceiling of the Odéon, 155
Massu, Jacques, General, 16, 220
Mathieu, Georges (artist), 125
Mathurin, Charles; his novel *Melmoth the Wanderer*, 141-142
Matin, Le (newspaper); on atrocities in Casablanca, 29-30
Matta, Sebastian (artist); at de Sade ceremony, 113-114, 118, 124
Mauriac, François (novelist); leading admirer of de Gaulle, 8; on the peaceful mission of France, 14; on police independence of de Gaulle, 41; protests against film project, 95, 127, 174, 213, 224
Maurois, André, 173
Maurras, Charles; converted to Nazism, 12; applauds round-up of Paris Jews (1942), 211, 224

Meissonier, Ernest (painter); depicts battles of Napoleon I, 19
Ménage, Gilles (grammarian); on "modesty" of French language (1672), 185
Mendès-France, Pierre (Prime Minister), 51
Ménilmontant (Paris), 75, 162
Mercure de France (newspaper), 20
Mermoz, Jean (flying hero), 202
Méryon, Charles (artist), 70, 76
Michel, Georges, 174
Michelet, Jules (historian), 227
Milhau, Jules, 173
Miller, Henry; and Paris, 68, 77, 223
Mirbeau, Octave (journalist and novelist), 29, 213
Mitterand, François (Minister of Interior); investigates "Communist plot", 51-52, 196
Moch, Jules (Minister of Interior), influence of, 49-50
Mohammed Ben Yussef (Sultan of Morocco), 54
Molière, 158, 217
Moltke, von (German Field Marshal); on French self-deception, 21, 193
Monde, Le (newspaper), 32, 40, 44, 97; on Houses of Culture, 158, 162, 186
Montluc, fortress of, 196
Montmartre (Paris), 68, 70
Montorgueil, Rue (Paris), 78
Montparnasse (Paris), 68, 70, 75, 87
Monsieur Hulot's Holiday (film), 176
Morand, Paul (academician); classical allusions of, 186; on the clarity of French, 188
Moreau, Jeanne, 86
Morin, Edgar, 113
Morocco, 28; horrors of its conquest, 29-31, 54
Mouvement Démocratique de Renovation Malgache (M.D.R.M.); campaigns for Malagasy independence, 33; accused of complicity in massacre of French settlers, 34-35

N

Nadeau, Maurice, 129, 175

Nancy; museum at, 153
Napoleon I, 6; gives culture a national basis, 10; symbolises the authentic France, 17; gives glamour to militarism, 18, 39, 58, 162
Napoleon III, 16; popular foreign adventures of, 17, 18; becomes Emperor, 27, 29, 58
Nef, La (review), 179
Nekmaria, caves of, 26
Nemours, Duke of, 26
Nerval, Gérard de, 117
Nesle, Tour de, 166
Nizan, Paul (writer); quoted against the bourgeoisie, 214–215, 229
Noailles, Marie-Laure de; partisan of Surrealist tradition, 121, 128
Nocher, Jean (real name Gaston Charon—writer and broadcaster); homespun philosopher of Gaullist régime, 8; as popular broadcaster, 195–203; background of, 196; his radio script "Platform 70", 196; supports Algerian war, 197; attacks destructive intellectualism, 197–198; on anti-militarism, 198; inveighs against enemies of France, 199; against the philosophy of the avant-garde, 199; against the artistic intelligentsia, 199; on women's fashions, 200; on the perversion of youth, 200; his programmes for youth and extract from, 200–202; counter-attacks detractors, 202; interview with, 203; representative of anti-France, 203; affinity with Pétain, 204; voices popular distrust of intellectuals, 204, 206, 211, 212, 213, 217, 222
Notre Dame (Paris), 69, 71, 72, 77, 78
Novel, the modern (see also under Eroticism, Paris, Surrealism and individual authors); the new intellectual novel, 147–148; its atmosphere of futility and despair, 149; lacks appeal to wide public, 149; its escapism, 150; novels reflecting modern French life, 174–175

O
Observateur, Le Nouvel (periodical), 97, 117, 133
Odéon, the (Paris), 155
Oeuvre Française, L' (anti-semitic organisation), 207
Opéra, the (Paris); ugliness of, 72; ceiling repainted by Chagall, 156
O.R.T.F. (French radio and television service), 180, 181

P
Palestro (Algeria); French colonists massacred at (1871), 27
Panizza, Oscar, 211
Panthéon, the (Paris), 72
Papon, Maurice (Paris Prefect of Police); writer on philosophy, 8; becomes Prefect, 52; early career of, 53–54; his arbitrary behaviour, 55; tolerates police violence, 56; joins Sud-Aviation company, 56; as writer and philosopher, 56–57; relations with *Prospective* group, 57–58, 60
Paris; the capital of thought, 12; Archbishop blesses Algerian colonists, 27; as spiritual heart of France, 64; supposed cultural centre of the world, 67–69; its alleged physical beauty, 69; phases in cultural history of, 69–71; ugly aspects of, 71–72; its "imposed" grandeur, 72–73; scarcity of private houses in, 74; old aspect disappearing, 74–75; vanishing picturesqueness, 76–78; violent history of, 78–79; discomfort of life in, 83–84; modern buildings, 84; drugstore disease, 86–87; restaurants and cafés, 87–88; femininity of, 88; myth of Parisian eroticism, 88; feminine elegance in, 89; prostitutes of, 90; the Mother of the Arts, 90–91; cosmopolitanism of, 93; its cultural life, 91–99; revived interest in English culture, 99–100; vogue of Americana, 100; last "golden age" of culture, 102; nostalgia for this

INDEX

age, 102–103; esoteric cultural atmosphere of, 141; new intellectual novel in, 147–149; clean-up of buildings under Gaullist régime, 154–155; House of Culture in, 156; residential status symbols, 168–169; new housing estates, 169-171
Parisians; rudeness of, 81; politeness campaign for tourists, 81; aggressive driving of, 81–82; falling for modernity, 85; in love with the recent past, 100–101; literary romanticism of, 135
Paris-Match (magazine), 168, 178
Paths of Glory (film); banned in France, 37
Paulhan, Jean; writes preface for *The Story of O*, 139, 140
Pauvert, Jean-Jacques; publisher of comic strip periodical *Giff-Wiff*, 123
Pauwels, Louis; his book *Le Matin des Magiciens*, 118
Paz, Octavio, 92, 113
Pélissier, Colonel, 26
Pellaert, Guy; his comic strip adventure "Jodelle", 146 *footnote*
Periodicals, literary; in Paris, 96
Pétain, Marshal, 39, 53, 58, 204, 211
Petit Parisien (newspaper), 30
Philip, André (Socialist minister), 36
Piaf, Edith, 70, 74
Picasso, Pablo, 160, 197, 200, 204
Pigalle, Place (Paris), 100
Pingaud, Bernard, 175
Pinter, Harold, 126
Pleven, René (Defence Minister), 51
Plexus (magazine), 120
Poher, Alain, 231
Poitiers, battle of, 187
Police, the French (see also under Compagnies Républicaines de Securité and Sûreté Nationale); increase of, after Liberation, 40; role of, under Gaullist régime, 40–53; record of, prior to de Gaulle, 41; examples of brutality, 42; behaviour during riots of 1968, 42–45; xenophobia of, 45; excesses officially condoned, 45–46; escapes government control, 46–47; powers of Prefect, 48; becomes right-wing, 48; politicising of, 49–51; plot against Fourth Republic, 51; police demonstration, 52; increased power of, in offences against "state security", 62
Pompidou, Georges; contributes to the Republic of Letters, 8; and the Parly II housing estate, 169, 196, 231
Pop art, 124; compared with modern French "realism", 125
Pradt, Abbé de; warns against military dictatorship, 26
Praz, Mario, 173
Prévert, Jacques, 74
"Printemps" (Paris store), 170
Prizes, literary, in France, 173
Prospective (literary review), 57–58

Q

Queneau, Raymond, 104, 108, 139
Queuille, Henri (Prime Minister, 1951), 50

R

Rabanne, Paco (dress designer), 90
Rabemananjara (Malagasy M.P.), 35–36
Racine, Jean, 190–191
Rakotondrabe (Malagery extremist), 35
Rakotonirina, Stanislas (Malagasy official), 35
Raseta (Malagasy M.P.), 35
Rassemblement du Peuple Français (R.P.F.); links with Paris police, 50, 196
Rauschenberg, Robert; exponent of pop art, 124
Ravoahangy (Malagasy M.P.), 35–36
Raynal, Henri (novelist), 146, 189
"rayonnement" (radiating); chauvinistic concept of France disseminating culture and civilisation, 6; by force of arms, 13; by conquest in Africa and the Far East, 20–23; at

"rayonnment" (radiating)—(cont.)
    work in Algeria, 27; its myth protected by censorship, 37, 63; lack of, from Paris to provinces, 153; French language its first instrument, 184
Réage, Pauline (see also *Story of O*); bestselling author, 139
Rébatet, Lucien (pro-Nazi journalist); 209; his career and book *Les Décombres*, 211
Reichshoffen; French cavalry charge at, 19
Réligieuse, La (film); banned by Gaullist régime, 63
Renoir, Auguste, 208
Rennes; dramatic centre at, 153
Republic, the First, 5, 15
Republic, the Third; golden age of French militarism, 18–20; democratic freedoms during, 223–224; reasons for survival of, 230
Republic, the Fourth, 8; attempts during, to bring culture to provinces, 153
Republic, the Fifth; balance of achievements, 231; aftermath of, 232
Retz, Gilles de, 117
Revel, Jean-François; his study of de Gaulle's language and mentality, 7
Revolution, the French; as disseminator of liberty, 13, 165; myths about achievements, 226–227
Reynaud, Paul; visits Indo-China as colonial minister, 30–31
Rights of Man, Declaration of, 227
Riley, Bridget (artist), 125
Rivarol (extreme Right-wing) newspaper), 211, 212
Rivette, Jacques (film director), 63, 164, 177
Robbins, Harold (author), 171
Rochefort, Christiane, 99
Rochelle, Drieu la (novelist); racist views of, 209
Rocque, Colonel de la; poses as representing France, 17; fights for a "purified" France, 224
Rodin, Auguste, 208

Romantics, the German, 129
Rond-Point de la Défense (outside Paris), 84, 167
Rossif, Frédéric (film director), 135
Rostand, Jean, 161
Roussel, Raymond, 95
Roy, Claude, 175
Rude, François; his bas-reliefs on Arc de Triomphe, 4–5, 13
Ryan, Cornelius (American historian); popularity of, in France, 172

S

Sacco-Vanzetti affair, the, 162, 171
Sacré-Coeur (Paris), 73
Sade, Marquis de; attraction of, in Paris cultural circles, 112; ceremony to commemorate anniversary of death, 113–115, 116–117, 118, 120, 141
Sagan, Françoise, 70
Saigon; trial of political suspects at, 32
Saint-Antoine; Faubourg (Paris), 74; Rue de, 79
Saint-Arnaud, General; helps Louis Napoleon, 27, 220
Saint Augustin; church of, 73
Saint-Cloud, Les Hauts de (Paris); new housing estate at, 170
Saint-Denis; Rue (Paris), 79; du Sacré Coeur (church), 80
Saint-Etienne; dramatic centre at, 153; quarrels over, 159; du Mont (church), 80
Saint-Exupéry, Antoine de; as a model for youth, 202
Saint-Germain des Prés (Paris), 68, 70; invaded by teenagers, 85–86; drugstore in, 86, 122; restaurants and cafés, 87; Cocteau on, 85; last "golden age" of culture centred in, 102–112
Saint-Michel, Boulevard (Paris), 89
Saint-Phalle, Niki de (artist), 121
Saint-Sulpice, Place (Paris), 87
Sainte Chapelle, the (Paris), 71–72
San-Antonio (thriller writer), 174
Sarcey, Francisque (theatre critic); reactionary views of, 213, 222

Sardou, Victorien (playwright), 222
Sartre, Jean-Paul, 70, 85, 104, 129; deplores American influence, 171, 175, 200, 204
Satory; prison camp at (1871), 221
Saunders, James (playwright), 100
Scientific Research, National Commission for, 35
Ségui (artist), 124
Senegal; ferocity of colonial troops from, 28, 33; massacres in, 29
Setif rising (Algeria, 1945), 28, 32, 54
"Shadoks, the" (French T.V. programme), 183
Simenon, Georges, 174
Singer, Gail (artist), 130
Slavik (decorator), his 19th century inspiration, 122-123, 169
Smidt, Colonel; quoted on frightfulness in Algeria (1841), 26
Sorbonne, the; student revolt at (1968), 112
Sous les Toits de Paris (film), 75
State Security, Court of (Cour de Sûreté d'Etat), its nature and powers, 62-63
Stéphane, Roger (Bonapartist writer), 183
Story of O; discussion of, 139-141
Strasbourg; dramatic centres at, 153
Streicher, Julius; his anti-Jewish newspaper *Der Stürmer*, 210
Stroessner, General (dictator of Paraguay), 172
Styron, William (writer), 172
Sud-Ouest (Bordeaux newspaper), 53
Sue, Eugène, 70
Sullivan Vernon—*see* Vian, Boris
Sunday Times, the; reports on Paris police brutality, 43
Sûreté Nationale (police organisation), officials of use torture in Algeria, 30; in Indo-China, 30-31; in Madagascar, 34-36; in Algeria, 36; politicising of, 49-51
Surrealism; trappings of still fascinate in Paris, 115; and de Sade, 116, 120; a potent cultural influence, 118-119; eroticism in, 120-122; in the theatre, 125-127, 141

T

Tananarive (capital of Madagascar); judical investigation into uprising at, 34-37
Tati, Jacques; his film *Playtime*, 178
Television, French, 178-183; under Gaullist régime, 179-181; lack of real life in, 181-182; French colour process, 182; audiences satisfied with chauvinism, 183
Temps Modernes (monthly review), 97, 104
Théâtre National Populaire (Paris), 153, 162, 171
Theodorakis, Mikis (Greek composer), 171
Theule, Joel le (Minister for Information), 178
Thiers, Louis (Prime Minister); supports Algerian war to avert French decadence, 23-24, 25, 27; on "triumph of civilisation" after Commune (1871), 221
Thonon; House of Culture at, 156, 159-160
Tixier-Vignancour, Jean-Louis (right-wing extremist), 52
Tocqueville, de (historian), on army hostility to French settlers in Algeria, 26
Tom Jones (film), 99
Tonking Delta, the, 29
torture; systematic use of, in French territories, 30; in Indo-China, 31-32; in Madagascar, 34-36; in Algeria, 36; used by Paris police (summer, 1968), 45
Toulouse; dramatic centre at, 133
Trehard, Jo (theatre director at Caen), 160, 161
Tribune Médicale (review); on effect of riot gas, 44
Tricontinental Conference (Cuba, 1966), 45
Triolet, Elsa, 137

Trouille, Clovis (artist), his erotic surrealist paintings, 119–120
Troyat, Henri (writer), 173
Truffaut (film director), 164
Truman, Harry (President), 60
Tuileries, the (Paris), 72
Turin, 69

U
Ungaretti, Giuseppe, 92
Utrillo, Maurice, 160

V
Vadim, Roger; his film *Vice and Virtue*, 116; flashy glamour of his films, 146; his *Liaisons dangereuses* a prohibited export, 177
Valéc, General; his moderate policy in Algerian campaign (19th cent.), 24
Vallat, Xavier (right-wing M.P.); insults Léon Blum, 210
Valmy, battle of, 15
Varda, Agnes: films of, 176–177
Vian, Boris (writer and musician), 70; early life and career, 103–107; discussion of his novels, 107–112; *Vercoquin et le Plancton*, 104, 108; *L'Ecume des Jours*, 104, 107–109; *L'Automne à Pekin*, 104, 106, 108; *J'irai cracher sur vos tombes*, 105, 107; *Les Fourmis* (short stories), 105; *L'Equarrissage pour tous* (play), 105; *L'Herbe rouge* (novel), 105, 108, 109–112; *L'Arrache-Coeur*, 106; *The Empire Builders* (play), 107; his contribution to culture, 112
Victoria, Queen, 29
Vidor, King (film director); his version of *War and Peace* cut in France, 37
Vigo; his film *Zéro de conduite* attacks bourgeoisie, 214

Villar, Jean, 153
Vinci, Leonardo da; his "Mona Lisa" loaned to Washington, 155
Viollis, Andrée (journalist); on French atrocities in Indo-China, 30–31
Vitrac, Roger, 95
Vogüe, Armand de (industrialist); contributes to *Prospective*, 57–58
Voltaire, 12, 187

W
Waldberg, Patrick; his history of Surrealism, 116
Walsh, Raoul; craze for his films in Paris, 100
Weingarten, Romain; failure of his play *L'Eté* in London, 97–98; his debt to Lewis Carroll, 125
Welles, Orson; his radio script *War of the Worlds*, 196
Werth, Alexander (historian), 4, 224
Wharton, Bryan (press photographer); on Paris police brutality, 43
Wilson, Edmund; on the post-war Sade cult, 115–116
Wilson, Georges; resigns from Théâtre National Populaire, 163
World Health Organisation, 84
World War, the First, 13, 17, 19, 20

X
Xenophobia (in France); of Paris police (summer 1968), 45; always latent in France, 207; anti-Algerian feeling, 207; anti-semitism, 207–212; approval of, among middle classes, 216

Z
Zola, Emile, 75, 213